INDIGENOUS RIGHTS

Changes and Challenges for the 21st Century

Edited by Sarah Sargent and Jo Samanta

Contributors:
Valentina Vadi, Lucas Lixinski, Sarah Sargent,
Jocelynne Scutt and Hephzibah Egede

University of Buckingham Press,
107-111 Fleet Street, London, EC4A 2AB
info@legend-paperbooks.co.uk | www.legendpress.co.uk

Contents © Sarah Sargent and Jo Samanta 2019
The right of the above author to be identified as the author of this work has been
asserted in accordance with the Copyright, Designs and Patents Act 1988. British
Library Cataloguing in Publication Data available.

Print ISBN 978-1-7895508-9-4
Ebook ISBN 978-1-7895509-0-0
Set in Times.

Publishers Note
Every possible effort has been made to ensure that the information contained in this
book is accurate at the time of going to press, and the publisher and author cannot accept responsibility for any errors or omissions, however caused. No responsibility for
loss or damage occasioned to any person acting, or refraining from action, as a result
of the material in this publication can be accepted by the editor, the publisher or any
of the authors.

CONTRIBUTORS' BIOGRAPHIES

Dr Hephzibah Egede

Dr Hephzibah Egede is Senior Lecturer in Law at the University of Buckingham. She is a dual qualified lawyer with admissions in England and Wales and Nigeria. In Nigeria, she worked as a commercial lawyer in Chris Ogunbanjo and Co, and with Mobil Producing Nigeria Unlimited (an Exxon-Mobil upstream subsidiary). She is currently co-director of the University of Buckingham Centre for Extractive Energy Studies (UBCEES) and pathway leader in the LLM International Oil and Gas Law in the School of Law, University of Buckingham. She previously worked with the ESRC Centre for Business Relationships, Accountability, Sustainability and Society (BRASS) at Cardiff University and acted as lead researcher to 'Law and Your Environment', a project funded by the United Kingdom Environmental Law Association (UKELA). The project led to the establishment of the Lord Nathan Memorial Fund for the Environment. Her research interests include Energy Governance and Natural Resource Management, Law and Development, Social Justice and Gender Empowerment, Legal Pluralism and Customary Governance in Sub-Saharan Africa.

Dr Lucas Lixinski

Dr Lucas Lixinski is Associate Professor at Faculty of Law, UNSW Sydney. He researches and writes extensively in the areas of international heritage law and international human rights law, often at the intersection of the two. He is Rapporteur of the International Law Association Committee on Participation in Global Heritage Governance, and sits on the Board of Editors of the International Journal of Heritage Studies, among other international journals. He is the author of *Intangible Cultural Heritage in International Law* (Oxford University Press, 2013) and *International Heritage Law for Communities: Exclusion and Re-Imagination* (Oxford University Press, 2019), as well as many other publications, which have appeared in leading journals like the American Journal of International Law, the European Journal of International Law, and the Leiden Journal of International Law, among others.

Professor Jo Samanta

Professor Jo Samanta is Emeritus Professor of Medical Law at De Montfort University, Leicester, UK. She was formerly Professor of Medical Law (2016-2018) and Reader (2014-2016) at De Montfort University. She has previously lectured at Nottingham Trent University and the Open University of Hong Kong. She has published widely, predominantly in the areas of medical law and ethics in top peer-reviewed journals including Medical Law Review, Cambridge Law Review, Journal of Law and Society, and the Journal of Medical Ethics. She has also published in high impact healthcare journals such as the BMJ, Nursing Ethics and Clinical Medicine. She has a particular area in empirical socio-legal studies and she has led and collaborated on a range of national and international funded projects. She is also a qualified solicitor, nurse and midwife with experience in the UK and South Africa.

Dr Sarah Sargent

Dr Sarah Sargent is a Reader in Critical Heritage Studies (Law) at the University of Buckingham. She is licensed to practise law (licenses currently inactive) in Colorado, Kansas, and Maryland, USA. Her legal practice focused on family law issues, including the rights of indigenous peoples under the Indian Child Welfare Act. She is currently the Chief Editor of the Denning Law Review and Director of the University of Buckingham Equine Law and Policy Research Centre. Her research interests include indigenous rights and intangible cultural heritage from an inter-disciplinary perspective.

Dr Jocelynne Scutt

Dr Jocelynne A. Scutt is Senior Teaching Fellow at the University of Buckingham. A barrister and human rights lawyer, she has advised and represented Indigenous Australians and Indigenous Australian organisations in cases relating to land rights, payroll tax, race discrimination, finance and credit, and criminal law. As a Judge and Judge of Appeal in Fiji, amongst others, she heard cases involving the customary law of the land. Her books include the *Artemis Women's Voices, Women's Lives* series (some 8 volumes), *The Incredible Woman – Power & Sexual Politics* (in 2 volumes), *Women & Magna Carta - A Treaty for Rights or Wrongs?* and *Women, Law & Culture – Conformity, Contradiction and Culture*. Her films include *Covered*, an installation addressing the controversy surrounding the hijab and burqa *The Incredible Woman* (with Karen Buczynski-Lee), and *A Greenshell Necklace* (with Deborah Hocking and Leah Brown).

Professor Valentina Vadi

Professor Valentina Vadi is a Professor of International Economic Law at Lancaster University, United Kingdom and Senior Grotius Fellow at Michigan Law School, United States. She was formerly a Reader in International Business Law at Lancaster University (2013-2015), an Emile Noël Fellow at the Jean Monnet Centre for International and Regional Economic Law at New York University

(2013-2014), and a Marie Curie Postdoctoral Fellow at Maastricht University (2011-2013). In addition, Professor Vadi lectured at Hasselt University (Belgium), the University of Rome III (Italy), the China EU School of Law (P.R. China) and Maastricht University (The Netherlands). She has published more than eighty articles in various areas of public international law in top journals, including the Harvard International Law Journal, the Vanderbilt Journal of Transnational Law, the Stanford Journal of International Law, the Columbia Human Rights Review, the European Journal of International Law, the Journal of International Economic Law and others. She is the co-editor (with Hildegard Schneider) of *Art, Cultural Heritage and the Market: Legal and Ethical Issues* (Springer: Heidelberg, 2014), and (with Bruno De Witte) of *Culture and International Economic Law* (Routledge, 2015). Valentina Vadi is the author of *Public Health in International Investment Law and Arbitration* (Routledge, 2012), *Cultural Heritage in International Investment Law and Arbitration* (Cambridge University Press, 2014), and *Analogies in International Investment Law and Arbitration* (Cambridge University Press, 2016).

INTRODUCTION

There has been a great deal written about the United Nations Declaration on the Rights of Indigenous Peoples—both before and after its approval in 2007 by the United Nations General Assembly. Prior to its approval, it faced a long and at times contentious drafting period. Just what were indigenous rights? How would they be understood alongside existing international legal regimes? Were these human rights or the rights of peoples? All of these issues were potential flashpoints in the drafting of the instrument, and the decisions made along the way by both states and non-state contributors to the Declaration have shaped the way in which indigenous rights are viewed today. The long drafting process was perhaps noteworthy. But equally noteworthy is the contribution that was made to the instrument by indigenous peoples themselves. Writing in 2009, Professor Aliza Organick notes that the involvement of indigenous peoples in the drafting process "ensured that the document is not wholly positive law, an extraordinary feat."[1] The content of the document then was something that "reflects and sets forth the principles, values, and aspirations"[2] of indigenous peoples.

There was, at the time of its approval, nearly unanimous optimism about the potential of the UNDRIP to make a real difference to the lives of indigenous peoples. Has this optimism been borne out? To what extent has the UNDRIP made a difference, and if so, how has it done so? These are important considerations in judging the ability of international law, including international human rights law, to achieve its aims.

As of the time of writing, indigenous rights are recognized as a category of human rights, mostly unproblematically. It may come as a surprise then to know that at one point in the drafting history of the UNDRIP, there was a fierce disagreement as to whether indigenous rights ought to be seen as human rights, or whether they were in fact, another species of rights altogether—more akin to the rights of peoples who were creating new states.

---

1. A Organick, "Listening to Indigenous Voices: What the UN Declaration on the Rights of Indigenous Peoples Means for US Tribes" (2009) 16(1) *University of California, Davis* 172, 174.
2. Ibid., 174.

The drafting process was a matter of deciding what indigenous rights would look like on paper, and also a matter of political expediency to ensure that sufficient state support existed to pass a resolution to approve the Declaration. Despite the inclusion of non-state drafting members, states remained the key to the approval of any Declaration.

Morgan traces the ways in which conceptions of indigenous rights changed over the long negotiations over the Declaration's content. She argues that there were three different ways in which indigenous rights were framed, with the first as a right to self-determination.[3] This proved to be a very contested way of interpreting indigenous rights, one that proved to be a threat to states, "due to the association of self-determination with the formation of independent states, and fears that its recognition [of indigenous peoples] could lead to secession and territorial dismemberment."[4] A second frame was that of "peace and security"[5] which urged a different understanding of self-determination which views it "as a *contribution* to peace and security"[6] rather than as a threat to states.[7] That this second frame was not internalized by states is evident in the delay and subsequent amendments to the Draft Declaration meant to alleviate fears about possible indigenous secession. The third frame is that of environmental rights, where "recognition of indigenous rights, particularly the right to self-determination with all its attributes, contributes to the ecologically sustainable use, management and preservation of the world's ecosystems."[8] Despite the stereotyping of indigenous peoples that occurs within the environmental frame,[9] it has proven to be a remarkably effective one for garnering international support and sympathy for indigenous rights. Morgan notes the high priority that the international community has placed on environmental issues[10] and suggests that the inclusion of indigenous rights within the environmental frame has meant that indigenous rights "have resounded with broader private and public concerns and understandings about the environment."[11]

Since its approval, the focus on the Declaration has changed from at times semantic debates about what rights ought to be, and instead has focused on what these mean in practice, and how they are to be interpreted. To what extent are these three frames, and the problems of interpretation and implementation implicit in each, active in the way in which the UNDRIP has been used since its 2007 approval?

---

3. R Morgan, "Advancing Indigenous Rights at the United Nations: Strategic Framing and Its Impact on the Normative Development of International Law" (2004) 13(4) *Social and Legal Studies* 481, 485-488.
4. Ibid., 482.
5. Ibid., 490.
6. Ibid., 490, emphasis in the original.
7. Ibid., 488-492.
8. Ibid., 492.
9. Ibid., 493-495.
10. Ibid., 495-496.
11. Ibid., 496.

The chapters in this book consider the practical impacts of the UNDRIP in a variety of settings and issues. A consistent theme is that the promise of UNDRIP has not been realized—that the potential of the instrument to make a positive difference in the lives of indigenous peoples in resolving issues, including those that pre-date the UNDRIP has fallen short. Indigenous concerns range from land rights, to the safeguarding of cultural heritage, to an understanding of what it means to be indigenous in the twenty-first century, to the ways in which indigenous rights intersect with the larger body of international law.

A predominant question addressed across the chapters is what the necessary interplay for realization of the rights in the UNDRIP is, what roles states should play, and what role they must play in a pragmatic sense for the delivery of rights. How far the UNDRIP can go to pressurise recalcitrant states into taking a positive and proactive stance on rights is examined across issues of economic development, cultural heritage, and land rights.

In the first chapter, Professor Valentina Vadi discusses the protection of indigenous rights within international economic law. She addresses the tensions that arise when economic development is in conflict with the safeguarding of indigenous culture. International indigenous rights intersect with many other areas of international law. Not all of these intersections are contentious. But the instance of the intersection discussed by Professor Vadi raises critical questions about the way in which international law should be utilised in attempting to resolve competing interests. She urges that it is possible for international economic law to take account of indigenous cultural rights. She recognizes that "a clash of cultures between the protection of indigenous heritage and the promotion of economic activities under distinct international law regimes"[12] but sees international law as holding promise in respecting local culture and traditions of indigenous people. One way forward, she argues, is the inclusion of indigenous rights within trade treaties which are subject to periodic negotiation and re-drafting. The possibilities of indigenous rights being recognized and safeguarded through treaties is in some ways redolent with argument about sovereignty and self-determination—and yet—this solution leaves states very much in the vanguard of indigenous rights realization—something that states historically have not demonstrated a willingness or reliability to do. This in no small part is what has led to the principle of self-identification and the lack of a definition within UNDRIP as to who is indigenous. These are themes that are picked up in subsequent chapters.

Lucas Lixinski's chapter likewise deals with the safeguarding of indigenous cultural heritage within international law. His chapter looks specifically at the intersection of the UNESCO Convention on the Safeguarding of Intangible

---

12. V Vadi, 33.

Heritage and the UNDRIP, using a case study of the Wayúu peoples of Venezuela and Colombia. Using the concept of "multi-sourced equivalent norms," he considers the ways in which norms found in both international instruments can work together to strengthen the safeguarding of intangible elements of indigenous cultural heritage. He turns again to the solution of local involvement in the implementation of international norms, arguing that "community involvement in heritage management at the international level holds the key for greater fairness in the safeguarding of indigenous cultures."[13]

Dr Sarah Sargent's chapter addresses the ability of the UNDRIP to provide a satisfactory resolution of long-standing indigenous land rights claims in the United States. Her chapter examines the claims raised about Western Shoshone land, rights which were protected by a treaty with the United States. Despite decisions that were favourable to the Western Shoshone claims from the Inter-American Court of Human Rights and the Committee for the Convention on the Elimination of All Racial Discrimination, the United States has done nothing to comply. This chapter considers whether the UNDRIP provides any potential means of resolving land disputes, and concludes that it represents an opportunity that was lost. The final rendition of the UNDRIP is frustratingly silent, rather than serving as a guide, on matters such as venue and forms of compensation. Indigenous frustration with the failure of the international legal system to provide an effective resolution to indigenous concerns has led to another reformulation of self-determination—this time in the form of "sustainable self-determination," as defined by indigenous groups, as a means of infusing this principle with indigenous normative meaning and as a means of safeguarding indigenous heritage—which is bound up inextricably with indigenous land. That land issues remain highly contentious is highlighted in the discussion of the Standing Rock Reservation issues which illustrate the continued need for a solution that recognizes and respects indigenous land rights and claims.

The fourth chapter, by Dr Jocelynne Scutt, addresses the ongoing indigenous rights struggle in Australia. Australia was notably one of the four states (along with Canada, New Zealand and the United States) which originally opposed the approval of the UNDRIP. It subsequently reversed its position to one of support for the UNDRIP. But as Dr Scutt asks, with what consequence? She argues that there remains a great deal of internal opposition to an effective implementation of the UNDRIP, a position that resonates against a backdrop of a history of colonization. She comments that "Almost 250 years of colonisation, settlement or invasion cannot be undone simply, if at all."[14] In the face of this legacy, the future of the UNDRIP's effectiveness within Australia remains uncertain.

---

13. L Lixinski, 53.
14. Scutt, 81

This chapter highlights the very formidable obstacles that stand in the way of realization of the rights within the UNDRIP.

Professor Jo Samanta examines another significant issue surrounding indigenous rights, namely that of indigenous knowledge-based claims and the relationships between indigenous peoples and third parties who seek to use that knowledge.[15] She explores the limitations of current international law in the safeguarding of indigenous interests in their traditional claims. Indigenous and traditional knowledge are potential sources of profit for pharmaceutical companies, leaving indigenous groups vulnerable to exploitation when laws do not provide an adequate base for safeguarding. The UNDRIP may hold real possibilities for better safeguarding, particularly when combined with other international law instruments which offer useful alternatives to the international intellectual property frameworks that are dominated by Western thinking. Here the strength of the UNDRIP is seen in its ability to be used in combination with other important international instruments that address indigenous and traditional knowledge interests and rights.

The safeguarding of indigenous interests in natural wealth and resources is raised by Dr Hephzibah Egede in her chapter. As with the chapter by Professor Samanta, she considers the usefulness of the UNDRIP in addressing indigenous rights and interests through an exploration of "how international regimes on indigenous rights such as the United Nations Declaration on the Rights of Indigenous Peoples (UNDRIP) 2007 can be deployed to promote the use of a homegrown 'African Legal ordering' in the transnational management of natural resources in Sub-Saharan Africa."[16] She argues that a system that is able to be inclusive of and comprised of African customary norms is necessary to protect community interests in natural resources and avoid exploitation by oil companies. The ability of the UNDRIP to be part of a transformative African-centric legal system demonstrates yet another avenue as to how this soft law instrument can be of enormous effect on the rights and daily lives of people. Returning to the frames for rights that Morgan has set forth, again and again, in these differing contexts and in different settings across the world, it is the first frame, that of self-determination, which predominates. Indigenous rights may have been framed in one way as a political package for garnering support, but the pragmatics of their exercise raises persistent questions about the role of states in providing human rights and the way in which the local indigenous community interacts with the state system and the international system to exercise those rights. In short, there is no escaping the prevalence of self-determination as the lynchpin for rights and the inclusion of indigenous communities in the post UNDRIP period.

---

15. Egede, 141.
16. Egede, 133

The UNDRIP contains unambiguous statements about the rights of indigenous peoples to internal self-determination, an internal self-determination shorn of any lingering suggestion that it carries with it any right to cede from the state. Setting limits on self-determination was a critical part of obtaining state approval. Providing a meaningful exercise for self-determination is a critical theme that runs throughout each chapter. How self-determination might be exercised varies in location and on the kind of issue being considered, but again and again, the importance, indeed, the necessity, of the active inclusion of indigenous communities resounds in each chapter. Although the UNDRIP is seen to have fallen short of what it might have been and might have done, the simple provision of a statement of indigenous rights to internal self-determination may yet be its most important contribution to the framework of indigenous rights, both at the international and state level. That the UNDRIP in combination with other international instruments or as a backdrop to the promotion and inclusion of non-Western norms in legal systems can be an effective way to promote indigenous rights demonstrates its undoubted potential to achieve what it set out to do in the first place.

GLOBAL V. LOCAL: THE PROTECTION OF INDIGENOUS HERITAGE IN INTERNATIONAL ECONOMIC LAW

Valentina Vadi[†]

INTRODUCTION

Indigenous cultural heritage plays an essential role in the building of the identity of indigenous peoples and thus its protection has profound significance for the realization of their human rights. Although the recognition of indigenous peoples' rights and cultural heritage has gained some momentum at the international law level since the adoption of the 2007 United Nations Declaration on the Rights of Indigenous Peoples (UNDRIP),[1] law and policy tend to prioritize macroeconomic notions of growth in spite of actual or potential infringements of indigenous entitlements.[2] Many of the estimated 370 million indigenous people around the world have lost or risk losing their ancestral lands because of the exploitation of natural resources.[3]

[†] The research leading to these results has received funding from the European Research Council under the European Union's ERC Starting Grant Agreement n. 639564. The Article reflects the author's views only and not necessarily those of the Union. The author wishes to thank Sarah Sargent and Jo Samanta for helpful comments on an earlier draft. The usual disclaimer applies.
1. United Nations Declaration on the Rights of Indigenous Peoples, A/RES/61/295 (2007).
2. L Barrera-Hernández, "Indigenous Peoples, Human Rights and Natural Resource Development: Chile's Mapuche Peoples and the Right to Water" (2005) 11 *Annual Survey of International & Comparative Law* 1.
3. N Pillay, "Let us Ensure that Development for Some is not to the Detriment of the Human Rights of Others", Statement by the United Nations High Commissioner for Human Rights, http://www.ohchr.org/EN/NewsEvents/Pages/DisplayNews.aspx?NewsID=11284&LangID=E (2011).

While the clash between economic development and indigenous peoples' rights is by no means new, this chapter approaches this well-known issue from a new perspective by focusing on international economic law. This chapter investigates the question of whether local indigenous ways of life can prevail over international economic governance. The protection of indigenous heritage has intersected with international trade law, creating clashes between indigenous culture and free trade. In parallel, a potential tension exists when a state adopts cultural policies that interfere with foreign investments as such policies may be deemed to amount to indirect expropriation or a violation of other investment treaty provisions. The key question of this study is whether international economic law has embraced a pure international economic culture or if, on the other hand, it is open to including cultural concerns in its operation. Until recently, international economic law had developed only limited tools for the protection of cultural heritage through dispute settlement.[4] However, recent arbitral awards have shown a growing awareness of the need to protect indigenous cultural heritage within investment disputes. The number of cases in which arbitrators have balanced the different values at stake is increasing.[5] In parallel, at the World Trade Organization (WTO), the case concerning the seal products ban adopted by the European Union (EU) has brought to the fore a veritable clash of cultures between moral concerns about animal welfare on the one hand, and indigenous cultural practices and free trade on the other.

This chapter proceeds as follows. *First*, it addresses the following issue: since indigenous heritage is "local" by definition, should its governance be purely local or should it pertain to international law? The latter approach is to be preferred in the light of historical reasons and relevant contemporary international law instruments. The international norms protecting indigenous cultural heritage will be scrutinized and particular reference will be made to the UNDRIP. *Second*, the chapter briefly sketches out the main features of international economic governance, referring to both the World Trade Organization and investment law regimes and their sophisticated dispute settlement mechanisms. *Third*, the chapter analyses and critically assesses relevant case studies. *Fourth*, this chapter offers some legal options to better reconcile the different interests at stake. *Fifth*, it draws some conclusions, arguing that the UNDRIP contributes significantly to the current discourse on indigenous heritage. This does not mean that further steps should not be taken. On the contrary, the collision between the protection of economic interests and indigenous entitlements in international law makes the case for strengthening the current regime in place for the protection of indigenous heritage. In particular, the participation of indigenous peoples in the decisions that affect their rights and heritage is crucial.

---

4. See generally V Vadi, "When Cultures Collide: Foreign Direct Investment, Natural Resources and Indigenous Heritage in International Investment Law" (2011) 42 *Columbia Human Rights Law Review* 797-889.
5. Ibid.

GLOBAL V LOCAL: THE INTERNATIONAL PROTECTION OF INDIGENOUS HERITAGE

As indigenous heritage is "local" by definition, should its governance be purely local or should it pertain to international law? Indigenous communities are geographically rooted in given places (*loci*), yet politically, historically, and legally situated between the national and the international spheres. Geographically, indigenous peoples are "*indigenous*" "because their ancestral roots are embedded in the lands on which they live … much more deeply than the roots of more powerful sectors of society living on the same lands."[6] They are "culturally distinctive societies that find themselves engulfed by settler societies born of the forces of empire and conquest."[7] They have been living in a given territory long before the establishment of the nation state under whose sovereignty they live today.[8]

Politically, indigenous peoples are situated between the national and the international arenas. For decades, indigenous peoples have been considered to be mere components of states rather than "legal unit[s] of international law."[9] They used to be subjects of domestic law only.[10] As Daes puts it, international law seemed to know no other subjects than states.[11]

Historically, however, indigenous nations have played a role in international relations, signed treaties, and used to be recognised as sovereign nations. The issues of "[indigenous] rights and sovereignty are rooted in the first encounters between the [tribes] and the colonial powers of the sixteenth and seventeenth centuries."[12] Historically, many scholars acknowledged the sovereignty and territorial rights of indigenous peoples, including Francisco de Vitoria (1483–1546) and Alberico Gentili (1552–1608) among others. They saw indigenous

---

6. J Anaya, *Indigenous Peoples in International Law*. (Oxford: Oxford University Press 2nd edition, 2004) 3.
7. Ibid.
8. Art. 1 of the ILO Convention 169 concerning Indigenous and Tribal Peoples in Independent Countries defines "indigenous peoples" "on account of their descent from the populations which inhabited the country, or a geographical region to which the country belongs, at the time of conquest or colonization or the establishment of present state boundaries and who, irrespective of their legal status, retain some or all of their own social, economic, cultural and political institutions."
9. *Cayuga Indians (Gr. Brit.) v. United States*, 6 Review of International Arbitral Awards 173 (1926) 176 (stating that an Indian tribe "is not a legal unit of international law.")
10. S Wiessner, "Indigenous Self-Determination, Culture, and Land: A Reassessment in Light of the 2007 UN Declaration on the Rights of Indigenous Peoples" in E Pulitano (ed.) *Indigenous Rights in the Age of the UN Declaration* (Cambridge: Cambridge University Press, 2012) 38. See also W Twining, *General Jurisprudence: Understanding Law from a Global Perspective* (Cambridge: Cambridge University Press, 2008) 362 (calling the assumption that domestic law consists of the state law and that public international law consists of the law of sovereign states as the "Westphalian duo"); R Dibadj, "Panglossian Transnationalism" (2008) 44 *Stanford Journal of International Law* 253, 256 (noting that as "a product of the Westphalian state-centered system of world law", international law "maintains that the states are the only subjects of international law…")
11. E-I Daes, "Indigenous Peoples' Rights to their Natural Resources" in A Constantinides and N Zaikos (eds.) *The Diversity of International Law* (Leiden/Boston: Martinus Nijhoff, 2009).
12. AF Kinney, "The Tribe, the Empire, and the Nation: Enforceability of Pre-Revolutionary Treaties with Native American Tribes" (2007-2008) 39 *Case Western Reserve Journal of International Law* 897, 898-99 (referring to the situation of indigenous tribes in Virginia).

sovereignty "as preventing land from being classified as *terra nullius*, or open to acquisition by mere occupation."[13] After "years of warfare, disease, and increasingly scarce natural resources," indigenous peoples likely assented to various treaties with colonial powers to prevent further encroachments of their sovereignty to "preserve what remained of their heritage and traditional way of life."[14] The aim of most treaties between the colonial powers and Aboriginal peoples "was to preserve Aboriginal self-government rather than cede sovereignty. The treaties were protective in nature, incorporating binding and effective clauses preserving Aboriginal rights in perpetuity."[15] Soon considered part of the new states, indigenous peoples "would encounter many difficulties in enforcing their treaty rights in either the municipal or international courts."[16]

The sovereignty of indigenous peoples has long been a matter of debate and "continues to be one of the most burning issues in domestic and international law today."[17] For indigenous peoples, indigenous sovereignty "has never been ceded or extinguished," and co-exists with the sovereignty of the state. For indigenous peoples, this parallel sovereignty is "a spiritual notion" representing the ancestral tie between the land, or "mother nature", and indigenous peoples.[18] Most indigenous peoples "seek not to secede from the territories in which they reside, but rather to wield greater control over matters such as natural resources, environmental preservation of their homelands, education, use of language, and [autonomy] … in order to ensure their group's cultural preservation and integrity."[19] Several countries have adopted notions of concurrent sovereignty, recognizing the sovereignty of indigenous peoples within their lands.[20] Within tribal sovereignty, cultural sovereignty has central relevance, as it enables "[p]rotecting and enjoying the fruits of tribal culture, and maintaining the power to decide how culture will be disseminated."[21]

Due to the failures of the early treaties and national law to address indigenous peoples' rights adequately, international law has increasingly regulated indigenous peoples' matters in the past decades, reaffirming their rights and various entitlements. The emergence of the human rights paradigm in the aftermath of WWII and the decolonization process have given momentum to the renaissance of indigenous rights at the international level by fostering the adoption of

---

13. J Cassidy, "Sovereignty of Aboriginal Peoples" 9 (1998) *Indiana International and Comparative Law Review* 65, 69.
14. Kinney, note 12, 902 (noting that these treaties "remained hardly more than empty words", proving to be "little more than a cessation of open hostilities".)
15. Cassidy, note 13, 96.
16. Ibid., 98.
17. Ibid., 69.
18. J. Brave Noise Cat, "Indigenous Sovereignty is on the Rise: Can it Shape the Course of History?" *The Guardian*, 30 May 2017 (quoting the "Uluru Statement from the Heart" issued by Aboriginal and Torres Strait Islander Tribes (2017)).
19. J Corntassel and T Hopkins Primeau, "Indigenous Sovereignty and International Law: Revised Strategies for Pursuing Self-Determination" (1995) 17 *Human Rights Quarterly* 343, 344.
20. Cassidy, note 13, 109.
21. E M. Genia, "The Landscape and Language of Indigenous Cultural Rights" (2012) 44 *Arizona State Law Journal* 653, 655.

international law instruments recognizing indigenous peoples' rights. There has been a paradigm shift in international law; and indigenous peoples have been deemed as "legal subjects" under the same.[22]

At the international level, indigenous peoples' rights have been protected and promoted in two complementary ways: on the one hand, the protection and promotion of indigenous peoples' rights remain embedded in the human rights framework. On the other hand, indigenous peoples have supported the creation of special forums and bodies that exclusively deal with their situation as well as the elaboration of legal instruments that focus on their rights.[23] For instance, the creation of the United Nations Permanent Forum for Indigenous Issues (UNPFII) reflects the efforts of indigenous peoples "to create space for themselves and their issues" within the United Nations machinery.[24] Analogously, both the 1989 International Labour Organization Convention Concerning Indigenous and Tribal Peoples in Independent Countries (ILO Convention No. 169)[25] and the United Nations Declaration on the Rights of Indigenous Peoples (UNDRIP)[26] are special instruments for the protection of indigenous peoples.

While a number of international law instruments protect different aspects of indigenous heritage, indigenous culture plays a central role in the UNDRIP. Drafted with the very active participation of indigenous representatives, the Declaration constitutes the outcome of two decades of preparatory work.[27] While this landmark instrument is currently not binding, this may change in the future to the extent that its provisions reflect customary international law.[28] The Declaration constitutes a significant achievement for indigenous peoples worldwide.[29] Not only does it re-empower indigenous peoples, but it also shifts

---

22. For a seminal study, see R L Barsch, "Indigenous Peoples in the 1990s: From Object to Subject of International Law" (1994) 7 *Harvard Human Rights Journal* (1994) 33. See also J Gilbert, *Indigenous Peoples' Land Rights under International Law: From Victims to Actors* (Ardsley: Transnational Publishers, 2006).
23. K Göcke, "Protection and Realization of Indigenous Peoples' Land Rights at the National and International Level" 5 *Goettingen Journal of International Law* (2013) 124.
24. S Sargent, "Transnational Networks and United Nations Human Rights Structural Change: The Future of Indigenous and Minority Rights" (2012) 16 *International Journal of Human Rights* 123-151, 136 (also noting that the membership composition of the UNPFII – of state and indigenous representatives on equal footing – "is a unique achievement in international indigenous rights, and indeed, in international law". Ibid., 139).
25. International Labour Organization Convention Concerning Indigenous and Tribal Peoples in Independent Countries (ILO Convention No. 169), 27 June 1989, 28 ILM 1382.
26. United Nations Declaration on the Rights of Indigenous Peoples (UNDRIP) G.A. Res. 61/295, U.N. Doc. A/RES/61/295 (13 September 2007). The Declaration was approved by 143 nations, but was opposed by United States, Canada, New Zealand and Australia. However, these four nations subsequently endorsed the Declaration.
27. Daes, n. 11, 31.
28. On the legal status of the Declaration, see M Barelli, "The Role of Soft Law in the International Legal System: The Case of the United Nations Declaration on the Rights of Indigenous Peoples" (2009) 58 *International and Comparative Law Quarterly* 957 (arguing that "regardless of its non-binding nature, the Declaration has the potential effectively to promote and protect the rights of ... indigenous peoples" and that "the relevance of a soft law instrument cannot be aprioristically dismissed." Ibid., 983).
29. E Pulitano, "Indigenous Rights and International Law: An Introduction", in E Pulitano (ed.) *Indigenous Rights in the Age of the UN Declaration* (Cambridge: Cambridge University Press, 2012) 25.

the discourse on their rights from the local to the international level with an intensity that was missing before. As Stavenhagen notes, "[t]he Declaration provides an opportunity to link the global and local levels, in a process of *glocalization*."[30]

Indigenous culture is a key theme of the Declaration.[31] Many articles are devoted to different aspects of indigenous culture; and the word "culture" appears no less than 30 times in its text.[32] Not only does the UNDRIP recognize the dignity and diversity of indigenous peoples' cultures, it also acknowledges their essential contribution to the common heritage of mankind.[33] The Declaration recognizes the right of indigenous peoples to practice their cultural traditions[34] and maintain their distinctive spiritual and material relationship with the land that they have traditionally owned, occupied or otherwise used.[35]

For indigenous peoples, land is the basis not only of economic livelihood, but also the source of spiritual and cultural identity.[36] Indigenous peoples maintain cultural and spiritual ties with the territory they have traditionally occupied,[37] not only due to the presence of sacred sites but also because of the intrinsic sacred value of the territory itself.[38] They "see the land and the sea, all of the sites they contain, and the knowledge and the laws associated with those sites, as a single entity that must be protected as a whole."[39] Although indigenous cultures vary across continents, "there is a common thread that runs through these diverse indigenous groups—a deep cultural and spiritual connection to the land, and a belief that the world is interconnected. Native peoples traditionally strive to live sustainably with the land, as stewards of it."[40] Because of the holistic worldview of indigenous peoples, a UN study insists that all the elements of indigenous

30. R Stavenhagen, "Making the Declaration Work" in C Charters and R Stavenhagen (eds.) *Making the Declaration Work: The United Nations Declaration on the Rights of Indigenous Peoples* (Copenhagen: IWGIA, 2009) 357.
31. S Wiessner, "The Cultural Rights of Indigenous Peoples: Achievements and Continuing Challenges" (2011) 22 *European Journal of International Law* 121, 139.
32. See Y Donders "The UN Declaration on the Rights of Indigenous Peoples. A Victory for Cultural Autonomy?" in I Boerefijn and J Goldschmidt (eds.) *Changing Perceptions of Sovereignty and Human Rights* (Antwerp/Oxford/Portland: Intersentia, 2008) 99.
33. UNDRIP, preamble.
34. UNDRIP, Article 11.
35. See eg. UNDRIP, preamble, Articles 8, 11, 12.1 and 13.1.
36. J Gilbert, "Custodians of the Land – Indigenous Peoples, Human Rights and Cultural Integrity" in M Langfield, W Logan and M Craith (eds.), *Cultural Diversity, Heritage and Human Rights* (Oxon: Routledge, 2010) 31.
37. Inter-Am. Ct. H.R., *Mayagna (Sumo) Awas Tigni Community v. Nicaragua*, Judgment of 31 August 2001, IACtHR Series C, No. 79, 75, para. 149 (clarifying that "For indigenous communities, relations to the land are not merely a matter of possession and production but a material and spiritual element which they must fully enjoy, even to preserve their cultural legacy and transmit it to future generations.")
38. Inter-Am. Ct. H.R., *Case of the Saramaka People v. Suriname*, Judgment on Preliminary Objections, Merits, Reparations and Costs, 28 November 2007, (ser. C) No. 172, para. 82.
39. C O'Faircheallaigh, "Negotiating Cultural Heritage? Aboriginal Mining Company Agreements in Australia" (2003) 39 *Development and Change* 27.
40. Genia, note 21, 659.

cultural heritage "should be managed and protected as a single, interrelated and integrated whole."[41]

Among the different theoretical models that have been proposed to deal with indigenous peoples' rights, the cultural integrity approach "emphasizes the value of traditional cultures in and of themselves as well as for the rest of society."[42] The cultural integrity model focuses on cultural considerations to protect indigenous peoples' identity, and acknowledges the dynamic nexus between indigenous peoples and their lands. More importantly, cultural integrity is essential to indigenous sovereignty. As a Native American scholar points out, indigenous sovereignty relies on a continued cultural integrity: "to the degree that a nation loses its sense of cultural identity, to that degree it suffers a loss of sovereignty."[43]

Some scholars criticize this approach, contending that an excessive emphasis on the cultural entitlements of indigenous peoples can lessen their political rights and restrain their claims to self-determination.[44] According to these authors, over-emphasizing culture risks undermining self-determination. Nonetheless, the protection of cultural rights and self-determination are not mutually exclusive and can be complementary. The cultural integrity approach is of fundamental importance for understanding and better protecting the culture and human rights of indigenous peoples in a holistic fashion.

Instead, a real limitation of the legal framework protecting indigenous cultural heritage is the absence – aside from the classical human rights mechanisms – of a special international court or tribunal, where indigenous peoples can raise complaints regarding measures that affect them.[45] In fact, while (national and regional) courts and (international) monitoring bodies have been extremely important in the process of enunciation and implementation of indigenous rights,[46] the lack of a dedicated world court allows indigenous heritage related cases to be dealt with by international (economic) courts and tribunals with limited if no mandate to adjudicate indigenous claims. The UNDRIP does not change this situation. Therefore, notwithstanding the major political merits of

---

41. E-I Daes, *Study on the Protection of the Cultural and Intellectual Property of Indigenous Peoples*, Sub-Commission on Prevention of Discrimination and Protection of Minorities, UN Doc. E/CN.4/Sub 2/1993/28.

42. L Westra, *Environmental Justice and the Rights of Indigenous Peoples* (London: Earthscan, 2008) 10.

43. V Deloria Jr., "Self-Determination and the Concept of Sovereignty" in JR Wunder (ed.) *Native American Sovereignty* (New York: Garland, 1996) 118.

44. See generally C Cutler "The Globalization of International Law, Indigenous Identity, and the 'New Constitutionalism'," in W Coleman (ed.), *Property, Territory, Globalization: Struggles over Autonomy* (Vancouver: University of British Columbia Press, 2010).

45. Human rights may be claimed before national courts and regional human rights courts, as well as through particular complaint mechanisms at the UN level. I Watson and S Venne, "Talking Up Indigenous Peoples: Original Intent in a Space Dominated by State Interventions" in E Pulitano (ed.), *Indigenous Rights in the Age of the UN Declaration* (Cambridge: Cambridge University Press, 2012) 106.

46. See generally G Pentassuglia, "Towards a Jurisprudential Articulation of Indigenous Land Rights" (2011) 22 *European Journal of International Law* 165-202.

the Declaration, "UNDRIP does not definitively resolve, but at best temporarily mediates, multiple tensions."[47]

INTERNATIONAL ECONOMIC GOVERNANCE AND THE DIASPORA OF INDIGENOUS CULTURE RELATED DISPUTES BEFORE INTERNATIONAL ECONOMIC *FORA*.

International economic law is a well-developed field of study within the broader international law framework and is characterized by sophisticated dispute settlement mechanisms. While the dispute settlement mechanism of the World Trade Organization[48] has been defined as the "jewel in the crown" of this organization,[49] investment treaty arbitration has become the most successful mechanism for settling investment-related disputes.[50] Currently the objects of vehement criticism, both investor-state arbitration and WTO courts are experiencing a phase of reflection and perhaps transformation.

The creation of the WTO Dispute Settlement Body determined a major shift from the political consensus-based dispute settlement system of the GATT 1947[51] to a rule-based, architecture designed to strengthen the multilateral trade system.[52] The WTO Dispute Settlement Mechanism (DSM) is compulsory and exclusive.[53] Panels and the Appellate Body interpret and apply the WTO treaties, preserving the rights and obligations of the WTO members. Accordingly, they cannot add to or diminish the rights and obligations provided in the covered agreements. Their decisions are binding on the parties, and the Dispute Settlement Understanding (DSU provides remedies for breach of WTO law. [54]

At the procedural level, only WTO member states have *locus standi* in the DSM, i.e. individuals cannot file claims before panels and the Appellate Body.[55] When cultural heritage-related trade disputes emerge, Article 23.1 of the DSU

---

47. See K Engle, "On Fragile Architecture: The UN Declaration on the Rights of Indigenous Peoples in the Context of Human Rights" (2011) 22 *European Journal of International Law* 163 (contending that "Most of the work that has been done on the declaration since its passage has been far from critical" and concluding that "If we are willing to examine it critically, the UNDRIP may have the potential to become an important site for the ongoing struggle over the meaning of human rights ...").
48. Marrakesh Agreement Establishing the World Trade Organization, Apr. 15th 1994. 33 ILM 1144 (1994).
49. A Narlikar, *The WTO: A Very Short Introduction* (Oxford: Oxford University Press, 2005).
50. See generally S Franck, "Development and Outcomes of Investor-State Arbitration" (2009) 9 *Harvard Journal of International Law* 435-489.
51. General Agreement on Tariffs and Trade, 30 October 1947, 55 UNTS 194.
52. See generally SP Crowley and JH Jackson, "WTO Dispute Procedures, Standard of Review, and Deference to National Governments" (1996) 90 *American Journal of International Law* 193.
53. P Van Den Bossche and W Zdouc, *The Law and Policy of the World Trade Organization* (Cambridge: Cambridge University Press, 4th edn, 2017).
54. *Understanding on Rules and Procedures Governing the Settlement of Disputes*, Marrakesh Agreement Establishing the World Trade Organization, Annex 2, 1869 UNTS 401, 33 ILM 1226 (1994) [hereinafter DSU].
55. H Andersen, "Protection of Non-Trade Values in WTO Appellate Body Jurisprudence: Exceptions, Economic Arguments, and Eluding Questions" (2015) 18 *Journal of International Economic Law* 391.

obliges Members to subject the dispute exclusively to WTO bodies.[56] In *US–Section 301 Trade Act*, the Panel held that members "have to have recourse to the DSU DSM to the exclusion of any other system."[57] In *Mexico–Soft Drinks*, the Appellate Body clarified that the provision even implies that "that Member is entitled to a ruling by a WTO panel."[58] Pursuant to WTO settled case law and Art. XXIII:1 of the GATT 1994, each WTO Member which considers any of its benefits to be prejudiced under the covered agreements can bring a case before a panel.[59]

In parallel, as there is no single comprehensive multilateral investment agreement, more than 3000 international investment agreements define investors' rights, in addition to customary law and general principles of law. International investment law provides extensive protection to investors' rights in order to encourage foreign direct investment (FDI) and to foster economic development. At the substantive level, investment treaties provide for *inter alia*: adequate compensation for expropriated property; protection against discrimination; fair and equitable treatment; full protection and security; and assurances that the host country will honour its commitments regarding the investment.

At the procedural level, investment treaties provide investors with direct access to an international arbitral tribunal. This is a major novelty in international law, as customary international law does not provide such a mechanism. The use of the arbitration model aims at depoliticizing disputes, avoiding potential national court bias, and ensuring confidentiality and effectiveness.[60] Arbitral tribunals review state acts in the light of their investment treaties, impelling states to conform to international investment law and to adopt principles of good governance.

As mentioned, both investor–state arbitration and WTO "courts" have become the objects of intense scrutiny in the past few years. Even if one assumes that foreign investment is not harmful *per se* and that it is desirable to promote it, the argument goes that some rules of international investment law can hurt host states by limiting the state's ability to protect its citizens against various harms.[61] Moreover, investor–state arbitration is based on a model of commercial arbitration that seems ill suited to deal with (international) public law issues. Because arbitral tribunals are not generally subject to an appeal mechanism, inconsistent awards have resulted. In response to these criticisms, countries and commentators have proposed a range of alternatives moving towards some

---

56. DSU, Article 23.1.
57. WTO Panel Report, *US–Section 301 Trade Act, United States–Section 301-310 of the Trade Act of 1974*, WT/DS152/R, adopted January 27th 2000, DSR 2000:II. para 7.43.
58. WTO Appellate Body Report, *Mexico–Taxes on Soft Drinks, Mexico–Tax Measures on Soft Drinks and Other Beverages*, WT/DS308/AB/R adopted March 24th 2006, para 52.
59. GATT 1994, Article XIII:1.
60. IFI Shihata, "Towards a Greater Depoliticization of Investment Disputes: The Role of ICSID and MIGA" (1986) 1 *ICSID Review–Foreign Investment Law Journal* 1-25.
61. S Ratner, "International Investment Law through the Lens of Global Justice" (2017) 20 *Journal of International Economic Law* 747-775.

judicialization of the system.[62] In turn, and perhaps paradoxically, WTO courts have been under siege for their alleged judicial activism, and for being too judicialized.[63] While a discussion of the various reform proposals is outside the scope of this chapter, it will suffice to mention the fact that some reforms can actually foster the consideration of important policy objectives before international economic courts.

Given the current structural imbalance between the dispute settlement mechanisms provided by human rights treaties, and the sophisticated dispute settlement mechanisms available under international economic law, cultural disputes involving investors' or traders' rights have often been brought before international economic law "courts." Obviously, this does not mean that these are the only available *fora*, let alone the best *fora* for this kind of dispute. Other courts and tribunals are available such as national courts, human rights courts, regional economic courts, and the traditional state-to-state *fora* such as the International Court of Justice or even inter-state arbitration. Some of these dispute settlement mechanisms may be more suitable than investor–state arbitration or the WTO dispute settlement mechanism to address cultural concerns. Given its scope, this study focuses on the jurisprudence of the WTO bodies and arbitral tribunals.

One may wonder whether the fact that cultural disputes are adjudicated before international economic law *fora* determines a sort of institutional bias. Treaty provisions can be vague and their language encompasses a potentially wide variety of state regulation that may interfere with economic interests. Therefore, a potential tension exists when a state adopts regulatory measures interfering with foreign investments or free trade, as regulation may be considered as violating substantive standards of treatment under investment treaties or the WTO covered agreements. Thus, the affected foreign investor may require compensation before arbitral tribunals or spur the home state to file a claim before the WTO panels.

More specifically, with regard to the WTO DSB, "It is quite uncontroversial that an adjudicatory system engaged in interpreting trade-liberalizing standards would tend to favour free trade."[64] According to some empirical studies, there is a consistently high rate of complainant success in WTO dispute resolution[65] and authors have theorised that "the WTO panels and the WTO Appellate Body have interpreted the WTO agreements in a manner that consistently promotes the goal of expanding trade, often to the detriment of respondents' negotiated and reserved regulatory competencies."[66] In particular, given the fact that WTO courts have

62. A Roberts, "Incremental, Systemic, and Paradigmatic Reform of Investor-State Arbitration" (2018) 112 *American Journal of International Law* 410–432.
63. G Shaffer, "A Tragedy in the Making? The Decline of Law and the Return of Power in International Trade Relations" (2018) *Yale Journal of International Law* 1–17.
64. JF Colares, "A Theory of WTO Adjudication: From Empirical Analysis to Biased Rule Development" (2009) 42 *Vanderbilt Journal of Transnational Law* 383, 387 referring to JP Trachtman, "The Domain of WTO Dispute Resolution" (1999) 40 *Harvard International Law Journal* 333–377.
65. J Maton and C Maton, "Independence under Fire: Extra Legal Pressures and Coalition Building in WTO Dispute Settlement" (2007) 10 *Journal of International Economic Law* 317.
66. Colares, n. 64, 388.

settled about 80% of the cases in favour of the claimant, Colares highlighted that "the DSB has evolved WTO norms in a manner that consistently favors litigants whose interests are generally aligned with the unfettered expansion of trade."[67]

This study questions whether the same "institutional bias" is present in investor–state arbitration. Some scholars perceive this mechanism as biased in favour of economic interests, and disrespectful of "vital" non-economic interests.[68] Certainly, given the architecture of the arbitral process, significant concerns arise in the context of disputes involving indigenous heritage. While arbitration structurally constitutes a private model of adjudication, investment disputes present international public law aspects.[69] Arbitral awards ultimately shape the relationship between the state, on the one hand, and private individuals on the other.[70] Arbitrators determine matters such as the legality of governmental activity, the protection of individuals' rights, and the appropriate role of the state.[71]

Investor–state arbitration, however, distinguishes between two types of non-state actors: 1) foreign investors; and 2) the FDI impacted non-state actors, including indigenous peoples.[72] While foreign investors have direct access to investor–state arbitration, thus bypassing local courts,[73] the communities that have been affected by a given investment do not have automatic access to the system. Rather, they have access to local courts, and eventually, regional human rights courts, and the complaints procedure of the Human Rights Council. Therefore, only the respondent state of which indigenous communities are nationals, not the individuals themselves, can raise counterclaims for eventual violations of domestic law protecting indigenous rights. Furthermore, the investor can challenge adverse court decisions in the host state upholding complaints brought by private parties against a foreign investor, by contending that such judgments constitute wrongful interference with the investment, thus amounting to a denial of justice of a judicial expropriation of the investment before an arbitral tribunal.[74]

The increasing impact of FDI on local communities has raised the question of whether the principle of access to justice, as successfully developed for the benefit of investors through the provision of binding arbitration, ought to be

---

67. Ibid., 387.
68. R Broad, "Corporate Bias in the World Bank Group's International Centre for Settlement of Investment Disputes – A Case Study of a Global Mining Corporation Suing El Salvador" (2015) 36 *University of Pennsylvania Journal of International Law* 854.
69. G Van Harten, "The Public-Private Distinction in the International Arbitration of Individual Claims against the State" (2007) 56 *International & Comparative Law Quarterly* 371, 372.
70. G Van Harten, *Investment Treaty Arbitration and Public Law* (Oxford: Oxford University Press, 2007) 70.
71. M Sornarajah, "The Clash of Globalizations and the International Law on Foreign Investment" (2003) 10 *Canadian Foreign Policy* 1.
72. N Gal-Or, "The Investor and Civil Society as Twin Global Citizens: Proposing a New Interpretation in the Legitimacy Debate" (2008-2009) 32 *Suffolk Transnational Law Review* 271-301.
73. F Francioni, "Access to Justice, Denial of Justice, and International Investment Law" in P-M Dupuy, F Francioni and E-U Petersmann (eds.) *Human Rights in International Investment Law and Arbitration* (Oxford: Oxford University Press, 2009) 72.
74. M Sattorova, "Denial of Justice Disguised? Investment Arbitration and the Protection of Investors from Judicial Misconduct" (2012) 61 *International and Comparative Law Quarterly* 223.

matched by a corresponding right to a remedial process for individuals and groups adversely affected by the investment in the host state.[75] While the recognition of multinational corporations (MNCs) as "international corporate citizens" has progressed,[76] by comparison, the procedural rights of indigenous peoples have remained limited. The paradox is that foreign investors and indigenous peoples lie at opposite ends of the same spectrum: international investment agreements protect foreign investors because of their foreignness; international law protects indigenous peoples because of their indigeneity.[77] At the same time, however, both foreign investors and indigenous peoples have clearly defined rights under international law.[78] The following section addresses the question as to whether indigenous peoples' cultural entitlements play any role in the context of international disputes before international economic courts.

WHEN CULTURES COLLIDE

Many of the estimated 370 million indigenous peoples around the world have lost, or are under imminent threat of losing, their ancestral lands because of the exploitation of natural resources.[79] Conflicts and disputes over the use of indigenous lands have escalated apace across the world.[80] In parallel, free trade may destabilize indigenous communities by commodifying their cultural heritage, transforming their lifestyles, and affecting their traditional cultural practices.[81] Indigenous peoples consider that trade liberalization and FDI "are creating the most adverse impacts on [their] lives" through environmental degradation, forced relocation, and deforestation among others.[82] For instance, in an open letter to the President of the World Bank, they stated: "For the World Bank and the WTO, our forests are a marketable commodity. But for us, the forests are a home, our source of livelihood, the dwelling of our gods, the burial grounds of our ancestors, the inspiration of our culture."[83] The letter concluded with the request not to exploit their forests.

---

75. Francioni, n. 73, 71.
76. P Muchlinski, "Global Bukovina Examined: Viewing the Multinational Enterprise as a Transnational Law Making Community" in G Teubner (ed.) *Global Law Without a State* (London: Dartmouth, 1997) 79.
77. M Langfield, "Indigenous Peoples are Not Multicultural Minorities: Cultural Diversity, Heritage and Indigenous Human Rights in Australia" in M Langfield, W Logan and M Craith (eds.), *Cultural Diversity, Heritage and Human Rights* (Oxford: Routledge, 2010) pp 135-152.
78. Vadi, n. 4, 797-889.
79. Ibid.
80. C Rodriguez-Garavito, "Ethnicity.gov: Global Governance, Indigenous Peoples, and the Right to Prior Consultation in Social Minefields" (2011) 18 *Indiana Journal of Global Legal Studies* 266.
81. See for example CG Gonzalez, "An Environmental Justice Critique of Comparative Advantage: Indigenous Peoples, Trade Policy, and the Mexican Neoliberal Economic Reforms" (2010-2011) 32 *University of Pennsylvania Journal of International Law* 723 and KC Kennedy, "Trade and Foreign Investment in the Americas: The Impact on Indigenous Peoples and the Environment" (2006) 14 *Michigan State Journal of International Law* 139.
82. See Indigenous Peoples' Seattle Declaration, on the Third Ministerial meeting of the World Trade Organization, November 30th–December 3rd 1999.
83. A Pha, "WTO Collapse: Win for People", *Guardian*, December 8th 1999.

The clash between economic interests and indigenous peoples' entitlements can (and has) be(en) explored from a number of different angles. Due to space limits, this chapter focuses on one of the many aspects of the collision between indigenous rights and economic globalization: the clash between the protection of indigenous cultural heritage and the promotion of economic interests in international economic law.

Indigenous cultural heritage is based on a holistic understanding of natural resources, cultural practices, and human development. According to General Comment 23, "Culture manifests itself in many forms, including a particular way of life associated with the use of land resources, especially in the case of indigenous peoples. [Culture] may include such traditional activities as fishing or hunting. . . . The enjoyment of those rights may require positive legal measures of protection and measures to ensure the effective participation of members of minority communities in decisions that affect them. . . . The protection of these rights is directed to ensure the survival and continued development of the cultural, religious and social identity of the minorities concerned, thus enriching the fabric of society as a whole."[84] By contrast, international economic law has fostered a culture of efficiency, productivity, and exploitation of natural resources in the pursuit of profit and development. Conflicts between indigenous rights and economic interests of investors and traders frequently occur on all continents of the world.[85] Moreover, "indigenous peoples potentially suffer a disproportionate burden in such a conflict" as loss of land can affect their human rights including their cultural entitlements.[86] After exploring a recent arbitration, this section focuses on the seal products dispute adjudicated before the WTO "courts."

(a) Indigenous Cultural Heritage and the Promotion of Foreign Investments

The development of natural resources is increasingly taking place in, or very close to, traditional indigenous areas. While development analysts point to extractive projects as anti-poverty measures, and advocate FDI as a major catalyst for development,[87] "for the most part, the peoples in the areas where the resources are located tend to bear a disproportionate share of the negative impacts of development through reduced access to resources and direct exposure to pollution and environmental degradation."[88] In particular, rising investment in the extractive industries can have a devastating impact on the life and culture of the indigenous peoples involved.[89]

---

84. UN Human Rights Comm., *General Comment No. 23: The Rights of Minorities* (art. 27), paras 7, 9, UN Doc. CCPR/C/21/Rev.1/Add.5, April 8th 1994.

85. M Krepchev, "The Problem of Accommodating Indigenous Land Rights in International Investment Law" (2015) 6 *Journal of International Dispute Settlement* 43.

86. Ibid.

87. OECD, *Foreign Direct Investment for Development* (Paris: OECD 2002) 3.

88. Barrera-Hernández, n. 2, 6.

89. K Tienhaara, "What You Don't Know Can Hurt You: Investor-State Disputes and The Protection of the Environment in Developing Countries" (2006) 6 *Global Environmental Politics* 73-100.

The linkage between economic globalization and indigenous peoples' rights has been discussed by domestic courts,[90] and regional and international human rights bodies.[91] This jurisprudence and the relevant literature are extensive; what is less known is the emerging jurisprudence of arbitral tribunals dealing with elements of indigenous cultural heritage. Given the impact that arbitral awards can have on indigenous peoples' lives, scrutiny and critical assessment of these arbitrations is of the utmost relevance. In general, investment disputes with indigenous cultural elements are characterized by the need to balance the protection of indigenous cultural heritage and the promotion of foreign investments by the host state.

To date, several investment disputes have involved indigenous cultural heritage elements.[92] For reasons of space, it is not possible to examine all these awards in the context of this contribution; this section will thus examine and critically assess an investment dispute concerning the Ngöbe-Buglé indigenous peoples in Western Panama.[93]

Ngöbe land originally extended from the Pacific Ocean to the Caribbean Sea.[94] When Christopher Columbus and his crew encountered the tribes in 1502, the Spanish *conquistadores* forced the Ngöbe into less desirable territories.[95] The largest indigenous group in Panama, the Ngöbe are predominantly subsistence farmers.[96] Nowadays these communities live in a *"Comarca"*, that is, a specially designated area.[97] The law establishing this indigenous region (*Ley 10/1997*, or *Ley de la Comarca*) recognizes the right of indigenous peoples to collective ownership of land within these zones and grants indigenous tribes a certain autonomy. For the former Special Rapporteur on the Rights of Indigenous Peoples, Professor James Anaya, the creation of *comarcas* is "one of the foremost achievements in terms of the protection of indigenous rights in the world."[98] Nonetheless, the domestic legal framework protecting indigenous entitlements

90. T Chapman "Corroboree Shield: A Comparative Historical Analysis of (the Lack of) International, National and State Level Indigenous Cultural Heritage Protection" (2008) 5 *Macquarie Journal of International & Comparative Environmental Law* 81-96
91. See generally L Westra, *Environmental Justice and the Rights of Indigenous Peoples* (London: Earthscan, 2008).
92. V Vadi, *Cultural Heritage in International Investment Law and Arbitration* (Cambridge: Cambridge University Press, 2014); V Vadi, "Natural Resources and Indigenous Cultural Heritage in International Investment Law and Arbitration", in K Miles (ed.), *Research Handbook on Environment and International Investment Law* (Cheltenham: Edward Elgar, 2019) 464–479.
93. C Trevino, "Panama Faces New ICSID Arbitration Over Thwarted Hotel Tourism Development," *Investment Arbitration Reporter*, April 24, 2015.
94. P.D Young, *Ngawbe: Tradition and Change among the Western Guaymí of Panama* (Urbana: University of Illinois Press, 1971) pp. 38-42.
95. Ibid.
96. P Young and J Bort "Ngöbe Adaptive Responses to Globalization in Panama" in W Loker (ed.), *Globalization and the Rural Poor in Latin America* (Boulder, CO: Lynne Reiner Publishers, 1999) 111.
97. Inter Am. Ct H.R., *Case of the Kuna Indigenous People of Madungandi and Embera Indigenous People of Bayano and Their Members v. Panama*, Preliminary Objections, Merits, Reparations and Costs. Judgment, 14 October 2014. Series C No. 284, para. 59.
98. UN General Assembly, Human Rights Council, Report of the Special Rapporteur on the Rights of Indigenous Peoples, James Anaya, *The Status of Indigenous Peoples' Rights in Panama*, July 3, 2014, para. 13.

in Panama remains "fragile and unstable in many regards" because "these lands continue to be threatened, particularly by tourism, real estate development, and mineral exploitation".[99]

In the pending case *Dominion Minerals Corp. v. The Republic of Panama*,[100] the claimant, a U.S. company, contends that Panama used allegedly spurious environmental pretexts to deny the renewal of a mining exploration permit to the local subsidiary of the company and this amounted to an indirect expropriation of the claimant's investment in Cerro Chorca, a mining property in western Panama.[101] For the investor, a subsequent law allowing foreign investments in the mineral sectors shows that the mineral moratorium aimed to expropriate the investment of the claimant rather than to end the extraction of mineral resources.[102] After a regulation permitted mining, however, "the Ngöbe-Buglé indigenous people ... staged a series of violent protests and road blockades" in opposition to such law, because they "[f]ear[ed] that [it] would allow foreign state-owned companies to undertake large-scale mining projects on indigenous lands."[103] Because the government "faced ... the threat of continuing social unrest," it finally placed "a moratorium on all mining activity within the ... regions inhabited by the Ngöbe-Buglé indigenous peoples, which included Cerro Chorca."[104]

The case shows a complex relationship between economic interests and cultural priorities. Indigenous peoples seem to lament the lack of power in influencing policies that shape their lives. Cultural loss, rather than mere material hardship, has become the medium through which indigenous people give shape to their concerns. For the indigenous peoples, "[t]hese mountains are sacred." Reportedly, "Ngöbe ancestors entombed evil spirits in these mountains so that they could not disturb the villages on the slopes below. To make sure the spirits remained imprisoned, the hills have been off-limits to farming, hunting, and logging for generations, in effect creating an ecological preserve that protects the natural resources on which the Ngöbe depend."[105] Therefore, for the Ngöbe, destroying Cerro Chorca would unleash the spirits imprisoned in it and upset the natural balance of the fragile mountain ecosystem. From an international investment law perspective, though, the Arbitral Tribunal will have to assess whether state action amounted to an indirect expropriation of the investor's property and respected the fair and equitable treatment standard.[106] As the case is still in an early phase, it is not yet possible to foresee the outcome.

Certainly, the investment law obligations of the state towards foreign investors do not justify violations of its human rights obligations towards indigenous

---

99. Ibid., paras 27 and 29.
100. *Dominion Minerals Corp. v. The Republic of Panama*, Request for Arbitration, March 29, 2016.
101. Ibid., para. 2.
102. Ibid.
103. Ibid., para. 42.
104. Ibid., para. 44.
105. Marian Ahn Thorpe, "The Other Side of the Mountain" *Cultural Survival*, June 2010.
106. *Dominion Minerals Corp. v. The Republic of Panama*, Request for Arbitration, para. 52.

peoples. In the *Sawhoyamaxa* case,[107] the Inter-American Court of Human Rights held Paraguay liable for violating various human rights of the Sawhoyamaxa indigenous community under the American Convention on Human Rights. These communities claimed that the state had, *inter alia*, violated their right to property, by failing to recognise their title to ancestral lands.[108] For its part, the state attempted to justify its conduct by contending that the lands in question belonged to German investors and were protected under the Germany-Paraguay bilateral investment treaty (BIT), which prohibited the unlawful expropriation of foreign investors' lands.[109]

However, after noting the linkage between land rights and the culture of indigenous peoples,[110] the Court clarified that the investment law obligations of the state did not exempt the state from protecting and respecting the property rights of the Sawhoyamaxa.[111] Rather, the Court noted that compliance with investment treaties should always be compatible with the human rights obligations of the state.[112] Moreover, the Court pointed out that the relevant BIT did not prohibit expropriation; rather it subjected it to several requirements, including the existence of a public purpose and the payment of compensation.[113] Therefore, the Court found a violation of Article 21 of the Convention[114] and ordered the government to return the "traditional lands" to the Sawhoyamaxa community.

(b) Indigenous Culture and the Promotion of Free Trade: The EU Seals Disputes

For the Inuit, a group of culturally similar indigenous peoples inhabiting the Arctic regions of Greenland, Canada, and Alaska, seal hunting is an integral part of their cultural identity, and contributes to their subsistence. In Canada, indigenous peoples' income from sealing "represents between twenty-five and thirty-five percent of their total annual income."[115]

However, as Europeans perceive the seal hunts as cruel, because of the way the seals are killed, the EU adopted a comprehensive regime governing

---

107. Inter-American Court of Human Right, *Case of the Sawhoyamaxa Indigenous Community v. Paraguay*, Judgment of March 29, 2006, Merits, Reparations and Costs.
108. Ibid., para. 2.
109. Ibid., para. 115(b).
110. Ibid., para. 118 (noting that "[t]he culture of the members of indigenous communities reflects a particular way of life, of being, seeing, and acting in the world, the starting point of which is their close relation with their traditional lands and natural resources, not only because they are their main means of survival, but also because they form part of their worldview, of their religiousness, and consequently, of their cultural identity.")
111. Ibid., para. 140.
112. Ibid.
113. Ibid.
114. Ibid., para. 144.
115. X Luan and J Chaisse, "Preliminary Comments on the WTO Seals Products Dispute: Traditional Hunting, Public Morals and Technical Barriers to Trade" (2011) 22 *Colorado Journal of International Environmental Law & Policy* 79, 82.

seal products.[116] The EU seal regime prohibited the importation and sale in the EU of any seal product except: (a) those derived from hunts traditionally conducted by Inuit and other indigenous communities, which contributed to their subsistence;[117] and (b) those that were by-products of a hunt regulated by national law and with the sole purpose of sustainable management of marine resources.[118] In addition, seal products for personal use might be imported but might not be commercialized.[119] The EU allowed the exception for indigenous hunting because of the international law commitments of its member states and of the UNDRIP.[120] In other words, it allowed seal products to be placed on the market where they resulted from hunts traditionally conducted by Inuit and other indigenous communities in recognition of the fact that sealing is an important part of the Inuit lifestyle.

Nonetheless, Inuit groups contested the ban. According to indigenous peoples' representatives, the "Inuit exemption" would not prevent the market for seal products from collapsing. Since the Inuit people did not export seal products themselves, but exported them via non-indigenous exporters, they alleged that the derogation in their favour would remain an "empty box." Furthermore, they stressed that the EU had adopted its seal regime without consulting the Inuit.[121] Therefore, they perceived the aboriginal exemption as inadequate to sustain cultural practices and praised the Canadian government for bringing the seal ban to the WTO.[122]

Canada and Norway brought claims against the EU before the WTO, contending that the EU seal regime was inconsistent with the European Union's obligations under the General Agreement on Tariffs and Trade 1994 (GATT 1994)[123] and under the Technical Barriers to Trade (TBT) Agreement.[124]

---

116. Regulation (EC) 1007/2009 of the European Parliament and of the Council of 16 September 2009 on Trade in Seal Products, 2009 OJ (L. 286) 36.
117. Ibid., Article. 3(1).
118. Ibid., Article 3(2)(b).
119. Ibid., Article 3(2)(a).
120. Ibid., preamble, point 14: "The fundamental economic and social interests of Inuit communities engaged in the hunting of seals as a means to ensure their subsistence should not be adversely affected. The hunt is an integral part of the culture and identity of the members of the Inuit society, and as such is recognised by the United Nations Declaration on the Rights of Indigenous Peoples. Therefore, the placing on the market of seal products which result from hunts traditionally conducted by Inuit and other indigenous communities and which contribute to their subsistence should be allowed."
121. E Barca, "Canada's Annual Seal Slaughter just Ended. Should there be Another?" *Vancouver Observer*, June 19th 2010.
122. "Canada Calls for WTO Panel in Seal Dispute with EU", 15 *Bridges Weekly Trade News Digest*, February 18th 2011.
123. General Agreement on Tariffs and Trade 1994, April 15, 1994, Marrakesh Agreement Establishing the World Trade Organization, Annex 1A, 1867 UNTS 187.
124. Canada initiated dispute proceedings in November 2009; and sought the creation of a panel in February 2011, after consultations failed to yield a resolution. The EU rejected the first request, but, as per WTO rules, could not do so a second time. See *European Communities–Measures Prohibiting the Importation and Marketing of Seal Products* (WT/DS400/4) Request for the Establishment of a Panel by Canada, February 14th 2011, available at http://www.worldtradelaw.net/pr/ds400-4(pr).pdf. See also *European Communities –Measures Prohibiting the Importation and Marketing of Seal Products* (WT/DS401/5) Request for the Establishment of a Panel by Norway, March 15th 2011, available at http://www.worldtradelaw.net/pr/

Canada and Norway argued, *inter alia*, that the indigenous communities condition (IC condition) violated the non-discrimination obligation under Article I:1 and III:4 of the GATT 1994.[125] According to Canada and Norway, such conditions accorded seal products from Canada and Norway treatment less favourable than that accorded to like seal products of domestic origin, mainly from Sweden and Finland, as well as those of other foreign origin, in particular from Greenland.[126] In fact, the majority of seals hunted in Canada and Norway would not qualify under the exceptions, "while most, if not all, of Greenlandic seal products are expected to conform to the requirements under the IC exception."[127] Therefore, according to the complainants, the regime would indirectly discriminate against Canadian and Norwegian imports of seal products,[128] as it would restrict virtually all trade in seal products from Canada and Norway within the EU.[129] Moreover, the complainants argued that while the EU measures did not prevent the trade in products derived from seals killed inhumanely,[130] they could prevent the commerce of products derived from seals killed humanely by commercial hunters.[131]

Canada pointed out that seal harvesting provided thousands of jobs in Canada's remote coastal and northern communities where few economic opportunities existed and had been an important part of the Inuit way of life for centuries. Moreover, Canada maintained that the EU's exemption for trade in traditional Inuit seal products would prove to be ineffective, particularly in the face of the collapse of the larger market, and the Inuit would suffer the effects. The trade ban would restrict virtually all trade in seal products within the European Union. According to Canada, the solution to this would be the restoration of full market access. In parallel, Norway claimed that since only certain countries have indigenous peoples, the measure would have an unequal impact and therefore it would not treat all of the WTO member states equally.[132]

The key question of the dispute was whether the seal products produced by indigenous peoples and those produced by non-indigenous peoples were like products.[133] If so, as the EU ban treated the two products differently, there would be discrimination, which was prohibited under GATT Article III. In the assessment of likeness, a key question was whether consumer preferences

---

ds401-5(pr).pdf.

125. General Agreement on Tariffs and Trade 1994, 15 April 1994, Marrakesh Agreement Establishing the World Trade Organization, Annex 1A, 1867 UNTS 187.

126. *European Communities–Measures Prohibiting the Importation and Marketing of Seal Products*, WT/DS400/R and WT/DS401/R, 25 November 2013, Reports of the Panel, para. 7.2.

127. Ibid., paras. 7.161 and 7.164.

128. Ibid., para. 7.141.

129. Ibid., para 7.46.

130. Ibid., para. 7.4.

131. Ibid., para. 7.226.

132. *European Communities–Measures Prohibiting the Importation and Marketing of Seal Products*, Request for the Establishment of a Panel by Norway.

133. See e.g. R Howse and J Langille, "Permitting Pluralism: The Seal Products Dispute and Why the WTO Should Accept Trade Restrictions Justified by Non-instrumental Moral Values" (2011) 37 *Yale Journal of International Law* 367, 402.

would matter in light of the *EC–Asbestos* case.[134] As is known, in that case, the Appellate Body considered asbestos-containing products and similar products without asbestos as different products that the EU could legitimately distinguish and regulate differently, because of consumer preferences. As consumers know that asbestos is harmful to health, and thus prefer products without asbestos, it is legitimate for a country to regulate products containing asbestos differently than other products. In the *Seal Products* dispute, the EU argued that consumer preferences mattered. Finally, if the panel nonetheless found that there was discrimination, it should examine the question as to whether the seal products regulation was justified under any of the exceptions under Article XX of the GATT 1994, and in particular under Article XX(a) on public morals.

The panel found that the seal products produced by indigenous peoples and those hunted by other actors were like products.[135] The panel acknowledged the existence of a number of international law instruments, including the UNDRIP, focusing on the protection of indigenous cultural heritage.[136] The panel also referred to a number of WTO countries adopting analogous Inuit exceptions.[137] Although the panel considered these sources as "factual evidence,"[138] it concluded that the design and application of the exception was not even-handed because the exception was available *de facto* to Greenland.[139] Therefore, the panel held, *inter alia*, that the exception provided for indigenous communities under the EU Seal Regime favoured seal products produced by indigenous communities over like domestic and foreign products.[140] The panel concluded that the same exception, *inter alia*, violated Articles I:1 and III:4 of the GATT 1994 because an advantage granted by the EU to seal products derived from hunts traditionally conducted by the Inuit was not accorded immediately and unconditionally to like products originating in Canada.[141]

Finally, the panel examined the question of whether the seal products regulation was justified under any of the exceptions under Article XX of the GATT 1994, and in particular under Article XX(a) on public morals. The panel found that the EU seal regime was necessary to protect public morals.[142] Yet, it determined that the regime had a discriminatory impact that could not be justified under the *chapeau* of Article XX(a) of the GATT 1994.[143]

---

134. *European Communities–Measures Affecting Asbestos and Asbestos-Containing Products*, WT/DS135/AB/R, adopted April 5th 2001, DSR 2001:VII.
135. *European Communities–Measures Prohibiting the Importation and Marketing of Seal Products*, Reports of the Panel, para. 7.136.
136. Ibid., para. 7.292.
137. Ibid., para. 7.294.
138. Ibid., footnote 475.
139. Ibid., para. 7.317
140. Ibid., para. 8(2).
141. Ibid., para. 8(3)(a).
142. Ibid., para. 7.409.
143. Ibid., para. 7.651.

Immediately after the release of the reports, Canada, Norway, and the EU each appealed certain legal interpretations developed in the panel reports. The Appellate Body *inter alia* confirmed that the EU seal regime *de facto* discriminated like products under Articles I:1 (Most Favoured Nation) and III:4 (National Treatment) of the GATT 1994. In particular, the EU Seal Regime was inconsistent with Article I:1 because it did not "immediately and unconditionally" extend the same market access advantage to Canadian and Norwegian seal products that it accorded to seal products originating from Greenland. The AB also upheld the Panel's finding that the EU Seal Regime was "necessary to protect public morals" thus confirming that the ban on seal products could be justified on moral grounds under GATT Article XX(a). However, it held that the regime did not meet the requirements of the *chapeau* of Article XX of the GATT 1994, criticizing the design and the implementation of the exception for Inuit.[144] The AB noted *inter alia* that the IC exception contained no anti-circumvention clause,[145] and pinpointed that "seal products derived from … commercial hunts could potentially enter the EU market under the IC exception."[146] The AB concluded that the EU Seal Regime was not justified under Article XX(a) of the GATT 1994.[147] Therefore, the EU was given a reasonable period to refine the seal regime in order to comply with the *chapeau* requirements. Ultimately, the flaws found by the panel and AB were not with the ban itself, but with the specific implementation of the ban's exception for indigenous peoples.

CRITICAL ASSESSMENT

The contribution of the UNDRIP to current discourse on indigenous heritage and rights in international law is significant. The UNDRIP adopts a holistic understanding of indigenous peoples' rights, considering them as an indivisible whole. The protection of the cultural identity of indigenous peoples constitutes its *raison d'être*[148] and "one can find the cultural rights angle in each article of the Declaration."[149]

The significant achievements of the UNDRIP to date do not mean that further steps are unnecessary. The UNDRIP constitutes the outcome of decades of work; at the same time it should also be seen as the point of departure for further

---

144. *European Communities–Measures Prohibiting the Importation and Marketing of Seal Products*, Reports of the Appellate Body, para. 5.339.
145. Ibid. para., 5.327.
146. Ibid. para., 5.328.
147. Ibid. para., 6.1(d)(iii).
148. F Francioni, "The Human Dimension of International Cultural Heritage Law: An Introduction" (2011) 22 *European Journal of International Law* 9 at 15.
149. E Stamatopoulou, "Taking Cultural Rights Seriously: The Vision of the UN Declaration on the Rights of Indigenous Peoples" in S Allen & A Xanthaki (eds.), *Reflections on the UN Declaration on the Rights of Indigenous Peoples* (Hart Publishing, 2011) 392.

analysis and action. The analysed case studies highlight several different clashes: the clash between international economic law and domestic law;[150] the clash between animal welfare and traditional cultural practices; and the clash between an international economic culture and a local indigenous culture. Of particular concern is the clash of cultures between the protection of indigenous heritage and the promotion of economic activities under distinct international law regimes. Economic globalization can affect indigenous peoples' way of life. The collision between the protection of indigenous heritage and the promotion of economic interests in international economic law makes the case for strengthening the current regime protecting indigenous heritage. The participation of indigenous peoples in the decisions that can affect their rights is crucial.[151] At the same time, as the seal products dispute shows, economic globalization can also empower indigenous peoples.[152]

International economic courts and tribunals may not be the most appropriate *fora* for adjudicating cultural heritage-related disputes.[153] At the procedural level, arbitral tribunals constitute an uneven playing field: while foreign investors have *locus standi* – i.e. the right to act or be heard – before these tribunals, indigenous peoples do not have direct access to these dispute settlement mechanisms. Rather, their home governments need to espouse their claims. Nonetheless, "for a variety of reasons, states cannot be reasonably expected to adequately represent the … rights of indigenous peoples."[154] In fact, the land claims and cultural entitlements of indigenous peoples often compete with the economic development plans of both investors and states. Therefore, despite the formal premise of equality between the parties, there are structural power asymmetries between companies and indigenous communities that governments rarely mitigate.[155] Not only does investor-state arbitration fail to take into account the eventual conflict of interest between the entitlements of indigenous peoples and the economic development plans of the state, but – like the WTO dispute settlement mechanism – it also confers distinct procedural advantages to foreign investors vis-à-vis other private actors.

---

150. P L Fitzgerald, "Morality May Not Be Enough to Justify the EU Seal Products Ban: Animal Welfare Meets International Trade Law" (2011) 14 *Journal of International Wildlife Law & Policy* 85, 89.

151. See Art. 18 of the UNDRIP ("Indigenous peoples have the right to participate in decision-making in matters which would affect their rights, through representatives chosen by themselves in accordance with their own procedures, as well as to maintain and develop their own indigenous decision-making institutions.")

152. On the importance of free, prior, and informed consent, see S Sargent, "What's in a Name? The Contested Meaning of Free, Prior and Informed Consent in International Financial Law and Indigenous Rights", in V Vadi and B De Witte (eds.), *Culture and International Economic Law* (London: Routledge, 2015) 87.

153. V Vadi, "Crossed Destinies: International Economic Courts and the Protection of Cultural Heritage" (2015) 18 *Journal of International Economic Law* 51.

154. W Shipley, "What's Yours is Mine: Conflict of Law and Conflict of Interest Regarding Indigenous Property Rights in Latin American Investment Dispute Arbitration" (2014) 11 *Transnational Dispute Management* 1.

155. See V. Vadi, "Heritage, Power and Destiny: The Protection of Indigenous Heritage in International InvestmentLaw and Arbitration" (2019) *George Washington International Law Review* 101.

While foreign investors are emancipated from the need to invoke diplomatic protection from their home state, affected indigenous communities remain subject to the procedural requirement that their claims be espoused by the state before international economic courts. While foreign investors are not required to exhaust the local remedies before recurring to investment treaty arbitration, indigenous peoples must exhaust the same before being able to pursue their own claims before an international tribunal. While indigenous peoples can (and have) present(ed) friend of the court (*amicus curiae*) briefs reflecting their interests, investment tribunals and the WTO panels and Appellate Body are not legally obligated to consider such briefs – rather, they have the faculty to do so should they deem it appropriate.[156] Generally, arbitral tribunals grant such requests if the friends of the court can demonstrate that they could assist tribunals without unduly delaying arbitrations.[157] As *amici curiae*, indigenous peoples cannot ask for final or interlocutory remedies to preserve their cultural entitlements and land rights before arbitral tribunals and the WTO DSM. They cannot appeal adverse decisions.

Finally, additional procedural and substantive issues seem to favour economic actors over indigenous communities. First, the procedural mechanisms that enforce international economic law seem more effective than those enforcing human rights law. Investors and traders' claims are adjudicated efficiently and effectively, and with greater potential for state liability than the human rights claims of indigenous peoples, which must exhaust domestic remedies first.[158] Second, "permanent alterations to landscape" or alteration of traditional cultural practices constitute irreparable harms to indigenous peoples that are difficult, if not impossible to quantify "by exclusively pecuniary measurements."[159] In fact, "any strictly pecuniary quantification of damages is likely to favour foreign investors" and traders at the expense of the competing interests of

---

156. The first *amicus curiae* submissions made by indigenous peoples before an international economic law panel were made in the Softwood Lumber case. See "WTO Members Comment on Indigenous Amicus brief in Lumber Dispute" *Bridges Trade BioRes*, 16 May 2002. Other *amicus curiae* submissions followed in subsequent arbitrations. See *Glamis Gold Ltd. v. United States of America, Quechan Indian Nation, Application for Leave to File a Non-Party Submission*, 19 August 2005. In the *Glamis Gold* case, an indigenous community was granted *amicus curiae* status. *Glamis Gold Ltd v. United States*, UNCITRAL (NAFTA) Award, 8 June 2009, para. 286. In the *Grand River* case, the Tribunal received a letter from the National Chief of the Assembly of First Nations, endorsing the UNDRIP "and the customary international law principles it reflects", and calling for indigenous rights to be "taken into account whenever a NAFTA arbitration involves First Nations investors or investments." See *Grand River Enterprise Six Nations Ltd. et al. v. United States of America*, Award, 12 January 2011, para. 60. The Tribunal did not explicitly qualify a letter from the National Chief of the Assembly of First Nations in Canada as an *amicus curiae* submission but noted that the claimants included the letter as "a supporting exhibit" and that "it was read and considered by the Tribunal." *Ibid*. In some cases, arbitral tribunals have denied the participation of indigenous non-disputing parties. See *Bernhard von Pezold and Others v. Zimbabwe*, ICSID Case No. ARB/10/15, Procedural Order No. 2, 26 June 2012, para. 49 (stating that *amici curiae* should be independent of the parties and "bring a perspective, particular knowledge or insight that is different from that of the parties.")
157. L Bastin, "Amici Curiae in Investor–State Arbitrations: Two Recent Decisions" (2013) 20 *Australian International Law Journal* 101.
158. Krepchev, n. 85, 53.
159. Ibid.

indigenous peoples.[160] Finally, the perceived tendency of the international economic regime to externalize the costs of carrying out economic activity by placing them fully on states and the fear of costly litigation can chill the willingness of states to adopt measures protecting indigenous entitlements (regulatory chill).[161]

At the substantive level, international economic *fora* are not the best courts, let alone the only courts, in which to adjudicate this collision of norms. They may not have a specific expertise on indigenous peoples' rights. Nor do they generally have the mandate to interpret and apply human rights treaties. They are tribunals of limited jurisdiction and cannot adjudicate on eventual infringements of indigenous peoples' rights. They generally lack the jurisdiction to hold states liable for breach of their human rights obligations unless states enable them to do so by including broad jurisdiction clauses in their international investment treaties.[162] Rather, they can only determine if the protections in the relevant investment treaty or WTO covered agreement respectively have been breached.

However, this does not mean that these *fora* cannot take into account other international law obligations of the host state. The collision between international economic law and other fields of international law can be solved through international economic law itself albeit to a limited extent. Three avenues can facilitate the consideration of indigenous entitlements in international economic disputes: 1) a treaty-driven approach; 2) a judicially driven approach; and 3) a mixed approach.

First, as states periodically renegotiate their international investment treaties, treaty drafters can expressly accommodate indigenous peoples' entitlements in the text of these treaties (i.e., a "treaty-driven approach").[163] A few investment treaties include general exceptions,[164] referring to human rights that certainly include indigenous entitlements.[165] Specific clauses protecting indigenous entitlements can be inserted too. For instance, Canada and New Zealand have inserted specific clauses protecting indigenous rights in their trade and

---

160. Ibid.
161. But see *Burlington Resources Inc. v. Republic of Ecuador*, ICSID Case No. ARB/08/5, Decision on Reconsideration and Award, 7 February 2017 (ordering Burlington to pay USD 41 million in compensation to Ecuador for environmental and infrastructure damage.)
162. See, e.g. *Urbaser S.A. and Consorcio de Aguas Bilbao Bizkaia, Bilbao Biskaia Ur Partzuergoa v. The Argentine Republic*, ICSID Case No. ARB/07/26, Award, 8 December 2016 (examining the counterclaims brought by Argentina).
163. Krepchev, n 85, 45.
164. See e.g. Article 18 of the 2014 Canada Model Foreign Investment Protection Agreement (FIPA).
165. See e.g. Article 24 of the 2016 Draft Pan-African Investment Code, entitled "Business Ethics and Human rights" (stating "The following principles should govern compliance by investors with business ethics and human rights:
    a. support and respect the protection of internationally recognized human rights;
    b. ensure that they are not complicit in human rights abuses;
    c. eliminate all forms of forced and compulsory labor, including the effective abolition of child labor;
    d. eliminate discrimination in respect of employment and occupation; and
    e. ensure equitable sharing of wealth derived from investments.")

investment agreements.[166] This explicit recognition of indigenous entitlements by international treaties can allow the state to protect indigenous groups without the fear of expensive claims. In parallel, investors can take into account the existence of protected groups when assessing the economic risks of the given investment.

Within the WTO framework, Article XX of the GATT 1994 includes a (closed) list of (limited) exceptions to fundamental trade standards. In some circumstances, the AB has sought guidance from other sources of law and international organizations to interpret and apply this provision. For instance, in the *Shrimp–Turtle* case, the AB referred to multilateral environmental agreements to define the scope of "exhaustible natural resources."[167] Analogously, the general exceptions listed in Article XX can be interpreted in light of international human rights instruments such as the UNDRIP.

Yet, only a few investment treaties include such a "general exceptions" clause or specific reference to the rights of indigenous peoples. Most international investment agreements were concluded some decades ago, "…when economic development was a primary concern over issues of environmental sustainability or cultural rights."[168] Moreover, the restrictive requirements of the introductory part (*chapeau*) of Article XX have *de facto* limited the successful application of Article XX of GATT 1994 to trade disputes. Notoriously, the *chapeau* of Article XX requires that the measures restricting trade must not be applied in a manner that would constitute a means of arbitrary or unjustifiable discrimination between countries where the same conditions prevail, and they must not constitute a disguised restriction on international trade.

A parallel inclusive way states can build some safeguards within international investment treaties is by requiring compliance with domestic law. For instance, states can clarify that the relevant investment treaty protects only those investments that comply with domestic law. Such a clause can enable an adaptation of the treaty to the social, cultural, and political needs of the state. Recent international investment agreements tend to add "legality requirements" – an obligation for foreign investors to conform to and respect the domestic laws of the host state (including human rights).[169] For instance, Article 15.3 of the 2012 Southern African Development Community Model BIT prohibits investors from operating their investment "in a manner inconsistent with international, environmental, labour and human rights obligations binding on the host state or the home state,

---

166. See, for instance, Article 15.8 of the New Zealand-Thailand Closer Economic Partnership Agreement of 2005 (reaffirming the government's capacity to accord special or more favourable treatment to Maori people); Article 23 of the Protocol on Investment to the New Zealand-Australia Closer Economic relations Trade Agreement of 2011 (same); Canada-Peru Free Trade Agreement, 29 May 2008, Annex II, Reservations for Future Measures, Schedule of Peru.

167. *Appellate Body Report, United States-Import Prohibition of Certain Shrimp and Shrimp Products,* WT/DS58/AB/R, 6 November 1998, para. 130.

168. Krepchev, n. 85, 67.

169. E De Brabandere, "Human Rights and International Investment Law", *Leiden Law School Grotius Centre Working Paper* 2018/75-HRL (2018) 1–22.

whichever obligations are the higher." Analogously, under Article 11 of the 2016 Indian Model BIT, "The parties reaffirm and recognize that: (i) Investors and their investments shall comply with all laws, regulations, administrative guidelines and policies of a Party concerning the establishment, acquisition, management, operation and disposition of investments."

Second, international economic courts can take into account indigenous entitlements within the current framework of international economic law (i.e., a "judicially driven approach").[170] International economic law is not a self-contained regime.[171] As a matter of treaty interpretation, Article 3.2 of the DSU enables panels and the AB to interpret WTO treaties in accordance with customary rules of treaty interpretation as reflected in Articles 31 and 32 of the Vienna Convention on the Law of Treaties (VCLT).[172] Analogous provisions appear in the text of several investment treaties. Notoriously, Article 31(3)(c) of the VCLT requires that "[t]here shall be taken into account, together with the context: … any relevant rules of international law applicable in the relations between the parties." Pursuant to Article 31(3)(c), "[e]very treaty provision must be read not only in its own context, but in the wider context of general international law, whether conventional or customary."[173] This provision expresses the principle of systemic integration within the international legal system, indicating that treaty regimes are themselves creatures of international law.[174] Therefore, both WTO adjudicative bodies and arbitral tribunals have some interpretative space to consider other international treaties when they collide with international economic law. In fact, customary rules of treaty interpretation require that international law protecting indigenous peoples' rights serve as an interpretive context if they are relevant to the interpretation of the respective international economic law provisions.

However, only rarely have WTO adjudicative bodies looked outside the WTO framework. For instance, in the *Seal Products* dispute, reference to international law instruments was made, but such instruments played a limited role, if any, in the final reports. Arbitral tribunals appear to be more open to referring to other international law instruments, looking to human rights law for analogies, or as

---

170. Krepchev, n. 85, 45.

171. WTO AB Report, *United States–Standards for Reformulated and Conventional Gasoline (US–Gasoline)*, WT/DS2/AB/R, adopted 20th May 1996, at 17 (affirming that WTO treaties are "not to be read in clinical isolation from public international law"); *Asian Agricultural Products Ltd v. Democratic Socialist Republic of Sri Lanka*, ICSID Case No. ARB/87/3, Award, 27 June 1990, para. 21 (highlighting that international investment law "is not a self-contained closed legal system . . ., but it has to be envisaged within a wider juridical context in which rules from other sources are integrated through implied incorporation methods, or by direct reference to certain supplementary rules, whether of international law character or of domestic law nature.")

172. Vienna Convention on the Law of Treaties, adopted 23 May 1969, in force 27 January 1980) 1155 UNTS 331 (VCLT).

173. I Sinclair, *The Vienna Convention on the Law of Treaties* (Manchester: Manchester University Press, 1984), 139.

174. C McLachlan, "The Principles of Systematic Integration and Article 31(3)(c) of the Vienna Convention" (2005) 54 *International and Comparative Law Quarterly* 279, 280.

an aid in constructing the meaning of investment treaty provisions, albeit the weight of such references in the final decision remains unquantifiable.

Finally, if certain indigenous rights have acquired the status of *jus cogens* norms, those norms should prevail in the case of conflict with international economic law.[175] International public order requires international economic courts to consider whether the proceedings do not violate competing international law obligations of a peremptory character. Yet, the present role of *jus cogens* norms in the context of investment arbitration remains unsettled at best and peripheral at worst. Rarely have the parties contended that a norm of *jus cogens* has been violated, and even when they have done so, arbitral tribunals have declined to adjudicate on the matter, stating that they have a limited mandate and cannot adjudicate on human rights claims.[176] Moreover, in some arbitrations, the host states have preferred to refer only to domestic constitutional provisions rather than relying on the alleged *jus cogens* nature of the rights involved. This is not surprising, as such pleadings may be considered to contribute to state practice, and states are very careful in invoking *jus cogens* as the same arguments could be used against them in other contexts, i.e. before national constitutional courts, regional human rights courts, and international monitoring bodies. For instance, with regard to indigenous peoples' rights, including the right to be consulted in matters affecting them or their religious rights, states have referred to domestic constitutional provisions.[177] The state's invocation of human rights to justify a given regulatory measure can serve as evidentiary record against the state itself in other proceedings, as it can be taken as an admission of its responsibilities towards indigenous peoples. Nonetheless, in recent practice, there have been far-sighted attempts to justify domestic measures in the light of the host state's human rights obligations.[178]

A third way to insert cultural concerns into the operation of investor-state arbitration is by raising counterclaims for eventual violations of domestic law protecting cultural entitlements. States have increasingly tried to assert counterclaims against investors, even though their efforts have tended not to be successful.[179] While most treaties do not have broad enough dispute resolution clauses to encompass counterclaims, "drafting treaties to permit closely related counterclaims would help to rebalance investment law".[180]

---

175. VCLT Article 64 (stating that treaties which violate peremptory norms are null and void).
176. *Biloune and Marine Drive Complex Ltd* v. *Ghana Investments Centre and the Government of Ghana* (UNCITRAL), Award on Jurisdiction and Liability, 27 October 1989, 95 ILR 184, at 203.
177. *Glamis Gold Ltd. v. United States of America*, ICSID/UNCITRAL, Award, 8 June 2009, para. 654.
178. V Vadi, "*Jus Cogens* in International Investment Law and Arbitration" (2015) 46 *Netherlands Yearbook of International Law* 357–388.
179. A.K. Bjorklund, "The Role of Counterclaims in Rebalancing Investment Law", *Lewis & Clark Law Review* 17 (2013) 464.
180. Ibid., 461.

CONCLUSIONS

The effective protection of indigenous cultural heritage benefits all humanity. Today, a growing number of international law instruments highlight cultural diversity as the common heritage of mankind,[181] and the UNDRIP has furthered the "culturalization of indigenous rights,"[182] enunciating a number of cultural entitlements of indigenous peoples, and highlighting the linkage between the preservation of their cultural identity and the enjoyment of their human rights. Although the Declaration *per se* is not binding, it may become so, insofar as it is deemed to reflect customary international law and/or general principles of law. At the very least, the UNDRIP constitutes a standard that states should strive to achieve.

The interplay between the promotion of free trade and foreign direct investment on the one hand, and the safeguarding of indigenous cultural heritage on the other in international economic law is an underexplored field.[183] This study has shed some light on this complex connection. The analysed case studies provide a snapshot of the clash of cultures between international economic governance and indigenous heritage protection. They also highlight a fundamental clash between local and global dimensions of governance. Indigenous heritage is local and it belongs to specific places; economic governance has an international character. At the same time, indigenous rights also eminently belong to the international discourse.

Economic disputes concerning indigenous cultural heritage have been brought before international economic "courts." Such disputes often involve the conflict between the protection of indigenous cultural heritage and the promotion of economic freedoms. These disputes can provide an important testing-ground for the degree to which adjudicators will read international economic law protections owed by states to foreign investors and traders in light of states' parallel international law obligations to their own indigenous peoples.

International economic courts may not be the most suitable tribunals to settle this kind of dispute, in that they may face difficulties in finding an appropriate balance between the different interests concerned. They are courts of limited jurisdiction, and cannot generally adjudicate on state violations of indigenous peoples' entitlements. This does not mean, however, that they should not (or do not) take cultural considerations into account. This chapter has explored three different yet complementary avenues for integrating cultural threads into the fabric of international economic law. First, *de lege ferenda*, since international

---

181. Universal Declaration on Cultural Diversity, November 2nd 2001, UNESCO Rec. Of. Gen. Conf., 31st sess., art. 1.

182. I Schulte-Tenckhoff, "Treaties, Peoplehood, and Self-Determination: Understanding the Language of Indigenous Rights" in E Pulitano (ed.), *Indigenous Rights in the Age of the UN Declaration* (Cambridge: Cambridge University Press, 2012) 64, at 67.

183. See, however, G K Foster, "Foreign Investment and Indigenous Peoples: Options for Promoting Equilibrium between Economic Development and Indigenous Rights" (2012) 33 *Michigan Journal of International Law* 627.

investment treaties are renegotiated periodically, there is scope for inserting *ad hoc* clauses within these treaties to protect indigenous entitlements. Second, *de lege lata*, international economic law is not a self-contained regime, but should be interpreted and applied in the light of international law. This is required by customary rules of treaty interpretation as restated by the VCLT. Third, Counterclaims can also help maintain a balance between economic interests and cultural heritage-related concerns. In this manner, the UNDRIP becomes relevant and indigenous cultural entitlements can be incorporated into the reasoning of international economic courts. Not only can these approaches promote the effectiveness of human rights instruments but they can also humanize and re-legitimize international economic law, fostering a sense of unity and complementarity between different competing subsets of international law.

In conclusion, FDI and free trade represent a potentially positive force for development. Still, decision makers in state policy and practice concerning economic activities must be mindful of the implications for the culture of indigenous peoples. Given the fact that international economic law adjudication can dramatically affect indigenous communities, international economic courts ought to hear the voices of these communities.[184]

---

184. For an analogous argument with regard to local communities in the context of European integration, see F Nicola, "Invisible Cities in Europe" (2011-2012) 35 *Fordham International Law Journal* 1285.

INDIGENOUS (INTANGIBLE) CULTURAL HERITAGE AND THE UNFULFILLED PROMISES OF RIGHTS DECLARATIONS

Lucas Lixinski

INTRODUCTION

Heritage is a part of identity, the importance of which is increasingly recognized by the law. A wide range of instruments has come into existence since the 1950s to protect various forms of heritage, and they all contain their own definitions of what 'heritage' is. Cultural heritage can be defined as the elements necessary for the maintenance over time of a certain cultural identity, important for the survival of a society. It is very difficult to define heritage in definite terms, and it has been stated that defining heritage is as difficult as defining beauty or art; heritage appeals to people's senses and emotions, and is therefore unfathomable.[1]

The 2003 Convention for the Safeguarding of the Intangible Cultural Heritage[2] creates the "Representative List of the Intangible Cultural Heritage,"[3] which

---

1. *See* R Lumley, "The Debate on Heritage Reviewed" in *Heritage Museums and Galleries: in Introductory Reader*, 15, 16 (G Corsane ed.) (Routledge, 2005).

2. Convention for the Safeguarding of the Intangible Cultural Heritage, Paris, 17 October 2003. Entry into force: 20 April 2006. States parties as of February 2018: 176 [hereinafter "The 2003 UNESCO Convention", or "ICH Convention"].

3. The relevant provision is Article 16: "1. In order to ensure better visibility of the intangible cultural heritage and awareness of its significance, and to encourage dialogue which respects cultural diversity, the Committee, upon the proposal of the States Parties concerned, shall establish, keep up to date and publish a Representative List of the Intangible Cultural Heritage of Humanity. 2. The Committee shall draw up and submit to the General Assembly for approval the criteria for the establishment, updating and publication of this Representative List."

allows for the inscription of "social customs and rituals."[4] Somewhat curiously, the ICH Convention only uses the word "indigenous" once, in its preamble.[5] According to its drafters, the otherwise lack of mention of indigenous peoples is attributable to a resistance to thinking of intangible heritage only in indigenous terms. By not mentioning indigenous peoples in the ICH Convention, the drafters reasoned, it would be clear that all peoples have their own intangible heritage, not only indigenous peoples. Further, this was considered to be a less problematic strategy for the negotiation of the instrument, in light of the difficult drafting process of the United Nations Declaration on the Rights of Indigenous Peoples (that had been nearly 20 years in its drafting when the 2003 UNESCO Convention was adopted).[6]

This strategy was largely successful, as manifestations of heritage inscribed on the intangible heritage lists are not all indigenous, and, in fact, indigenous heritage is only a small fraction of those manifestations inscribed. Among the manifestations of indigenous heritage inscribed in the list is the Wayúu normative system, applied by the Pütchipü'üi or "*palabrero*." The Wayúu are an indigenous group in Northern Colombia and Venezuela, and the Wayúu legal system is the dispute resolution system adopted within the community, and fully endorsed by the 1991 Colombian Constitution, which contains mechanisms for the recognition and enforcement of indigenous jurisdictions.

The Wayúu normative system was inscribed on the representative list in November 2010 in the domain of "social customs and ritual," because of its promise of cross-cultural dialogue. However, there may be implications resulting from this inscription. If, on the one hand, it may be hailed as a means of enhancing the visibility of the legal system, on the other there is a certain risk of "folklorisation" of the legal system. This folklorisation would mean not only a potential risk of freezing the legal system in time, but, perhaps more importantly, would turn the system into a "cultural token", a cultural performance

---

4. The relevant provision is Article 2: "For the purposes of this Convention, 1. The "intangible cultural heritage" means the practices, representations, expressions, knowledge, skills – as well as the instruments, objects, artefacts and cultural spaces associated therewith – that communities, groups and, in some cases, individuals recognize as part of their cultural heritage. This intangible cultural heritage, transmitted from generation to generation, is constantly recreated by communities and groups in response to their environment, their interaction with nature and their history, and provides them with a sense of identity and continuity, thus promoting respect for cultural diversity and human creativity. For the purposes of this Convention, consideration will be given solely to such intangible cultural heritage as is compatible with existing international human rights instruments, as well as with the requirements of mutual respect among communities, groups and individuals, and of sustainable development. 2. The"intangible cultural heritage", as defined in paragraph 1 above, is manifested *inter alia* in the following domains: (a) oral traditions and expressions, including language as a vehicle of the intangible cultural heritage; (b) performing arts; (c) social practices, rituals and festive events; (d) knowledge and practices concerning nature and the universe; (e) traditional craftsmanship. ..."
5. The preamble clause reads: "Recognizing that communities, in particular indigenous communities, groups and, in some cases, individuals, play an important role in the production, safeguarding, main-tenance and re-creation of the intangible cultural heritage, thus helping to enrich cultural diversity and human creativity."
6. See J Blake, *Commentary on the 2003 UNESCO Convention on the Safeguarding of the Intangible Cultural Heritage* 12 (2006).

to be gazed at, but containing no meanings, significance or practical implications that could be taken to heart.

This chapter uses the listing of the Wayúu system to discuss the ways in which (intangible) cultural heritage regimes interact with the rights of indigenous peoples, particularly through two aspects. First, the chapter looks at the implications of inscribing a sophisticated system of dispute resolution in a necessarily less-nuanced cultural heritage list, and uses this example as an allegory of practices surrounding the packaging of "the other" in debates about culture in international law. Second, the chapter examines the extent to which the system created by the ICH Convention can work in coordination with two soft law instruments on the rights of indigenous peoples: the United Nations Declaration on the Rights of Indigenous Peoples (UNDRIP) of 2007; and the Organization of American States' American Declaration on the Rights of Indigenous Peoples (ADRIP) of 2016. These instruments contain several provisions with regard to the protection of indigenous culture and heritage, and generally the potential of heritage protection as a foundation for larger claims about autonomy and self-determination. For the analysis of these two declarations in conjunction with the ICH Convention, I partly rely on the idea of Multi-Sourced Equivalent Norms (MSENs) in international law, or the idea of "two or more norms which are … similar or identical in their normative content; and … have been established through different international instruments or 'legislative' procedures or are applicable in different substantive areas of the law."[7] These are "norms which on their face are presumed to be mutually reinforcing, even though at some level of analysis and with certain factual patterns there might emerge an inconsistency between them."[8]

In light of this framework, and also considering the broader political debates about the implementation of heritage norms, this chapter contains two parallel theses: firstly, I argue that, despite the many shortcomings of the use of heritage protection systems as an indigenous advocacy tool, there is still some potential to be explored in this strategy, especially as a backdoor to institutional and legal reluctance to offer recognition, and in spite of the many shortcomings of framing culture, and rights claims based on culture, as heritage. Secondly, I also argue that MSENs can work to the advantage of indigenous peoples in this context because they help translate advocacy potential from instruments like the UNDRIP and ADRIP into the interpretation of instruments like the ICH Convention. Despite there being some inconsistencies among these instruments, they can be avoided by focusing on the broader politics of heritage and its potential.

This chapter will proceed as follows: Section 2 will briefly examine the listing mechanism of the ICH Convention. Section 3 will focus on the Wayúu normative system, its status in domestic constitutional frameworks (as a means

---

7. T Broude and Y Shany, "The International Law and Policy of Multi-Sourced Equivalent Norms" in *Multi-Sourced Equivalent Norms in International Law* 1, 5 (T Broude and Y Shany, eds.) (Hart Publishing, 2011).
8. Ibid., 9

to assess its legal and political status before local polities), and the reception of UNESCO status by the Wayúu community and other political and legal actors. Section 4 will address the structure of the UNDRIP and ADRIP with regard to the protection of indigenous heritage, and contrast the inscription of the Wayúu legal system under the UNESCO instrument to what seem to be the potentials of the UNDRIP and ADRIP with respect to the politics of heritage. Section 5 concludes the paper.

INTANGIBLE HERITAGE LISTING

The purposes of the ICH Convention, as determined in Article 1, are four: (1) to safeguard ICH; (2) to ensure respect for the ICH of communities, groups and individuals; (3) to raise awareness; and (4) to provide international cooperation and assistance. This provision lays down the foundations of the safeguarding system created by the Convention. A full exploration of the system created by this Convention is beyond the purposes of this paper,[9] but the listing mechanism is central to our purposes, and needs to be discussed in some detail.

The safeguarding of intangible heritage at the international level happens primarily through intangible heritage lists. One of them is the "Representative List of the Intangible Cultural Heritage of Humanity" (Article 16), while the other is the "List of Intangible Cultural Heritage in Need of Urgent Safeguarding" (Article 17). When the ICH Convention was being drafted, the listing mechanism was opposed by some States, most notably Norway. The Norwegian delegation expressed the view that a list-based mechanism would create a hierarchy of manifestations of heritage (the "listed", which would somehow be "better", and the "unlisted"). They argued that a catalogue of best practices in the safeguarding of intangible heritage alone would suffice to accomplish the objectives of the Convention. The Indian delegation, on the other hand, thought that the listing approach was an effective one, even though it should be approached carefully so as not to create any sort of hierarchy. This argument was generally accepted, as the listing would help in the awareness-raising that was necessary for the achievement of the Convention's objectives. Further, as highlighted by the Brazilian delegation, the listing mechanism at the international level mirrored the national obligation of inventorying, thus being also a desirable means to implement the Convention.[10]

The criteria for inscription of manifestations of heritage in these lists have been the object of discussion of the Intergovernmental Committee (one of the bodies responsible for implementing the ICH Convention). A first set of criteria

---

9. For a longer discussion and critique of the system created by the ICH Convention, *see* L Lixinski, "Selecting Heritage: The Interplay of Art, Law and Politics" (2011) 22(1) *European Journal of International Law* 81.
10. See J Blake, *Commentary on the UNESCO 2003 Convention on the Safeguarding of the Intangible Cultural Heritage* 79 (Institute for Art and Law 2006).

has already been approved into the operational directives for implementation of the Convention (and has been amended in 2010, 2012 and 2014).[11]

The criteria for inscription on the representative list are slightly different from those for the urgent safeguarding list,[12] and in many ways impose a lesser burden on States seeking inscription. The criteria for inscription on the list of representative intangible heritage, which must be met by all States seeking inscription, are: (1) that the manifestation of heritage falls within the concept of Article 2 of the Convention; (2) that the inscription will contribute to the visibility and awareness of the significance of ICH and will encourage dialogue, thereby entangling cultural diversity and being a testimony to human creativity; (3) that safeguarding measures are elaborated to protect and promote the element; (4) free, prior and informed consent of the affected communities, groups and individuals; and (5) that the element is present in one of the inventories required from States Parties.[13] Also, communities must be involved in the preparation of the nominations for this list.[14]

The manifestation of heritage to be inscribed must be described in reference to its significant features in the present (that is, the Committee is clearly aware that the element may, and probably will, change in the future),[15] also including discussion of its social and cultural functions. The history of the element is not a required element.[16] The free, prior and informed consent of the communities, groups or individuals must also be secured and proven, in the same fashion as the consent for inscription in the urgent list.[17]

Seventy-six manifestations of heritage have been inscribed during the first round of inscriptions in October 2009, and that list has since ballooned to over 500 elements in more than 120 countries. Among these, a few are noteworthy, including Tibetan opera, the Tango, Chinese sericulture and silk craftsmanship, an Afro-Uruguayan cultural practice called "Candombe" and the cultural space associated with it (which is but a few blocks in a neighborhood in Montevideo), and a traditional dispute settlement mechanism for water disputes in Southern Spain, among many others.[18] These first inscriptions indicate that the range of

---

11. *Intergovernmental Committee for the Safeguarding of the Intangible Cultural Heritage, Fifth Session – Nairobi, Kenya, Decision 5.COM 10.1*, Doc. ITH/10/5.COM/CONF.2002/Decisions, of 19 November 2010.
12. For a comparison, *see Intergovernmental Committee for the Safeguarding of the Intangible Cultural Heritage, Second Extraordinary Session* (Sofia, Bulgaria, 18-22 February 2008), Decision 2.ext.com 17 (Report of the Intergovernmental Committee for the Safeguarding of the Intangible Cultural Heritage on its Activities between the First and Second Sessions of the General Assembly of the States Parties to the Convention, paras. 11-19).
13. *General Assembly of States Parties to the Convention for the Safeguarding of the Intangible Cultural Heritage, Operational Directives for the Implementation of the Convention for the Safeguarding of the Intangible Cultural Heritage* (June 2008), *available at* www.unesco.org/culture/ich. Rule 19.
14. Ibid., Rule 21.
15. See UNESCO, *Report on the Expert Meeting on Criteria for Inscription on the Lists Established by the 2003 Convention for the Safeguarding of the Intangible Cultural Heritage* (Paris, 5-6 December 2005).
16. See Form ICH-02 (2009) – Representative List. Explanatory Note, para. 2.
17. Ibid., at para. 5.b.
18. All the documents referring to these inscriptions are available at UNESCO Intangible Heritage Convention, the Intangible Heritage Lists, available at http://www.unesco.org/culture/ich/index.php?p-

safeguarding initiatives to be adopted under the Convention is very wide, and can go from the preservation of tangible elements necessary for the perpetuation of the activity, the enactment of specific laws, the institution of national holidays aimed at celebrating the cultures that served as the source for the manifestations of heritage inscribed, to educational and awareness-raising activities. Traditional norms of the involved communities have been taken into account when discussing community involvement, and also as important starting points for the preservation of the practices themselves.

Notably, the ICH Convention's definition of ICH precludes from inscription any manifestations of heritage that are incompatible with universally recognized human rights.[19] This connection to human rights, because it is framed negatively, would lead to the impression that rights strategies on the basis of ICH would only work inasmuch as they conformed to a mainstream view, which would sit at odds with the claims of minority groups, such as indigenous peoples, to recognition, since claims to recognition are often based on assertions of distinctiveness. Nevertheless, the practice of nominations into the ICH Convention lists shows that the organs of the Convention have been far more amenable to recognizing intangible cultural heritage that challenges prevailing assumptions about universalist human rights,[20] and thus the potential remains for ICH manifestations to be used in the pursuance of rights claims.

Amidst this wide array of manifestations of heritage inscribed by UNESCO is the Wayúu normative system. Inscription was proposed by Colombia, even though the Wayúu live in a territory both in Colombia and Venezuela. But what is this system, and what does it mean that it was inscribed in a heritage list?

THE WAYÚU NORMATIVE SYSTEM AS HERITAGE

The Wayúu are an indigenous people living in the La Guajira peninsula, between Colombia and Venezuela. The Wayúu normative system is one that revolves around the Pütchipü'üi (the *palabrero*), who is the person "in charge of administering the words" (in Spanish, *palabras*, or, in Wayúu, pütchikalü).[21] This

---

g=00011&inscription=00003&type=00002.

19. ICH Convention, Article 2(1). For a commentary on the history of this definition, see Francesco Francioni, "Article 2(1): Defining Intangible Cultural Heritage," in J Blake and L Lixinski (eds.), *The 2003 Intangible Heritage Convention: A Commentary* (Oxford University Press, forthcoming 2019).

20. For this discussion, see Lucas Lixinski, "The Convention for the Safeguarding of the Intangible Cultural Heritage and Human Rights: Relativism and Collectivism 2.0", in Janet Blake and Lucas Lixinski (eds.), *The 2003 Intangible Heritage Convention: A Commentary* (Oxford University Press, forthcoming 2019).

21. Most of this account is drawn from interviews with *palabreros* available on YouTube. See http://www.youtube.com/watch?v=XnWuldfC-0w (first of a three part series of an interview with a *palabrero*); http://www.youtube.com/watch?v=fojEsmitk8M (interview with a historian specializing in Wayúu history); and http://www.youtube.com/watch?v=V_vM_i4yorA (a video prepared to support the UNESCO nomination). Another important source is an audio interview with the *palabrero* Guillermo Ojeda Jayariyu (also coordinator of the main body of *palabreros*, the Junta Mayor Autónoma de Palabreros Wayúu) on the Colombian National Radio's website, highlighting the risks and advantages of inscription on the UNESCO list. See

figure arises historically from a need to resolve disputes within the community, and is a figure of authority. The *palabrero* is chosen on an ad hoc basis, taking into account an individual's social and economic status within the community. It is this status (including social connections) that creates and legitimates the authority of the *palabrero*. Gradually, the administration of justice role of the *palabrero* demanded that the *palabrero* prove stronger cultural connections and awareness of how their decisions impacted on the social status of the group as a whole (which is connected to knowledge of history and a form of precedent within the community). Elder councils in the communities have a bearing on the activities of *palabreros*. Elder councils are the precedent library from which the *palabrero* draws. The Wayúu normative system collectivizes law, as traditionally the decisions of the *palabrero* have effects not only on the individual who is found guilty of misconduct, but on the individual's entire family or clan (Eirukü).

Relating a murder case he presided over, a *palabrero* discussed how the family of a murder victim took upon themselves to avenge the murder, and invaded property belonging to the social group from which the murderer came, ransacking and looting property. This was deemed illegitimate, but it would be allowed if the looting had been determined by a *palabrero* (which would then make the looting the payment of compensation). The procedure for handling a murder, for instance, is to bring together the entire family of the deceased. The elders in the group have the final word in what happens, and the reparations expected. Reparations that are determined must be paid by the entire clan, seeing as it is the clan that is held responsible for the murder, rather than any individual. The clan found guilty pays reparations often in livestock (to be then sacrificed), or in necklaces made of carved stones, which are classified according to purity (the purer the necklace, the more valuable it is). A necklace represents repentance and the collective willingness to reproach the conduct of the individual within their clan who perpetrated the action. The necklaces have a cultural worth only, not being really available in the market. Wearing the necklaces shows acceptance of the reparations, and forgiveness for the wrongdoing. Once reparations are paid, it is up to the family of the victim to determine whether they are satisfied or not (which then ends the process). If the family is not satisfied with the reparations, it is considered that the word was not carried through, and it amounts to a declaration of war between the two clans.

The Wayúu normative system does not admit imprisonment as a punishment; it instead translates punishment into economic penalties (deprivation of property, including future inheritance). Ostracism is also a possibility, albeit always temporary, until the person found guilty proves that their behavior has changed, and will no longer occur. Often, ostracized delinquents find their way to neighboring countries, most notably Venezuela, where they have no social ties that remind them of their crimes.

---

http://www.fonoteca.gov.co/index.php?option=com_topcontent&view=article&id=2280:ique-venga-el-pal-abrero&catid=62:sonar-despierto

The decisions of the *palabrero* are final and binding. The *palabrero* is seen as a conciliator, a peace-maker. The *palabrero* in the video indicates that it is now time to put the Wayúu normative system in writing, to allow it to be preserved for future generations. In discussing compatibility with the Colombian Constitution, he explains that whenever a person is subject to the system, they renounce all access to ordinary Colombian courts.

The judicial process with a *palabrero* depends on how many people's *palabras* are heard. The process for homicide is the fastest one, almost immediate. In other instances, the process may take up to eight days. The process with a *palabrero* has an economic cost to the parties, which historically consisted of part of the reparations paid to the victims. The *palabrero* could choose amongst the livestock given in reparation. Currently, the person who seeks out the *palabrero* has to cover travel and accommodation costs, in addition to a share of the reparations determined. Also, currently some of the compensations determined are monetary, which is pointed out as partly responsible for the erosion of the Wayúu culture (because it excludes women from the process, who would otherwise be responsible for the animal sacrifice in this matrilineal culture), alongside the fact that the proceedings now sometimes also happen in Spanish, instead of the Wayúu language.

For the most part, *palabreros* and Wayúu communities showed appreciation for the listing before UNESCO, as it raised the profile of their normative system and their culture, which means increased awareness of their existence, translatable into preservation measures and some degree of recognition. Notably, a Venezuelan *palabrero*, attending a ceremony in Colombia celebrating the UNESCO inscription, stated that the recognition by UNESCO amounted to recognition of the Wayúu nation independently of the boundaries of the two countries over which the Wayúu people are spread (Colombia and Venezuela).[22] The safeguarding plan presented to UNESCO, in this sense, goes beyond the protection of the *palabrero* system alone. The aspirations of the Wayúu with respect to safeguarding under UNESCO encompass measures aimed at the Wayúu language, spirituality, social organization, understanding of territory, and traditional economy.[23]

The Colombian Minister of Culture, by contrast, discussing the inscription on the UNESCO list, highlighted the possibilities of exploring the inscription of the Wayúu normative system as a means to promote cultural tourism,[24] which is

22. See J Luis De la Hoz, 'Ministra de Cultura entregó el reconocimiento Patrimonio de la humanidad a los *palabreros* Wayúu', *El Informador* (30 November 2010), *available at* http://www.el-informador.com/index.php?option=com_content&view=article&id=8243:ministra-de-cultura-entrego-el-reconocimien-to-patrimonio-de-la-humanidad-a-palabreros-wayuu&catid=77:la-guajira&Itemid=420
23. See audio interview with the *palabrero* Guillermo Ojeda Jayariyu (also coordinator of the main body of *palabreros*, the Junta Mayor Autónoma de Palabreros Wayúu) on the Colombian National Radio's website, *available at* http://www.fonoteca.gov.co/index.php?option=com_topcontent&view=article&id=2280:ique-venga-el-palabrero&catid=62:sonar-despierto
24. See J Luis De la Hoz, "Ministra de Cultura entregó el reconocimiento Patrimonio de la humanidad a los palabreros Wayúu", *El Informador* (30 November 2010), *available at* http://www.el-informador.com/index.php?option=com_content&view=article&id=8243:ministra-de-cultura-entrego-el-reconocimien-

a peculiar means of exploiting the system, and one which further ceremonialises and folklorises it. The risk of folklorisation was highlighted by Guillermo Ojeda Jayariyu, coordinator of the main body of *palabreros*, the Junta Mayor Autónoma de Palabreros Wayúu.[25] In his statement, Ojeda Jayariyu pointed to the negative consequences of folklorisation for the survival of the Wayúu culture in the long run.

These two contrasting statements point to the different potentials various stakeholders see in heritage. On the one hand, heritage holders seem to find in the recognition of their heritage the potential for broader claims about cultural, legal and even political autonomy. For the Colombian government (Executive branch), on the other hand, the potential of this recognition lies in cultural tourism, in the packaging of the Wayúu legal system and its selling to tourists under the label of "heritage as experience." One of the main problems with the listing mechanism of the UNESCO Convention is how it risks freezing the manifestation of heritage in time, which would be particularly problematic in the case of an entire legal system. The possibility of exploring the Wayúu system for cultural tourism further risks mummifying it, and turning it into a performance for tourists, as opposed to a current means of conflict resolution.

Add to these two perspectives (Wayúu in Venezuela and the Colombian Executive branch) that of the Judiciary (both in Venezuela and in Colombia), who think of the Wayúu legal system as part of the law of the land, and nothing more (therefore taking the Wayúu normative system at face value, not instrumentalising it as a means to reach some other objective). As far as the recognition of the Wayúu normative system in Venezuela goes, though, there is little legal value placed on it. The Venezuelan legal system does not recognize Wayúu law, and indeed criminalizes significant parts of it. For instance, that the entire clan is responsible for paying compensation for wrongdoing is seen by Venezuelan criminal courts as extortion.[26] Hence, at least in Venezuela, Wayúu law is riddled with a certain sense of foreign-ness that is difficult to overcome. This "otherness" is somewhat reminiscent of how one Australian court has addressed the issue of the normative value of indigenous law. In *Bulun Bulun & Anor v R & T Textiles Pty Ltd*, an important Australian case on intellectual property law, the court said that indigenous law (the "others" law) was not to be considered part of the colonizers' legal system; rather, it was to be considered part of the case's "factual matrix."[27] In saying that, the court turned the entire legal system

---

to-patrimonio-de-la-humanidad-a-palabreros-wayuu&catid=77:la-guajira&Itemid=420
25. See audio interview with the *palabrero* Guillermo Ojeda Jayariyu (also coordinator of the main body of *palabreros*, the Junta Mayor Autónoma de Palabreros Wayúu) on the Colombian National Radio's website, *available at* http://www.fonoteca.gov.co/index.php?option=com_topcontent&view=article&id=2280:ique-venga-el-palabrero&catid=62:sonar-despierto (initials here?)
26. See audio interview with the *palabrero* Guillermo Ojeda Jayariyu (also coordinator of the main body of *palabreros*, the Junta Mayor Autónoma de Palabreros Wayúu) on the Colombian National Radio's website, *available at* http://www.fonoteca.gov.co/index.php?option=com_topcontent&view=article&id=2280:ique-venga-el-palabrero&catid=62:sonar-despierto (initials here?)
27. 41 IPR 513 at 530.

of the Ganalbingu people into a performance to be interpreted by the ultimate authority, the white Australian judge. The Australian posture is still one step ahead of the Venezuelan response (to the extent that Ganalbingu law at least is not criminalized), but both instances orientalise indigenous law and deny it real application. The lack of judicial recognition of Wayúu law may partly explain why Venezuelan Wayúus are so keen to use the UNESCO listing as a springboard for broader political claims (a reaction that does not seem to occur on the Colombian side of the border).

The 1991 Colombian Constitution,[28] on the other hand, fully recognizes indigenous jurisdictions such as the Wayúu. Article 246 and 248 of the Constitution determine that indigenous authorities may exercise jurisdictional functions within their territories, in accordance with their norms, as long as they are not contrary to the Constitution, and that the Colombian judicial system will enforce final and binding decisions arising from these jurisdictions.[29] The Constitutional Court of Colombia has determined that the constitutional provisions do not "habilitate" indigenous law, but rather accepts it, and determines that coordination mechanisms be put in place.[30] It has also determined that indigenous law, when being enforced by Colombian courts, should be interpreted in the way that gives these communities the greatest possible autonomy.[31]

The Wayúu legal system is then to be enforced and interpreted by Colombian courts in a way that is conducive to their autonomy, which is certainly different from creating the "other." It seems, thus, that Colombian legal practice is not yet ready to ceremonialise Wayúu law in the same way as cultural authorities, and to actually treat it as a living, integral part of the Colombian normative system. The dissonance in the expectations about the uses of UNESCO recognition (or, more broadly, of the status of Wayúu law and culture as heritage) still remains, however. And a third layer is added to the mix: now, in addition to the Venezuelan Wayúu's autonomy aspirations and the Colombian Executive's economic hopes, one must add judicial perceptions: on the one hand, there is the Venezuelan Judiciary's attitude (in response to the political Constitution of Venezuela), largely orientalising Wayúu law and denying it any real legal effects; on the other, the Colombian Judiciary is ready to step in as an enforcer at face value, and in a means conducive to autonomy.

A schematic of these relationships would look as follows:

---

28. For a more detailed account of the evolution of Latin American Constitutionalism with regards to the protection of indigenous peoples, see L Lixinski, "Constitutionalism and the Other: Multiculturalism and Indigeneity in Selected Latin American Countries" (2010) 14 *Anuario Iberoamericano de Justicia Constitucional* 235-266 (2010).

29. The relevant provisions are the following: "Article 246. The authorities of indigenous peoples may exercise jurisdictional functions within their territories, in accordance with their own rules and procedures, as long as they are not contrary to the Constitution and laws of the Republic. The law shall establish the forms of coordination of this special jurisdiction with the national judicial system." and "Article 248. Only convictions in final judgments qualify as criminal precedents in all legal orders."

30. Cited by E Solano González, *La Jurisdicción Especial Indígena ante la Corte Constitucional Colombiana*, 159-177, 160, *available at* http://www.bibliojuridica.org/libros/3/1333/11.pdf.

31. Ibid.

Fig. 1 – Perceptions of the Wayúu Legal System

If one considers the interplay of the relationships within each country, there is something to be said about reactions to the listing being, at least in part, responses to pre-existing Judicial branch attitudes. In Venezuela legal enforceability is denied to the Wayúu normative system (which is only symptomatic of broader problems of non-recognition of indigenous autonomy in the country), and the response is to find a backdoor for political claims (enter the UNESCO listing). In Colombia, on the other hand, where legal enforceability has long been recognized (alongside broader political recognition), there is no perceived need to make a case for autonomy on the basis of UNESCO recognition. However, the government official's attempt to appropriate Wayúu law for economic purposes only is received coldly, in what can be seen as an exercise of the autonomy the Wayúu already seemingly enjoy in Colombia. Furthermore, a different reading of the Colombian government official's attempt at highlighting the economic potential can simply be read as a complement to the judicial recognition. In other words, if the Wayúu in Colombia no longer need to make a political and legal bid for recognition, they might as well now turn to the economic potential of their heritage, and decide whether to exploit it as an exercise of their autonomy. The fact that the Colombian authorities are hopeful of that exploitation may be seen simply as opening the door for that discussion. In both countries the reactions to the listing seem to respond to Judicial perceptions of the Wayúu normative system (again, judicial perceptions here acting as a proxy for broader political and or legal recognition issues). Except that in Venezuela the response contains within it a revolutionary spark, whereas in Colombia it is by and large a mutually supportive set of attitudes.

Bearing in mind all of these relationships, what role, if any, can the United Nations Declaration on the Rights of Indigenous Peoples and the American Declaration on the Rights of Indigenous Peoples play in mediating these tensions? The next section explores some of these possibilities.

THE UNDRIP, ADRIP, AND THE POLITICS OF HERITAGE

The Wayúu in Venezuela chose to piggyback on the Colombian inscription on the UNESCO intangible heritage list and use the opportunity to promote broader debates about their political and legal status. As is the rule with indigenous advocacy (at least in Latin America),[32] "culture" became the banner behind which political claims of indigenous peoples could be gathered and articulated. And, in this case, culture translated as heritage.

The most significant problem with the idea of protecting culture as heritage is the very commodification that necessarily ensues, in a way that "cultural heritage becomes revered over, and disembodied from, the very peoples associated with it."[33] The UNDRIP and ADRIP both protect indigenous heritage and legal systems, containing several provisions on these themes.

Out of the two main provisions on indigenous heritage in the UNDRIP,[34] only one of them seems to say something about the idea of legal systems as heritage, and only inasmuch as a legal system can be treated as a ceremony. It seems to be the case that the Wayúu legal system could be treated as a set of ceremonies, at least by UNESCO, given the domain of intangible heritage under which it was inscribed in the list ("social customs and rituals").

By contrast, there are three core provisions in the UNDRIP regarding indigenous legal systems. One of them affirms the right of indigenous peoples to have their own legal systems while at the same time being able to (if they choose to) participate in the political and social life of the state in whose territory they are situated.[35] The second one affirms indigenous peoples' right to develop their own legal systems (as long as they do not contradict international human

---

32. See generally K Engle, *The Elusive Promise of Indigenous Development: Rights, Culture, Strategy* (Duke University Press, 2010).

33. Ibid.

34. The full provisions are as follows: "Article 11. 1. Indigenous peoples have the right to practise and revitalize their cultural traditions and customs. This includes the right to maintain, protect and develop the past, present and future manifestations of their cultures, such as archaeological and historical sites, artefacts, designs, *ceremonies*, technologies and visual and performing arts and literature. 2. States shall provide redress through effective mechanisms, which may include restitution, developed in conjunction with indigenous peoples, with respect to their cultural, intellectual, religious and spiritual property taken without their free, prior and informed consent or in violation of their laws, traditions and customs." (emphasis added) and "Article 31. 1. Indigenous peoples have the right to maintain, control, protect and develop their cultural heritage, traditional knowledge and traditional cultural expressions, as well as the manifestations of their sciences, technologies and cultures, including human and genetic resources, seeds, medicines, knowledge of the properties of fauna and flora, oral traditions, literatures, designs, sports and traditional games and visual and performing arts. They also have the right to maintain, control, protect and develop their intellectual property over such cultural heritage, traditional knowledge, and traditional cultural expressions. 2. In conjunction with indigenous peoples, States shall take effective measures to recognize and protect the exercise of these rights."

35. The full provision is as follows: "Article 5. Indigenous peoples have the right to maintain and strengthen their distinct political, legal, economic, social and cultural institutions, while retaining their rights to participate fully, if they so choose, in the political, economic, social and cultural life of the State."

rights norms).[36] And the third one determines that, if such a legal system exists, the state will adopt measures to ensure these legal systems are recognized.[37]

The ADRIP, by contrast, benefits from close to ten years of use of the UNDRIP (not to mention it did not have the African bloc's last-minute push against self-determination),[38] and therefore has somewhat more sophisticated provisions on these matters. The key provisions on heritage[39] are somewhat similar in tone to those in the UNDRIP. Further, the ADRIP also contains provisions on the recognition of indigenous legal systems,[40] a provision on the resolution of

---

36. The full provision is as follows: "Article 34. Indigenous peoples have the right to promote, develop and maintain their institutional structures and their distinctive customs, spirituality, traditions, procedures, practices and, in the cases where they exist, juridical systems or customs, in accordance with international human rights standards."

37. The full provision is as follows: "Article 27. States shall establish and implement, in conjunction with indigenous peoples concerned, a fair, independent, impartial, open and transparent process, giving due recognition to indigenous peoples' laws, traditions, customs and land tenure systems, to recognize and adjudicate the rights of indigenous peoples pertaining to their lands, territories and resources, including those which were traditionally owned or otherwise occupied or used. Indigenous peoples shall have the right to participate in this process."

38. For this history, see K Engle, "On Fragile Architecture: The UN Declaration on the Rights of Indige-nous Peoples in the Context of Human Rights" (2011) 22(1) *European Journal of International Law* 141

39. The full provisions are as follows: "SECTION THREE: Cultural identity. Article XIII. Right to cul-tural identity and integrity. 1. Indigenous peoples have the right to their own cultural identity and integrity and to their cultural heritage, both tangible and intangible, including historic and ancestral heritage; and to the protection, preservation, maintenance, and development of that cultural heritage for their collective continuity and that of their members and so as to transmit that heritage to future generations. 2. States shall provide redress through effective mechanisms, which may include restitution, developed in conjunction with indigenous peoples, with respect to their cultural, intellectual, religious and spiritual property taken without their free, prior and informed consent or in violation of their laws, traditions and customs. 3. Indig-enous people have the right to the recognition and respect for all their ways of life, world views, spiritual-ity, uses and customs, norms and traditions, forms of social, economic and political organization, forms of transmission of knowledge, institutions, practices, beliefs, values, dress and languages, recognizing their inter-relationship as elaborated in this Declaration." And "Article XXVIII. Protection of Cultural Heritage and Intellectual Property 1. Indigenous peoples have the right to the full recognition and respect for their property, ownership, possession, control, development, and protection of their tangible and intangible cul-tural heritage and intellectual property, including its collective nature, transmitted through millennia, from generation to generation. 2. The collective intellectual property of indigenous peoples includes, inter alia, traditional knowledge and traditional cultural expressions including traditional knowledge associated with genetic resources, ancestral designs and procedures, cultural, artistic, spiritual, technological, and scien-tific, expressions, tangible and intangible cultural heritage, as well as the knowledge and developments of their own related to biodiversity and the utility and qualities of seeds and medicinal plants, flora and fauna. 3. States, with the full and effective participation of indigenous peoples, shall adopt measures necessary to ensure that national and international agreements and regimes provide recognition and adequate protection for the cultural heritage of indigenous peoples and intellectual property associated with that heritage. In adopting these measures, consultations shall be effective intended to obtain the free, prior, and informed consent of indigenous peoples."

40. The relevant provision is as follows: "Article XXII. Indigenous law and jurisdiction 1. Indigenous peoples have the right to promote, develop and maintain their institutional structures and their distinctive customs, spirituality, traditions, procedures, practices and, in the cases where they exist, juridical systems or customs, in accordance with international human rights standards. 2. The indigenous law and legal systems shall be recognized and respected by the national, regional and international legal systems. 3. The matters referring to indigenous persons or to their rights or interests in the jurisdiction of each state shall be conducted so as to provide for the right of the indigenous people to full representation with dignity and equality before the law. Consequently, they are entitled, without discrimination, to equal protection and benefit of the law, including the use of linguistic and cultural interpreters. 4. The States shall take effective measures in conjunction with indigenous peoples to ensure the implementation of this article."

conflicts between indigenous and non-indigenous law,[41] with a further declaratory provision underscoring the relevance of using indigenous legal systems in all decisions affecting them.[42] A notable difference between the UNDRIP and the ADRIP is that the language in the latter, precisely benefitting from activity under the former, is more assertive in some respects. For instance, whereas the UNDRIP says states shall implement systems of recognition of indigenous law, the ADRIP says that indigenous legal systems are recognized domestically, regionally, and internationally. It is a somewhat subtle change in phrasing, but one that testifies to a degree of consensus being built around indigenous norms. With respect to heritage, the provisions are very similar, with the most notable difference being the ADRIP's stronger emphasis on control over heritage, as well as reparations and restitution, which are more tentatively addressed in the UNDRIP.

These three instruments (the ICH Convention, the UNDRIP, and the ADRIP), all being applicable to the Wayúu context, call into question the extent to which they can be considered MSENs. At first glance, the differences in language, and the broader scope of the UNDRIP and ADRIP (which contain more provisions applicable in one way or another to the Wayúu normative system, as opposed to the one provision on the definition of intangible heritage that can be found in the ICH Convention) would suggest there is no relationship to be found among these instruments. However, because they all, in this situation, serve the purpose of emancipating indigenous peoples by celebrating their cultural diversity (to a certain extent), they can be considered to be equivalent norms (even if the UNDRIP and ADRIP are not formally binding, whereas the ICH Convention is).

And MSENs have the potential to create legitimacy deficits, as Claire Charters argues.[43] Most significantly, these parallel provisions dilute their own normative value through institutional competition aggravated by procedural opacity. But, at the same time, not only are these legitimacy concerns mitigated by dialogic attempts, but they also create more opportunities for the establishment of more responsive institutions, as they become open to input from the outside.[44] In this sense, UNESCO can have a positive influence on the implementation of the UNDRIP and ADRIP by nation states, and the two Declarations may

---

41. The relevant provision is: "Article XXXIV In case of conflicts and disputes with indigenous peoples, states shall provide, with the full and effective participation of those peoples, just, equitable and effective mechanisms and procedures for their prompt resolution. For this purpose, due consideration and recognition shall be given to the customs, traditions, norms or legal systems of the indigenous peoples concerned."
42. The relevant provision is: "Article XXIII. Contributions of the indigenous legal and organizational systems 1. Indigenous peoples have the right to full and effective participation in decision-making, through representatives chosen by themselves in accordance with their own institutions, in matters which affect their rights, and which are related to the development and execution of laws, public policies, programs, plans, and actions related to indigenous matters. 2. States shall consult and cooperate in good faith with the indigenous peoples concerned through their own representative institutions in order to obtain their free, prior and informed consent before adopting and implementing legislative or administrative measures that may affect them."
43. C Charters, "Multi-Sourced Equivalent Norms and the Legitimacy of Indigenous Peoples' Rights under International Law" in *Multi-Sourced Equivalent Norms in International Law* 289, 289 (T Broude and Y Shany eds.) (Hart Publishing, 2011).
44. Ibid.

positively influence the implementation of the ICH Convention when it comes to indigenous peoples. The fact that the UNDRIP and ADRIP are not binding, and therefore dispense with ratification processes, means they can in fact be a lot more pervasive, given the tradition of judicial recourse to non-binding international instruments to shed light on binding rules of international law, especially in the area of human rights.[45]

In light of the existence of two sets of norms (the ones on heritage, and the ones specific to indigenous legal systems) in the UNDRIP and ADRIP, one must wonder why the Wayúu would want to assert their rights before UNESCO (and, therefore, turn their legal systems into heritage). Beyond the fact that the UNDRIP and ADRIP have no enforcement mechanisms, whereas UNESCO is a ready and available international forum, one possible reason would be an assertion (echoed by the Venezuelan Wayúu leader) of the transboundary character of the Wayúu people, and ultimately their (symbolic) independence from Colombia or Venezuela. But that is very unlikely an agenda, given that the nomination was made only by Colombia, despite the fact that Venezuela is, too, a party to the ICH Convention (and in fact became a party almost a full year before Colombia).

But it does seem, in opinions expressed by Wayúu leaders in the aftermath of the inscription, that what is at stake for them is the survival of their culture in general, not the enforceability or recognition as a valid system of law (a matter that, however important, is only part of the question of Wayúu survival, and one that seems to be largely settled, at least in Colombia). In this sense, the inscription in the UNESCO list becomes an advocacy tool, despite the fact that it is the nominating state before UNESCO that gets to determine the content of the nomination file (and, ultimately, the very content and meaning of the heritage, at least in this international forum).[46]

For the purposes of the survival of a culture, culture as heritage is still seen as an effective (or at least appropriate) advocacy tool, despite the grave risk of commodification and folklorisation, one that has already come to the fore even in the celebration of the Wayúu inscription. The objective of cultural survival seems to fit well within the limits of self-determination in the UNDRIP and ADRIP.[47] By translating self-determination into cultural development (alongside

---

45. With respect to the uses of non-binding instruments and generally the application of international human rights treaties by domestic courts, see B Conforti and F Francioni (eds.), *Enforcing International Human Rights in Domestic Courts* (Brill, 1997); and D L Sloss (ed.), *The Role of Domestic Courts in Treaty Enforcement: A Comparative Study*, Cambridge University Press (2009). On the specific behavior of domestic courts of one country in the use of soft law, see C Lima Marques and L Lixinski, "Treaty Enforcement by Brazilian Courts: Reconciling Ambivalences and Myths?"*(2009)* 4(1) *Brazilian Yearbook of International Law* 138-169 (2009).

46. For this critique in more depth, *see* L Lixinski, "Selecting Heritage: The Interplay of Art, Law and Politics"*(2011)*. 22(1) *European Journal of International Law* 81-100.

47. The full provision is as follows: "Article 3. Indigenous peoples have the right of self-determination. By virtue of that right they freely determine their political status and freely pursue their economic, social and cultural development." For a broader discussion of heritage listing as self-determination, coupling the Wayúu example with Ladakh Buddhist Chanting in India, see L Lixinski, "Heritage Listing as Self-de-

the economic development that seems to be the target of the Colombian Executive branch), one waters down the political potential of self-determination, and the recognition of Wayúu culture and identity becomes the recognition of culture for culture's own sake. While this may not be the full extent of the Wayúu agenda (in that they clearly want to attribute significance to their culture beyond the recognition of culture for its own sake), it seems to be possible to inscribe the culture as a first step, to then re-discuss its meaning and the implications of the inscription once it is a done deal (which seems to be happening with the Wayúu, if one takes the Venezuelan side of the border's statements as representative of the wider Wayúu people).

But, because recognition of a legal system as a manifestation of heritage seems to receive more attention than the judicial enforceability of that system, is that to say the UNDRIP (and, more recently, the ADRIP) have failed the Wayúu people? It would seem that it did not, on the Colombian side of the border. The opinions of Colombian Wayúu representatives in the aftermath of the inscription seemed to express much more concern about cultural survival than with broader claims for political autonomy, a goal which seems to be served by inscription of their legal system as heritage. On the other hand, Venezuelan Wayúu claims for greater legal and political autonomy seem to indeed fall flat in the context of the inscription of the Wayúu normative system in the UNESCO intangible heritage list. The UNDRIP and ADRIP do not seem to have successfully penetrated, at least in this instance, the implementation of the 2003 ICH Convention. But that is not to say that, in the long run, this interpenetration will not happen; much to the contrary, there are reasons to believe that the ICH Convention has the potential to become more sensitive to the UNDRIP and ADRIP in other contexts, particularly as the Declarations gain more recognition and more avenues for community participation are opened before UNESCO. Considering Claire Charters' claim that indigenous participation in international fora is by and large responsible for the development of more just norms for indigenous peoples across the spectrum of international institutions,[48] community involvement in heritage management at the international level holds the key for greater fairness in the safeguarding of indigenous cultures.

CONCLUDING REMARKS

Listing a legal system as a manifestation of intangible heritage under UNESCO cuts both ways: if on the one hand it becomes a platform to promote greater autonomy for a legal system and an indigenous people, on the other it risks mummifying the culture and focusing on its ceremonial aspects as a means to create a performance that can attract tourists. All in all, the Wayúu example, and

termination", in A Durbach and L Lixinski (eds.), *Heritage, Culture, and Rights: Challenging Legal Discourses* 227-249 (Hart Publishing, 2017).
48. n. 41.

the dissonance between the Judicial (through the Colombian Constitutional Court) and Executive (through the Colombian Ministry of Culture) branches' treatment of the *palabrero* system, illustrates tensions in the creation and packaging of the other. It reveals that, behind every packaging, there may (and should) run a deeper political agenda that is capable of subverting attempts at commodification of culture (and legal systems) in favor of the promotion of cultural diversity and understanding across borders.

The commodification of culture is a constant risk when it comes to attempts at legally protecting or safeguarding heritage, but it is one that seems to go largely unrecognized in the existing legal frameworks. This happens in part because these frameworks are purposefully open-ended, because constricting legal safeguarding is one means of commodification. But, by avoiding legal commodification at the international level, the result is that these instruments leave the door open for commodification in all other possible levels, and local authorities and communities themselves, unaware of the unintended consequences of some of the strategies and policies they may adopt towards their own heritage, put these cultural manifestations at risk. There does not seem to be much of a risk with commodification when heritage governance stems organically from the communities themselves, because they are certainly interested in the long-term survival and social engagement with the manifestations of heritage. However, when external actors are involved, the risk is greater, because the value they perceive in heritage is often short-term and economically driven.

Despite the risks associated with involving external actors, communities cannot dispense with them, particularly because heritage listing is seen as a means to generate awareness from those external actors themselves. In this sense, the value of heritage listing is relational, and UNESCO listing is only important to communities to the extent it is perceived by them as a tool to present their heritage to the outside world, while at the same time claiming ownership and control over it. The former goal is easily accomplished, the latter is the more difficult one, because of the monopoly states have when it comes to listing, which can give them a falsely inflated stake in that heritage. States should act here only as mediators, not as co-owners of heritage being listed.

These tensions come further to the fore when one speaks of indigenous heritage, given the fragility of those communities to begin with, and the many political issues on the table at any given time. The UN Declaration on the Rights of Indigenous Peoples and the OAS American Declaration on the Rights of Indigenous Peoples are attempts to articulate these issues, and they include several provisions on heritage. However, the UNDRIP and ADRIP have, so far, largely failed to make their way into UNESCO, despite its many provisions on indigenous heritage. But that is one instance, in which the claims of the Colombian Wayúus (the ones receiving the UNESCO blessing) were modest and fell squarely within the goals of the heritage system. The UNESCO listing has managed to generate some discussion from Wayúus in Venezuela (where greater recognition is needed) about the potentials of the recognition of their culture as platforms for their political agendas. So, despite UNESCO not having taken the UNDRIP into account at the time of inscription, indigenous advocates can still creatively use heritage listing as a platform for more pervasive advocacy.

RIGHTS AND REPARATIONS: AN ASSESSMENT OF THE UNDRIP'S CONTRIBUTION TO AMERICAN INDIAN LAND CLAIMS

Sarah Sargent

One of the most complex questions that arises in indigenous rights is that of adequate reparations for lost land. Land plays a very specific and central role in indigenous culture. It is the focal point of indigenous identity, religious and cultural beliefs. Safeguarding indigenous rights to land and providing appropriate and effective reparation for land that has been lost is one of the most contentious areas of jurisprudence in this area.

Indigenous land claims in the United States have been the subject of domestic, regional and even international litigation. The result of those cases in domestic courts has rarely been satisfactory to indigenous claimants, even in those exceptional instances where rulings favoured indigenous claims. In some instances, awards of monetary damages go uncollected for years, rejected by the indigenous community as unsatisfactory compensation for the loss of its land.

Favourable decisions in regional or international forums may be unenforceable. The much-anticipated 2007 United Nations Declaration on the Rights of Indigenous Peoples (UNDRIP) has proven to be very disappointing as it offers little to help resolve the problems of indigenous claims on aspects of enforcement, adequate reparations and providing direction on an appropriate forum in which to raise these claims.

The UNDRIP in its approved form is a "compromise"[1] document that falls short of the promise demonstrated in its drafting phases. It might have been

---

1. S Wiessner, "The Cultural Rights of Indigenous Peoples: Achievements and Continuing Challenges" (2011) 22 (1) *European Journal of International Law* 121, 131.

able to provide stronger guidance and direction in some contentious areas of land claims. In the end, the UNDRIP's contribution to provide for adequate reparations disappoints and adds little to the already existing reparations available in the Inter-American and UN systems of human rights. It also does nothing to clarify issues about the appropriate venue in which to raise claims.

Land rights have become a contentious issue on a number of levels. One of these has to do with simple pragmatics—that, as discussed further in this chapter, the land is needed for sustaining life, for hunting, fishing, and perhaps grazing of livestock. On another level, perhaps no less an issue for survival, is the way in which the land is inextricably linked to indigenous identity and culture. This is also further discussed within the chapter. States, for their part, are reluctant to recognise indigenous land rights when these might interfere with development or extraction of resources. This is the situation with the Western Shoshone lands. The recognition of land claims, and the basis on which these are recognised, can also determine whether or not the state is responsible for compensating indigenous groups for land wrongfully taken.

This chapter uses the land claims of the Western Shoshone as a case study to evaluate the effects of the UNDRIP. These claims have been brought to the U.S. Supreme Court, to the Inter-American Commission of Human Rights and to the Committee on the Elimination of all Racial Discrimination (CERD) through its innovative Early Warning and Urgent Action Procedure. The examination of land claims through this case study highlights the persistent and pervasive problems that indigenous groups face when trying pursue legal action.

This chapter proceeds as follows. Firstly, it examines the importance that land has to indigenous groups in the United States. This centrality of land to indigenous identity, culture and well-being is a vital part of the significance of indigenous land claims. Second, it considers the contradictory and complex legal doctrines that have evolved in the United States on the nature of indigenous land interest, and when and whether that interest can be extinguished, and whether any loss of land interest is compensable. The third section considers the case study of the Western Shoshone land claims brought through the United States legal system, and then to the Inter-American regional human rights system, and finally to the international human rights system of the United Nations Convention on the Elimination of All Racial Discrimination. The fourth section evaluates the effectiveness of the UNDRIP in addressing the difficulties highlighted in the Western Shoshone case study. Finally, some concluding thoughts are offered.

SECTION ONE: IMPORTANCE OF LAND TO INDIGENOUS PEOPLES IN THE UNITED STATES

Land is of critical importance to indigenous peoples. It forms a core of their cultural and spiritual identity, as well as providing, in some instances, the means of sustenance and livelihood through hunting, fishing and ranching.[2] Land is much more than the physical space of where indigenous peoples live, or where ancestors lived. Often the identity of a particular indigenous group is inextricably intertwined with a specific landscape. This is poignantly demonstrated in the reaction of the Navajo peoples in returning to their homelands after they were forcibly removed:[3]

> "The nights and days were long before it came time for us to go to our homes", Manuelito said. "The day before we were to start we went a little way towards home, because we were so anxious to start... When we saw the top of the mountain from Albuquerque we wondered if it was our mountain, and we felt like talking to the ground, we loved it so, and some of the old men and women cried with joy when they reached their homes."[4]

The indigenous relationship to land is not merely a relic from the past. It remains very much a matter of concern in the contemporary construction of indigenous rights. Land rights underpin the ability to exercise many other indigenous rights. The International Law Association Committee on the Rights of Indigenous Peoples[5] notes that land rights are part of "the crucial element of indigenous self-determination as well as cultural identity and integrity".[6]

Specific localities are significant to indigenous groups as vital to indigenous identity and spirituality. This means that specific areas of land are unique and because of this, replacement of that land with other land or the provision of monetary compensation for its loss, can fail as an adequate measure of reparation.

But there is another fundamental consequence to the loss of access to ancestral and traditional lands. Loss of land means the loss of access to resources that meet basic needs of survival, such as clean water, hunting and fishing, as well as to spiritual and cultural resources.[7] This is true of the Western Shoshone, as highlighted in the claims that were raised to the Committee on the Elimination

---

2. See for instance, "Inter-American Commission on Human Rights, Indigenous and Tribal Peoples" Rights Over Their Ancestral Lands and Natural Resources, Norms and Jurisprudence of the Inter-American Human Rights System" (2010) 35(2) *American Indian Law Review* 263, 296-300 ("Norms and Jurisprudence").
3. The Navajo peoples were removed from their homelands in the Southwestern part of the present day United States after a protracted conflict with the United States. Finally, they were permitted to return to their homelands, albeit to a greatly reduced land mass, in 1868. See D Brown, "The Long Walk of the Navahos", in *Bury My Heart at Wounded Knee: An Indian History of the American West* (Vintage, 1991).
4. D Brown, *Bury My Heart at Wounded Knee: An Indian History of the American West* (Vintage, 1991) 34-36. Manuelito was commenting on the Navajo return to their land in 1868. See also Valentina Vadi, Chapter 1 this book at 13-40.
5. The International Law Association has "consultative status, as an international non-governmental organisation, with a number of the United Nations specialised agencies." Website for the International Law Association, "About Us" at http://www.ila-hq.org/en/about_us/index.cfm.
6. Interim Report, Rights of Indigenous Peoples, International Law Society (2010) 10-11. ("Hague Conference Report").
7. Norms and Jurisprudence, n. 2, 299-300.

of All Racial Discrimination.[8] This loss can lead to poor health and housing standards, and contribute to the low life expectancy and high mortality rates that many indigenous groups experience.[9]

Access to and the ability to use land can be important for indigenous peoples' livelihood, even for those activities that are no longer strictly traditional. That indigenous peoples' lives, culture and activities change over time is a point that should not be lost in the consideration of adequate reparations for the use of land. Culture by its very definition is something that changes. Thus, to limit indigenous interests in land or activities to that which has been traditional is fraught with problems. This does not account for instances of forced assimilation, often necessary to simply survive, or adapting activities to what can be supported on marginal land, due to the taking of more valuable land.

Nor does this approach account for cultural change that inevitably occurs, rendering the land no less valued or needed. A good example of this is that of the ranching activities of the Dann sisters, whose litigation about Western Shoshone land rights is discussed later in this chapter. This pastoral form of livelihood is not divorced from traditional use of land and resources; it is a change of pastoralism which has had to be adapted to meet changes in indigenous circumstances over more than one hundred years.[10] It would be wrong to view it as having no link to traditional activities.[11] Using a classification of "traditional" activities as defining indigenous interests in land and resources ignores the fact that changes may have had to occur in activities to ensure basic survival of peoples faced with changed circumstances and harsh living conditions.

SECTION TWO: INDIGENOUS LAND CLAIMS IN THE UNITED STATES

This section evaluates the legal doctrines of the United States that are raised in land claims and in defining indigenous land interests in respect to determining whether these are compensable; and if compensable, what form the reparations should take. The United States has created a contradictory and complex set of federal law doctrines that set out the relationship between indigenous groups and the federal government, determining what interest in land indigenous groups are said to hold, and setting limits around the compensability of claims when land has been wrongfully taken.

A starting point for discussion is understanding the nature of land interest that United States federal law and policy deem American Indian tribes hold.

---

8. See discussion, *infra*.
9. Norms and Jurisprudence, n. 2, 299-300.
10. See S Sargent, "Unfulfilled promises: Safeguarding the horse culture of American Indians", *Transnational Dispute Management* TDM 2 (March 2014)
11. *Amended Request for Urgent Action under the Early Warning Procedure, by the Yomba Shoshone Tribe and the Ely Shoshone Tribe of the Western Shoshone Peoples* (Amended Request) para 3, https://law2.arizona.edu/iplp/outreach/shoshone/documents/WSCERDAmendedRequest.pdf

It is one of use and possession, and not of fee simple title. This is referred to as "Indian title" or "native title." Under this form of title, tribes do not have the ability to sell their land. The Doctrine of Discovery says that Indian tribes' interest in land was converted by the arrival of Europeans to the shores of the so-called New World. Whatever interest Indian tribes had was transformed, according to this doctrine, to a limited right of possession. It is a doctrine that perhaps surprisingly is still relied upon today as the basis of American Indian land interests.

The United States Supreme Court still relies on the much discredited[12] "Doctrine of Discovery" for finding that indigenous interest in land is not fee title, but simply one of use and possession. As recently as 2005, this was cited with approval by the United States Supreme Court as the basis for establishing land interests of the federal government and Indian tribes. In the decision of *Sherrill v Oneida Indian Nation of New York*,[13] a footnote in the majority decision written by Justice Ginsberg explains:

> Under the "doctrine of discovery", fee title to the lands occupied by Indians when the colonists arrived became vested in the sovereign — first the discovering European nation and later the original States and the United States. In the original 13 States, fee title to Indian lands or the pre-emptive right to purchase from the Indians was in the State.[14]

Commentators trace some contemporary U.S. positions on Indian title to the trilogy of decisions from the U.S. Supreme Court written by Chief Justice Marshall, known as the "Marshall trilogy."[15] These cases represent Marshall's efforts to interpret the doctrine of discovery in litigation about disputed claims to lands in which American Indians had an interest. There is not a settled position on what these cases ultimately provide,[16] and this is complicated by the lack of consistency between the decisions themselves. Debate centres around what residual form of rights American Indians have after the arrival of Europeans on these lands. Given the tangle of contradictory legal reasoning in these cases, it is not surprising that understanding the U.S. position can be difficult. There is also a split of views as to what the current position *is* and what it *should be*.[17]

Watson has offered a clear and concise explanation of the at-times bewilderingly contradictory and complex positions that have been taken to

12. See, for instance, *UN Permanent Forum on Indigenous Issues Discusses Theme: The Doctrine of Discovery*, 2012, https://www.unngls.org/index.php/un-ngls_news_archives/2012/350-un-permanent-fo-rum-on-indigenous-issues-discusses-theme-the-doctrine-of-discovery
13. 544 US 197 (2005).
14. *Sherrill v Oneida Indian Nation of New York*, 544 US 197 (2005), footnote 1.
15. *Johnson v McIntosh*, 21 US 543 (1823); *Cherokee Nation v Georgia*, 30 US 1 (1831); *Worcester v Georgia*, 31 US 515 (1832).
16. See B Watson, "The Doctrine of Discovery and the Elusive Definition of Native Title" (2011) 15(4) *Lewis and Clark Review* 995, 999-1000.
17. See Watson, n. 16, generally on this point.

the U.S. courts on the nature of Indian title. In particular Watson notes that the U.S. Supreme Court decisions have taken two main views of Indian title: that of "limited possessor"[18] versus "limited owner."[19] Firstly, is the one put forward in *Johnson v McIntosh*[20], which is the mainstream position followed in U.S. Supreme Court decisions today. Watson describes this:

> The indigenous inhabitants continue to possess the land they occupy, but after discovery, no longer own the lands they occupy. The discoverer owns the land subject to native title, i.e. the right of possession (or occupancy). The discoverer/owner can transfer ownership notwithstanding the native title. The discoverer/owner has the exclusive (pre-emptive) right to extinguish the native title. Once the native title is extinguished, the discoverer/owner of the lands also has the right of possession.[21]

In contrast is the view of the "limited owner" that was put forward by the *Worcester v Georgia*[22] decision:

> The indigenous inhabitants continue to own the lands they occupy but, after discovery, cannot sell their lands to whomsoever they please. The discoverer holds a "right of pre-emption" giving the discoverer the exclusive right to acquire the property rights of the indigenous inhabitants.[23]

Clearly, as Watson emphatically notes, the limited owner view gives more rights to indigenous groups and as in the later *Worcester v Georgia* case, modifies the position that was taken in *Johnson v McIntosh*.[24] But the U.S. Supreme Court continues to follow the *Johnson* precedent, effectively ignoring the *Worcester* case, and never reconciling the contradictory positions.[25]

This line of legal reasoning exists alongside a view that American Indians have "inherent sovereignty"—that is a sovereignty that is not derived from any constitutional or legal positions, but something that was an innate quality of such groups. However, confusingly and contradictorily, this inherent sovereignty can be unilaterally abrogated by Congress at any time.[26] Thus, to the extent

---

18. Ibid., 999.
19. Ibid., 999.
20. 21 US 543 (1823).
21. Watson, n. 16, 998-999. Emphasis in the original.
22. 31 US 515 (1832).
23. Watson, n. 16, 998. Emphasis in the original.
24. See generally Watson, n. 16.
25. See Watson, n. 16, generally. See also B Watson, "The Impact of the American Doctrine of Discovery on Native Land Rights in Australia, Canada, and New Zealand" (2011) 34 *Seattle University Law Review* 507, 507-512.
26. On the doctrine of discovery, see R A Williams Jr, *The Colonist's War for America*, in *The American Indian in Western Legal Thought: The Discourse of Conquest* (Oxford University Press, 1990), particularly

that such inherent sovereignty would give sovereign-like claims to land—those that would be needed, for instance, to enter into treaties where the land is the subject—the ability of Congress to unilaterally terminate sovereignty of indigenous groups belies any need for treaties. The concept of inherent sovereignty itself contradictorily exists alongside doctrines that view American Indian tribes as "wards" or "domestic dependents"[27] of the federal government, such that the federal government acts as a trustee for tribes, including on matters of land.

The sum and substance of the complex legal views taken of indigenous interest in land is that indigenous interest, if found to exist, is non-proprietary, with the effect that the taking of the land is easily accomplished and requires no compensation unless there has been a breach of the trustee duties of the United States federal government. There are few instances where American federal law would support payment of compensation or reparation for the loss of land.

TREATY DISPUTES: DOMESTIC LAW OR INTERNATIONAL LAW?

Should claims arising under treaties be brought as a matter of domestic or international law? The U.S. position has been unfailingly that these are a matter of domestic jurisdiction, based on the positions in the Marshall decisions, positions that are again based on the doctrine of discovery.[28]

Scholars advance contrary arguments that treaty disputes should be viewed as a matter for international, rather than domestic, resolution.[29] Dorr, for instance, comments on the historical account that regarded American Indian nations as "fully sovereign",[30] such that treaties between the U.S. federal

---

312-319 and V Deloria Jr, "The Doctrine of Discovery", in *Behind the Trail of Broken Treaties: An Indian Declaration of Independence* (University of Texas Press, Austin, 1985). On plenary power, see V Deloria Jr, "The Plenary Power Doctrine", in *Behind the Trail of Broken Treaties: An Indian Declaration of Independence* (University of Texas Press, Austin, 1985).

27. See, for instance, the discussion by M Sundquist, "Worcester v Georgia: A Breakdown in the Separation of Powers" (2010) *35 American Indian Law Review* 239, 244, where the United States Supreme Court notes the existence of both an inherent sovereignty of the Cherokee Nation and its status as a "denominated domestic dependent nation…" in its decision in *Worcester v Georgia*. See also V Deloria, Jr, who comments that "John Marshall's offhand remark that the relationship between the Indians and the United States resembled "that of a guardian to its ward" was transformed by the federal courts and Congress into a full-blown theory of wardship under which Congress had unlimited and plenary power to dispose of the lives and property of Indians without any more justification than it had the power and, by definition, the wisdom to do so.", "Dependent Domestic Nations", in *Behind the Trail of Broken Treaties: An Indian Declaration of Independence* (University of Texas Press, Austin, 1985), 134.

28. For a full discussion on this see S Wiessner, "American Indian Treaties and Modern International Law" (1995) 7 *St Thomas Law Review* 567.

29. Ibid., 587-588.

30. D Dorr, "The Background of the Theory of Discovery" (2013) 38(2) *American Indian Law Review* 477, 492.

government and the American Indian should be "regarded as internationally binding."[31]

Wiessner continues in this vein when he comments on the legal sleight of hand that has served the interests of the United States government in making American Indian tribes subordinate and subject to federal policy, and in making legal questions about treaty terms matters of domestic law. In so commenting, he reveals inconsistencies in the doctrines that are used, which makes understanding American federal Indian policy at times very difficult:

> Another argument for the international character of these treaties
> is that tribal governments in the United States are not bound by
> the United States Constitution, in particular its Bill of Rights.
> On the other hand, Congress, on questionable constitutional
> basis articulated first by Chief Justice Marshall, has made the
> sweeping claim to "plenary power" over the Indians, coupled
> with the characterization of the federal-Indian as a guardian-ward
> relationship. In conjunction with the "domestic dependent nation"
> metaphor, this has served to cloud the understanding of the original
> treaty obligations as purely domestic.[32]

As this chapter discusses, even those treaty claims that have advanced into the regional and international human rights sphere have not fared well as the United States cannot be compelled to implement decisions made against it. International law lacks a direct enforcement mechanism, and there is very often little to nothing that can be done to make a state implement measures it does not wish to. Even if indigenous treaties were determined to be international rather than domestic in nature, the intractable problem of compliance and enforcement would not have been solved.

SECTION THREE: CASE STUDY: LITIGATION OF WESTERN SHOSHONE LAND CLAIMS

Just as the legal doctrines that control the relationship with the federal government and Indian nations are multifarious, so are the histories of long-running litigation on Indian land claims. The histories of these cases reflect the changing federal policy on Indians and the difficulty of accommodating the land claims created by treaties in a way that is consistent with the attributes an Indian nation had to enter into a treaty in the first place—that of a sovereign legal personality.[33]

---

31. Ibid., 492.
32. Wiessner, n. 28, 587-588.
33. S Sargent and G Melling, "The Exercise of External Self-determination by Indigenous Groups: An examination of the Republic of Lakotah and the inherent sovereignty of American Indigenous Peoples" (2015) 1 *Sri Lanka Journal of International and Comparative Law* 49.

The domestic jurisdiction of the U.S. in itself conflicts with the idea of Indian nations as sovereign, in that the legal system of the U.S. subsumes any of the Indian nation, making the U.S. system the dominant one. Secondly, the U.S. system has devolved doctrines that limit the ability of the American Indian nations to assert any claims whatsoever.

The domestic history of litigation about the Western Shoshone efforts to preserve their land rights is a long and complex one. There are several cases that have been brought, all of which assert the Western Shoshone claims, none of which have been successful in the United States courts, in having that land restored to them. The decisions are consistent in their denial of Shoshone rights. One claim brought through the Indian Claims Court—a court specially created to hear Indian litigation about land rights[34]—found that the Shoshone had lost legal title to the land that had been granted to them through the Treaty of Ruby Valley.[35] The basis for this loss was the presence on the land of non-Indians. This presence, referred to as "gradual encroachment"[36] was repeatedly asserted by the federal government as sufficient to divest the Western Shoshone of their land rights, despite the terms of the treaty and their own continued presence and use of the land.[37] This continued presence of the Western Shoshone and the use they made of the land resulted in allegations of trespass against two Western Shoshone sisters, Mary and Carrie Dann.[38] The trespass claim was due to their use of the land to graze livestock, without having a federal permit.[39] The Dann position was that they were not required to have a permit, as their livestock was on tribal land.[40] This law suit was to make its way to the U.S. Supreme Court,[41] and then to the Inter-American Commission on Human Rights.[42]

The United States Supreme Court decision upheld prior findings that the Western Shoshone interest in the land had been extinguished through the gradual encroachment onto it, and that any compensation due had been completed through payment to the U.S. federal government as the trustee for the tribe.[43] Commentators raise concerns about the position that the U.S. Supreme Court took regarding the extinguishment of Western Shoshone land title, that "gradual encroachment" of non-Western Shoshone onto the land in violation of the terms of the treaty could somehow serve to violate the Shoshone land interests under

---

34. D Schaaf and J Fishel, "*Mary and Carrie Dann v United States* at the Inter-American Commission on Human Rights: Victory for Indian Land Rights and the Environment (2002) 16 *Tulane Environmental Law Journal* 175, 178-179.
35. Ibid., 178-179.
36. Ibid., 179.
37. Ibid., 179-180.
38. Ibid., 179.
39. Ibid., 179.
40. T Luebben and C Nelson, "The Indian Wars: Efforts to Resolve Western Shoshone Land and Treaty Issues and Distribute the Indian Claims Commission Judgment Fund (2002) 42 *Natural Resources Journal* 801, 804.
41. Schaaf and Fishel, n. 34, 180.
42. Ibid., 181.
43. Ibid., 179- 180.

that treaty. Schaaf and Fishel note a failure to "discuss how the ICC [Indian Claims Commission] acquired legal authority to extinguish Western Shoshone land rights"[44] and the Supreme Court failure to recognise that "such gradual encroachment does not ordinarily suffice under U.S. law to extinguish Indian land rights."[45]

A second issue is noted by the former United Nations Special Rapporteur on Indigenous Issues, Professor James Anaya. He comments that the U.S. Supreme Court decision failed to even rule on the merits of the Western Shoshone claim, choosing instead to affirm the underlying rulings regarding the loss of land title by the gradual encroachment upon the land. Anaya notes that:

> The U.S. Supreme Court refused to consider the merits of the case—whether or not the Western Shoshone still had title to the land in question. Often people mistakenly assume that the Supreme Court resolved the underlying ownership dispute, but it did not even consider the question...[46]

These criticisms were to resurface in the decisions against the United States in the Inter-American regional human rights system and in the international human rights system.

INTER-AMERICAN SYSTEM ON HUMAN RIGHTS

It should be noted here, to avoid confusion in nomenclature, that the Inter-American system is a regional system of countries in North, Central and South America, and not a domestic system of the United States.

The Inter-American system provides a forum for individuals to bring human rights complaints about the state. The system is made up of two different organs, the Commission and the Court, who have different but inter-related jurisdiction and power to hear matters.[47] All matters begin before the Commission. The Commission can only issue non-binding decisions, but it does permit individuals to lodge complaints against states.[48] Some matters can proceed to the Court from the Commission[49]—and are then subject to one of two jurisdictional powers

---

44. Ibid., 180.
45. Ibid., 180.
46. J Anaya, "Keynote Address: Indigenous Peoples and their Mark on the International Legal System" (2006-2007) 31(2) *American Indian Law Review* 257, 265.
47. J Pasqualucci, "Advisory Practice of the Inter-American Court of Human Rights: Contributing to the Opinion of the Evolution of International Human Rights Law" (2002) 38 *Stanford Law Journal* 241, 247.
48. T Helton, "Introduction to the IACHR Report on Indigenous and Tribal Peoples' Rights Over Their Ancestral Lands and Natural Resources: Norms and Jurisprudence of the Inter-American Human Rights System" (2010) 35(2) *American Indian Law Review* 257, 260-262. See also Pascqualucci (2002) n. 47, 248.
49. Helton, n. 48, 261.

of the Court—its binding, or contentious jurisdiction, and its non-binding, or advisory jurisdiction.[50] It is part of the Organisation of American States (OAS).[51]

This regional human rights system has been very influential in setting legal standards for reparations in indigenous land claims.[52] Its decisions incorporate its own regional instruments and normative interpretations, as well as making reference to international instruments and norms.[53] These decisions have challenged state-centric views by recognising indigenous systems of land tenure on the same footing as state land title registration systems. This has opened up new avenues of legal thinking and response on indigenous land claims.

There are two organs that can address human rights complaints: the Inter-American Commission on Human Rights (Commission) and the Inter-American Court on Human Rights.[54] Intricately linked to the function of these two organs are two human rights instruments, the American Declaration on the Rights and Duties of Man and the American Convention on Human Rights.[55] Broad jurisdictional allowances create a wide scope for bringing human rights claims against states. This is accomplished through the application of the American Declaration on the Rights and Duties of Man to all member states of the OAS.[56] This allows individuals to file human rights complaints against member States in the Commission. This permits bringing indigenous land claims against States that have not signed onto the American Convention.[57] The *Dann* case, was brought against the United States using this provision for Commission jurisdiction.[58] It was filed in 1993 with the decision delivered in 2002.[59]

The Inter-American Commission found against the United States on several important points of law. The complaint to the Commission raised issues about the way in which the U.S. federal government had justified the extinguishment of Western Shoshone interest in land. This was done, the complaint argued,

---

50. Pasqualucci (2002) n. 47, 249.
51. Helton, n. 48, 260.
52. See generally Pasqualucci (2002), n. 47; J Pasqualucci, "The Evolution of International Indigenous Rights in the Inter-American Human Rights System" (2006) 6 *Human Rights Law Review* 281; J Pasqualucci, "International Indigenous Land Rights: A Critique of the Jurisprudence of the Inter-American Court of Human Rights in Light of the United Nations Declaration on the Rights of Indigenous Peoples (2009) 27(1) *Wisconsin International Law Journal* 5. Pasqualucci (2006) comments "...the Inter-American Court of Human Rights and the Inter-American Commission on Human Rights have developed a progressive case law on indigenous peoples' rights." 283.
53. *Norms and Jurisprudence*, n. 2, 273. This states, "The IACHR [Commission] and the Inter-American Court may look to the provisions of other international human rights treaties in interpreting the American Declaration and the American Convention in cases that concern indigenous and tribal peoples. The IACHR has clarified that the provisions of other multilateral treaties adopted within and outside of the framework of the Inter-American system are relevant to interpreting the American Declaration of the Rights and Duties of Man....The IACHR and the Court have also had recourse to the interpretations of the United Nations human rights organs and mechanisms, in respect to the rights enshrined in the international treaties monitored by these organs and mechanisms.", 273-274.
54. Helton, n. 48, 260.
55. Ibid., 260.
56. Pasqualucci (2009), n. 52, 52
57. Pasqualucci (2002), n. 47, 251.
58. See, for instance, Pasqualucci (2006), n. 52, 282.
59. Schaaf and Fishel, n. 34, 181.

"without due process of law and without compensation."[60] The Commission's decision agreed with this, finding that the U.S. had taken Western Shoshone land without due process.[61] The Commission found that the actions of the U.S. were a violation of human rights, and contrary to international human rights standards.[62]

There was a great deal of optimism that this decision had opened up an avenue for legal protection for American Indian land rights.[63] It seemed that a venue had been found that would force the U.S. government to change its doctrines, and respect the land rights it once had promised to in treaties.[64]

In the wake of the Commission's decision it might well have been expected that the U.S. would review and change its domestic policies and doctrines with respect to indigenous rights, and ensure that indigenous property rights were properly protected in light of its comments. Indeed, the Inter-American decision contemplated that the United States would ensure that the Danns were given a remedy that was comport with its decision and that there would be reform to the U.S. domestic system.[65] But as further discussion in this chapter shows, this hopeful promise of change was not to be realized.

RELATED CLAIM OF YOMBA SHOSHONE TO CERD

The Western Shoshone land claims were also brought to an international forum. In contrast with the non-binding jurisdiction of the Inter-American Commission on Human Rights, the forum to which this claim was brought is able to issue binding decisions against states who are members of the Convention. The Yomba Shoshone, a tribe of the Western Shoshone, brought a claim with the Committee for the Elimination of all Racial Discrimination in 1999. This committee is the treaty body for the binding Convention for Elimination of All Racial Discrimination (CERD). This claim was pending during the Inter-American litigation, with the Committee delivering its decision in 2006, some four years after the Inter-American decision.

The CERD has been the site of the development of an international jurisprudence on the rights of indigenous peoples. The Committee has developed statements on positions on the way in which indigenous rights are protected and promoted within the language of the Convention, a Convention that is heavily focused on "equality." In 1997, the Committee issued General Recommendation 23 that addresses the rights of indigenous peoples under the Convention. The

---

60. Ibid., 181.
61. Ibid., 181.
62. Ibid., 181.
63. Ibid., 186-187.
64. Ibid., 182.
65. *Mary and Carrie Dann v United States*, Case 11.140, Report No. 75/02, Inter-Am. C.H.R., Doc. 5 rev. 1 at 860 (2002). para 171 and para 172, online at https://www1.umn.edu/humanrts/cases/75-02a.html

General Recommendation specifically addresses land rights, and the appropriate form of reparations when land has been lost:

> The Committee especially calls upon States parties to recognize and protect the rights of indigenous peoples to own, develop, control and use their communal lands, territories and resources and, where they have been deprived of their lands and territories traditionally owned or otherwise inhabited or used without their free and informed consent, to take steps to return those lands and territories. Only when this is for factual reasons not possible, the right to restitution should be substituted by the right to just, fair and prompt compensation. Such compensation should as far as possible take the form of lands and territories.[66]

This Recommendation provided a basis for believing that the Committee might be sympathetic to American Indian land claims, especially those where challenges were made to the adequacy of the U.S. form of compensation through money damages paid to the U.S. government as a trustee.

CERD has several mechanisms by which claims alleging a state has violated its provisions can be brought before the Committee. One of these permits states to bring claims against other states, through the provisions of Article 11. Another permits claims to be brought by individuals against states via the provisions of Article 14. Article 14 requires that a state acquiesce to this jurisdiction. If a state does not, then an individual cannot bring a claim against a state through this provision.[67] The United States has not acquiesced to the Committee's jurisdiction to hear complaints against it under Article 14 and so this mechanism was not available for the Yomba Shoshone complaint. One difficulty to be surmounted was that of finding a way to bring a claim against the U.S. before the Committee. This was accomplished through an innovative mechanism available to bring a complaint about a state to the Committee. This is the Early Warning and Urgent Action Procedure that the Committee established under Article 10 of the Convention—asserting that this was a procedure that was permitted under the terms of the Convention.[68] The Early Warning and Urgent Action procedure allows complaints about states to be brought before the Committee, even where a state has not assented to the Committee's competence under Article 14. Article 10 notes that the Committee has the power to "adopt its own rules of procedure,"[69] and it was under this aegis that the Early Warning and Urgent Action Procedure was created. A claim brought under this procedure requires no additional acquiescence from

---

66. General Recommendation Number 23, Indigenous Peoples, August 18, 1997. A/52/18, annex V.
67. See Article 14.
68. See Early Warning Procedure, http://www.ohchr.org/EN/HRBodies/CERD/Pages/EarlyWarningProcedure.aspx#about.
69. Convention on the Elimination of All Forms of Racial Discrimination, Article 10(1).

the state. The Committee deems, as discussed below, that a state party to the Convention is subject to the jurisdiction of the Committee for this procedure. Thus, it was under this procedure that the Western Shoshone land claims were brought before the CERD Committee.

The Yomba Shoshone, a tribe of the Western Shoshone, later joined by another tribe of the Western Shoshone, the Ely Shoshone, alleged that the actions of the United States in its taking of the Western Shoshone land violated the equality provisions of CERD. The Yomba Shoshone claimed that the United States "determined in a discriminatory manner that those rights have been extinguished."[70] Its amended request highlights the continued presence of the Western Shoshone on the lands in question, and the ongoing use of the land for traditional activities needed for sustenance and survival, such as hunting and fishing,[71] as well as use for traditional religious practices, and plant gathering for medicinal purposes.[72] Other, non-traditional practices that had evolved as a necessity of adapting to changing circumstances, such as cattle grazing, were also part of the Western Shoshone use of the land.[73]

The claims of discrimination are based on the way in which the United States has dealt with the question of indigenous interest in land, and the doctrines that were used to assert the Western Shoshone had lost any interest in the land. These were argued to be violations of CERD provision on equality. The amended claim states that:

> … there was a lack of procedural safeguards, and due process for the Western Shoshone was not equal to what non-indigenous people ordinarily receive in United States courts. These discriminatory elements of the claims process constitute violations of Western Shoshone rights to equality under the law.[74]

After protracted proceedings, CERD issued a decision in 2006 against the United States which condemned U.S. provisions for indigenous rights as not meeting international legal standards.[75] This decision against the United States was again a ground-breaking one in international law for indigenous rights as it was:

> … the first time a United Nations Committee has issued a full decision against the United States with respect to its highly controversial federal Indian law and policy.[76]

---

70. Amended Request. n. 11, para 3.
71. Ibid., para 7.
72. Ibid., para 8.
73. Ibid., para 7.
74. Ibid., para 35.
75. Committee for the Elimination of Racial Discrimination, Sixty-eighth session, Geneva, February 20-March 10, 2006, Early Warning and Urgent Action Procedure, Decision 1(68) United States of America (Early Warning and Urgent Action Procedure).
76. J Fishel, "United States Called to Task on Indigenous Rights: The Western Shoshone Struggle and

The Early Warning and Urgent Action Procedure Decision 1(68) issued in April 2006 called for the United States to take immediate temporary steps to:

> (a) Freeze any plan to privatize Western Shoshone ancestral lands for transfer to multinational extractive industries and energy developers;
> (b) Desist from all activities planned and/or conducted on the ancestral lands of Western Shoshone or in relation to their natural resources, which were being carried out without consultation with and despite the protests of the Western Shoshone peoples;
> (c) Stop imposing grazing fees, trespass and collection notices, horse and livestock impoundments, restrictions on hunting, fishing and gathering, as well as arrests, and rescind all notices already made to that end, inflicted on Western Shoshone people while using their ancestral lands.[77]

These were not intended as final resolutions, but rather steps to be taken while a final resolution could be reached. These temporary steps were seen as ones that would limit or prevent any further risk to the Western Shoshone peoples and their lands.

The decision also criticised the legal doctrines and processes which the United States had relied upon to assert there was no longer any Western Shoshone interest in the land. The use of "gradual encroachment" and the procedure used in the Indian Claims Commission were found to be problematic. The decision notes the findings made by the Inter-American Commission decision in the *Dann* case:

> The Committee is concerned by the State party's position that Western Shoshone peoples' legal rights to ancestral lands have been extinguished through gradual encroachment, notwithstanding the fact that the Western Shoshone peoples have reportedly continued to use and occupy the lands and their natural resources in accordance with their traditional land tenure patterns. The Committee further notes with concern that the State party's position is made on the basis of processes before the Indian Claims Commission, "which did not comply with contemporary international human rights norms, principles and standards that govern determination of indigenous property interests", as stressed by the Inter-American Commission on Human Rights in the case *Mary and Carrie Dann versus United States (Case 11.140, 27 December 2002).*[78]

Success at the International Level" (2006-2007) *American Indian Law Review* 619, 621.
77. Committee for the Elimination of Racial Discrimination, Sixty-eighth session, Geneva, 20 February-10 March 2006, Early Warning and Urgent Action Procedure, Decision 1(68) United States of America. Early Warning and Urgent Action Procedure, n.75, para 10.
78. Early Warning and Urgent Action Procedure, n.75.

The United States argued that the Early Warning and Urgent Action Procedures were not part of the Convention, and that the Committee was acting without authority in creating this venue.[79] The Committee countered this, saying that Article 10 of the Convention allows it to create such rules as were needed to implement the Convention, and that the Committee's ability to implement the Early Warning and Urgent Action Procedures was thus authorized within the text of the Convention. The Committee discounted the position of the U.S., that the Committee lacked jurisdiction to hear complaints about the U.S. The U.S. argued that the Early Warning and Urgent Action procedures were without a basis in the Convention. The Committee responded that the U.S. signed onto the Convention after the implementation of the Early Warning and Urgent Action procedures, thus accepting these.[80]

Just as the decision from the Inter-American Commission had been hailed as a ground-breaking one that would make a difference for indigenous groups asserting land claims, so was this seen as a pioneering decision. It was met with a great deal of hope and enthusiasm, which was also to be proved misplaced. James Anaya remarked on the decision as important for its use of the equality provisions of CERD to require states to have "respect for cultural diversity, based upon respect of the integrity of indigenous cultures."[81] Anaya argued that the implications of the decision were far-reaching and set a new international law precedent to support indigenous rights: "This decision clearly represents that international law applies to indigenous peoples today and does so through a model of equality that supports indigenous peoples' plan of self-determination."[82]

The U.S., however, has taken no steps to comply with the CERD decision. This is made clear in a letter of 11 March 2011 from the Chairperson of the Committee on the Elimination of Racial Discrimination. The letter expresses continuing "concern over the slow progress in the implementation of [CERD's] decision 1(68)... regarding traditional rights to land of the Western Shoshone."[83] The letter further requests that CERD "would be grateful to receive information on effective measures taken... in order to find a solution acceptable to all on Western Shoshone ancestral lands, in its seventh, eight [sic] and ninth periodic reports due on 20 November 2011."[84]

---

79. Report to the United Nations Committee on the Elimination of Racial Discrimination In Response to United States Period Report Annex II Early Warning and Urgent Action Procedure Decision 1(68) (Western Shoshone) Submitted by the Western Shoshone National Council, the Timbisha Shoshone and the Yomba Shoshone Tribe December 2007, para 6. https://law2.arizona.edu/iplp/outreach/shoshone/documents/WSResponsetoUSPeriodicReport.pdf.
80. Ibid., para 6.
81. J Anaya, "Keynote Address: Indigenous Peoples and their Mark on the International Legal System" (2006-2007) 31(2) American Indian Law Review 257, 260.
82. Ibid., 260.
83. Letter from Chairperson of the Committee on the Elimination of Racial Discrimination, March 11, 2011, at http://www2.ohchr.org/english/bodies/cerd/docs/USA_11March2011.pdf
84. Ibid.

What was a promising breakthrough for solving indigenous land claims in international human rights law in fact has not delivered what was hoped for. State recalcitrance to comply with international human rights law is something to which, to date, no effective solution has been found.

UNITED NATIONS DECLARATION ON THE RIGHTS OF INDIGENOUS PEOPLES

Writing prior to the approval of the UNDRIP in 2007, one commentator sums up the position of the Western Shoshone and where their litigation in the Inter-American system and through CERD has left them—with favourable rulings that cannot be put into effect in the face of an unwilling United States:

> No remedy is available in the American courts. The international forums with jurisdiction to review the violations of Western Shoshone human rights by the United States, CERD, and the IACHR have rendered opinions that are precedent-setting but unenforceable.[85]

It was this impasse on the recognition of indigenous land rights and the ability to enforce rights, even and perhaps especially where states were unwilling to recognise them where UNDRIP stood poised to make a difference. While various solutions were proposed for inclusion in the UNDRIP during its drafting stages, the final document's content is silent in many areas where promising innovations were under consideration during the long drafting stage of the Declaration. The 2007 approval of the UNDRIP occurred in the aftermath of these notable decisions, where it was apparent that their promise was not going to be immediately actualised. Was it too much to expect the UNDRIP to respond to this? The UNDRIP itself had struggled to get to the floor of the UN General Assembly for a vote. Its advocates may have been trying to avoid jeopardising its tenuous journey to a vote, given the long years spent in drafting, and the 2006 bloc against a vote.[86] It is useful to recall here the observation made by Wiessner that the final UNDRIP document is one that is a "compromise."[87] The following discussion reveals the implications of this in the silence or ambivalence in critical articles of the instrument. Only Article 28 emerges with a strong statement that helps to resolve issues about adequate reparation, by placing monetary compensation at the bottom of a hierarchical list of preferences.

---

85. Luebben and Nelson, n. 40, 133.
86. M Davis, "To Bind or Not to Bind: The United Nations Declaration on the Rights of Indigenous Peoples Five Years On" (2012) 19 *Australian International Law Journal* 17, 20-23.
87. Wiessner, n. 1, 131.

LAND CLAIMS: STATE OR INTERNATIONAL CLAIM?

Perhaps the biggest disappointment is the failure of the final version of the UNDRIP to address to what forums indigenous land claims should be brought. The UNDRIP represents a lost opportunity to clarify in what forum—domestic, international or both—treaty-based land claims should be brought.

Article 37 is silent on where indigenous land claims are to be raised. It does not clarify whether claims are a matter of domestic or international law. Draft versions of this article attempted to address this, by offering various solutions as to when and whether land claims should be a matter of international rather than domestic law.

Article 37 does not deal with land claims generally, but rather "treaties, agreements and other constructive arrangements".[88] Many, if not all, land claims of American Indians can arise through treaties and other agreements[89] and so the silence on where these are to be resolved weakens any effective guidance that the UNDRIP has on resolving land disputes. Without a clear indication of where land disputes are to be resolved, the value of its other detailed provisions on the resolution of land claims are ineffective. An important, albeit contentious, piece of the equation for resolution of indigenous land claims has been left out of the UNDRIP. The overall result is that the UNDRIP then fails to provide useful guidance for the resolution of indigenous land claims. This section evaluates four issues with respect to the contribution that the UNDRIP might have made in the resolution of American Indian claims: whether treaty claims should be brought to an international or domestic forum, establishing indigenous interests in land, the form that reparations or compensation should take, and the inherent weakness of formulating indigenous rights as human rights.

TREATY CLAIMS: INTERNATIONAL OR DOMESTIC JURISDICTION?

A 2004 report on the drafting process indicated that indigenous land claims arising through treaties and agreements were matters of domestic, rather than international, concern. The report notes that "Disputes that arise under such treaties and agreements should be resolved pursuant to any processes specified in the treaties, agreements, and other constructive arrangements, or otherwise *submitted to competent domestic bodies or processes* for timely resolution in accordance with principles of justice and equity..."[90]

---

88. UNDRIP Article 37(1).
89. S Wiessner, "Rights and Status of Indigenous Peoples: A Global Comparative and International Analysis" (1999) 12 *Harvard Human Rights Journal* 57, 94-97.
90. E/CN.4/2004/79m 9g. 69, emphasis added.

In 2005, the language of the draft article remained contested. The original language provided that "conflicts and disputes which cannot be otherwise settled should be *submitted to competent international bodies agreed to by all parties concerned*".[91] The Chairman's summary of proposals shows that there was continued resistance to the idea that indigenous treaties should be resolved at the international level:

> Disputes should be submitted to competent domestic bodies or processes for timely resolution. Where such resolution is not possible and the concerned parties agree, disputes may be submitted to competent international bodies.[92]

In other words, submission to international bodies was only to be made with the agreement of all parties concerned—something that might be difficult to attain where one of the parties was a state insistent on the domestic nature of such disputes. It might be viewed that this language—while perhaps not palatable to those who view indigenous land treaties as subject to international jurisdiction rather than domestic—is better than nothing. While the content might be objectionable, at least some direction and hierarchy of venue is given.

But the final approved version of the UNDRIP contains neither a provision for domestic or international resolution. This leaves open the question of whether indigenous treaties are subject to international law and resolution or domestic law. In the end, these greatly contested issues were resolved by silence on the matter.

This does not settle the issue of whether those American Indian claims that arose through treaties, such as the Western Shoshone claims, are a matter of international or domestic jurisdiction. The Western Shoshone claims have been raised in both domestic and international forums, with the international decision from the CERD Committee being highly condemning in its view of the doctrines and the processes that the United States uses to make findings about land claims. There is a clear divide between what the U.S. courts find as acceptable legal doctrine and what the regional and international position on those doctrines are. Very different results come about – with domestic decisions finding against American Indian interests and regional and international decisions finding in support of them. These differences were established ahead of the approval of the UNDRIP—but in the end the UNDRIP fails to address the appropriate forum for bringing treaty based land claims.

---

91. Report of the Working Group established in accordance with Commission on Human Rights Resolution 1995/32 of 3 March 1995 on its tenth session, September 1, 2005, E/CN.4/2005/WG.15/2, 45. Emphasis added.
92. Ibid., 45. Emphasis added.

ESTABLISHING INDIGENOUS INTERESTS IN LAND

UNDRIP Articles 26 and 27 discuss the basis of indigenous rights to land and the processes by which states are to determine land claims and recognise indigenous land rights. Article 26 reiterates the position of the Inter-American system whereby indigenous connection to land is that which is "possess[ed] by reason of traditional ownership or other traditional occupation or use, as well as those that they have otherwise acquired."[93] Article 27 requires states to give "due recognition to indigenous peoples' laws, traditions, customs and land tenure systems"[94] in determining land claims. But these two articles read together also have notable differences from the Inter-American provisions. The "due recognition" that states are required to give falls far short of the Inter-American requirement that indigenous norms are to be considered in their own right, independent from and equal to state laws on land. These articles suggest that state law might trump indigenous norms, even though no clear weighting on differing legal norms is provided.

Whatever shortcomings these articles have, however, they are not supportive of the U.S. doctrines used to determine American Indian interest in land. Gradual encroachment does not provide the due recognition of traditional ownership, occupation or use required by the UNDRIP, nor of indigenous land tenure systems. But the UNDRIP does not go so far as to condemn those doctrines such as gradual encroachment that fail to give at least this level of recognition to indigenous land interests. There is still the possibility of the state deciding to give more weight to its own legal doctrines, having considered those of the indigenous group, with an end result that is no different than if a doctrine such as gradual encroachment had been used.

FORMS OF REPARATION

Article 28 is noted by the International Law Association as being UNDRIP's "most important provision for dealing with reparation."[95] This article creates a hierarchy of reparations in land claims. Monetary compensation is the least preferred remedy, and the return of the land that has been taken is the preferred remedy. The International Law Association's interpretation of this Article notes:

> ...restitution [of the land taken] is the form of redress to be granted any time that it is actually practicable. When it is not practicable, then it must be replaced by compensation, which must be "just, fair and equitable"; the combination of all these terms denotes that

---

93. UNDRIP Article 26(2).
94. UNDRIP Article 27(2).
95. Hague Conference Report, n. 6, 41.

compensation must take a form that is perceived as just, fair and equitable by the indigenous communities concerned.[96]

In this, the UNDRIP delivers perhaps its most powerful content in favour of American Indian land claims. The compensation has to be one that is seen as acceptable by the indigenous group. If it is not, then it arguably does not meet the requirement of this UNDRIP article. Thus, where indigenous groups such as the Western Shoshone have rejected monetary compensation, the U.S. practice of deeming such monetary awards accepted when these are paid to the U.S. government in its role of trustee would not be permitted. This then would make it impossible to say that a land claim can no longer be litigated because compensation has been accepted. In this article the UNDRIP has delivered a powerful antidote to the U.S. practice of deeming compensation accepted and all land claim disputes resolved when the U.S. pays itself as the trustee of American Indian tribes—despite tribes refusing to accept the monetary compensation.

ENFORCEABILITY: UNSATISFACTORY CONSEQUENCES OF CASTING INDIGENOUS LAND RIGHTS AS HUMAN RIGHTS

By definition, a soft law instrument such as the UNDRIP is not enforceable against states. The UNDRIP, therefore, cannot be seen as deficient for not providing mechanisms to directly enforce its provisions. But the construction of indigenous land rights as human rights—with the rights obligations and protections flowing through the state—raises some intractable problems. Should indigenous land rights be cast as human rights? Or is there another way of constructing these rights that might actually effectively increase state compliance and enforcement?

Aponte Miranda points out that the choice to cast international indigenous rights as human rights was a strategic, political choice.[97] But this has not been without its negative consequences.[98] One of the most unsatisfactory consequences of indigenous rights being seen as human rights is that the state remains a gate-keeper for most rights, and rights are construed to be something provided through and by states.[99] This sets up at best a precarious situation for the enforcement of indigenous rights and a dubious formula for states to

---

96. Ibid., 41.
97. L Aponte Miranda, "Uploading the Local: Assessing the Contemporary Relationship Between Indigenous Peoples' Land Tenure Systems and International Human Rights Law Regarding the Allocation of Traditional Lands and Resources in Latin America"(2008) 10 *Oregon Review of International Law* 419, 428.
98. But not all scholars agree. Some very powerful arguments are put forward as to the benefits of a human rights regime. See S James Anaya, "Divergent Discourses About International Law, Indigenous Peoples, and Rights over Lands and Natural Resources: Toward a Realist Trend" (2005) 16 *Colorado Journal of International Environmental Law and Policy* 237.
99. See, for instance, J Corntassel, "Cultural Restoration in International Law: Pathways to Indigenous Self-Determination" (2012) 1(1) *Canadian Journal of Human Rights* 94.

implement and accept judicial or other legal findings against them which require them to make reparations to indigenous peoples for land. This is the classic formula for international human rights, but one that has been discarded in the Inter-American approach to indigenous land rights.

A second danger in relying upon states to deliver indigenous rights in a satisfactory way is the occurrence of state paternalism.[100] This is a paternalism that is also present in the international system and that serves to limit the possibilities of indigenous self-determination and autonomy at many levels, as noted by Lenzerini:

> ... Governments, for their part, rather than working to recreate the requisite conditions to allow indigenous peoples to pursue and realize their expectations, prefer to increase the dependency of such communities on the way in which state institutions manage their affairs.[101]

Lenzerini points out that paternalism operates to disempower indigenous peoples and keeps them dependent upon states for their very survival.[102] This situation is the very antithesis of what a realisation of indigenous rights would entail, and is one of the fundamental barriers towards adequate reparations for indigenous lands claims. State paternalism seems geared towards forcing indigenous assimilation rather than indigenous self-determination. The inadequacy of a rights approach because of the positionality of states within that approach is noted by indigenous scholar Corntassel. He argues instead for the necessity to be free of state gate-keeping on the delivery of indigenous rights, which, he notes, in the same vein as Lenzerini, only serves to keep indigenous rights dependent upon the state.[103]

Given the omnipresent state paternalism towards indigenous peoples, states are likely to remain recalcitrant in the return of indigenous lands it has taken. This raises then the question of what is necessary to make reparations effective. Different views and suggestions for a resolution have been put forward. Lenzerini identifies what is specifically needed to have an effective system for land claim reparations. He argues that a very high priority must be given to the return of land to indigenous peoples, despite the practical difficulties that this action might entail.[104] Both the Inter-American system and the UNDRIP provisions provide an emphasis on the return of land as reparation for land claims.

---

100. F Lenzerini, "The Trail of Broken Dreams: The Status of Indigenous Peoples in International Law" in F Lenzerini (ed.), *Reparations of Indigenous Peoples: International and Comparative Perspectives* (Oxford University Press, 2009) 81.
101. Ibid., 81.
102. Ibid., 81.
103. Corntassel, n. 98, 96. Emphasis added.
104. Lenzerini, n. 100, 618.

Others insist that the legal system must be inclusive of indigenous perspectives in order to provide rights in place of rhetoric.[105] Solutions to this seemingly intractable problem might lay in institutions that can deliver norms reflective of indigenous views and not that of states. Teubner and Fischer-Lescano, for example, argue for the creation of a system of indigenous norm production, which "would be law *sui generis,* worthy of the name".[106] Alfred and Corntassel make a similar argument for the need for a system that produces indigenous norms. But rather than such a system being a part of the existing international community, they argue forcefully that indigenous peoples should instead implement what they need instead of being reliant upon states and a state-driven international system:

> We do not need to wait for the colonizer to provide us with money or to validate our vision of a free future; we need only to start to use our Indigenous languages to frame our thoughts, the ethical framework of our philosophies to make decisions and to use our laws and institutions to govern ourselves.[107]

This point is made strongly in the Conclusions and Recommendations of the International Law Association Committee on the Rights of Indigenous Peoples report of 2012:

> States must comply with the obligation—according to customary and, where applicable, conventional international law—to recognize and fulfil the right of indigenous peoples to reparation and redress for the wrongs they suffered, in particular their lands taken or damaged without their free, prior and informed consent. Effective mechanisms for redress –established in conjunction with the peoples concerned—must be available and accessible in favour of indigenous peoples. Reparation must be adequate and effective, and according to the perspective of the indigenous communities concerned, actually capable to repair the wrongs they have suffered.[108]

This in turn puts an increased spotlight upon the calls for an indigenous solution, for a solution that turns its back upon state and international systems as ineffective and non-responsive. The real way forward for the realisation of indigenous land rights may in fact lay there—for the crafting of solutions there. Although great strides have been made in both regional and international systems

---

105. G Teubner and A Fischer-Lescano, "Cannabilizing Epistimes: Will Modern Law Protect Traditional Cultural Expressions?" in C Graber, *Traditional Cultural Expressions in a Digital Environment* (London, Edward Elgar Publishing, 2008) 1, 11.
106. Ibid., 12.
107. T Alfred and J Corntassel, "Being Indigenous: Resurgences against Contemporary Colonialism" (2005) *Government and Opposition* 597, 614.
108. International Law Association Committee on the Rights of Indigenous Peoples (Sofia 2012), Final Report, 31. Emphasis added.

for establishing the legal rights of indigenous peoples to their lands, the inability to enforce these remains greatly problematic. The legitimacy of indigenous land rights as international customary law may provide some impetus for an indigenous solution. Increasingly, it would seem that an indigenous solution is the only way that indigenous land rights will be effectively realised. The regional and international systems may have been pushed as far as they can go.

In summation, it has to be asked whether the UNDRIP is equipped to deal with the remediation of past injustices that arose in the taking of American Indian land by the U.S. federal government. Or is this too much to ask of any international instrument, particularly one that is soft law? The problems with the U.S. positions stem back to the Marshall trilogy of cases that set up the now well ingrained positions about domestic dependents and the "limited possessor" rights of American Indians. These are based on the doctrine of discovery which is itself a troubling relic of an age of conquest that hardly seems compatible with modern regional and international human rights law.

Despite the approval of the UNDRIP and the CERD and Inter-American decisions that condemned the U.S. practices and legal positions, the problem of recognition of Western Shoshone interest in land has not been solved. The U.S. practices of reparation and rights recognition have not changed. The UNDRIP has not made any inroads into curbing or changing these practices. In this, it is no different than the Inter-American and CERD systems, which went as far as they could in pushing the boundaries of legal principles. But when a state such as the United States wishes to ignore these pronouncements, it certainly can do so. Perhaps the hope for the change in these doctrines and practices can be found in the words of former UN Special Rapporteur James Anaya:

> The Declaration provides a new grounding for understanding
> the status and rights of indigenous peoples, upon which the legal
> doctrines of conquest and discovery must be discarded as a basis for
> decision-making by judicial and other authorities.[109]

Only when, and if, the United States is willing to abandon the doctrine of discovery and its legacy in terms of the ways in which American Indian land rights are determined, is there likely to be any wholesale change in the rights and reparations in domestic courts for American Indian land claims. Despite the apparently promising results from the Inter-American Commission and the CERD Committee, no change in the underlying U.S. domestic policy or law has been achieved. The UNDRIP might have gone further in providing some resolution to the issues the U.S. positions on opposing these decisions, but in

---

109. Statement of United Nations Special Rapporteur on the Rights of Indigenous Peoples, James Anaya, Upon Conclusion of Visit to the United States, May 4, 2012, online at http://unsr.jamesanaya.org/visit-to-usa/statement-of-the-united-nations-special-rapporteur-on-the-rights-of-indigenous-peoples-james-anaya-upon-conclusion-of-his-visit-to-the-united-states.

the final estimation it seems that the real value to the UNDRIP is in challenging the legitimacy of the basis on which the U.S. positions are based. Only when the doctrine of discovery and its legacy are abandoned and repudiated will it be possible to establish adequate rights and reparations for American Indian land interests.

It is of note that the international efforts to condemn the doctrine of discovery and to address its legacy continue. The CERD Committee, in its Concluding Observations to the Holy See[110] (which has the status of a state party to the Convention), in January 2016, specifically takes the Holy See to task over the doctrine of discovery. The Committee notes that a "high-level dialogue [that] is scheduled to take place in Rome to address the concerns raised by indigenous peoples."[111] The Committee calls for information on "the outcome of the meeting and concrete follow-up measures taken."[112] The highly visible criticism of the doctrine of discovery by the CERD Committee keeps the debate over the doctrine and its damaging legacy alive. But this alone, at the international level, is not going to be sufficient to over-ride those effects in the legal doctrines of the United States. Thus far, the United States has been impervious to the international and regional criticisms of its domestic laws on American Indian land claims. The CERD Committee's pressure on the Holy See about the doctrine of discovery may in time widen to a renewed focus on the doctrines based on this within the United States. Whether this pressure may in time build to push a change within the United States, or whether matters will remain on the course charted thus far of ignoring the calls for change, will remain to be seen.

The CERD Committee criticism of the Doctrine of Discovery in 2016 has not thus far brought about any change in the position of the United States government with respect to indigenous land rights. This does not mean that international pressure to address American Indian land rights has ceased. But it does point out that the United States continues to be impervious to international pressure, even while the international community continues to focus on indigenous land rights. In addition, a new land rights crisis broke out at the Standing Rock Reservation over plans to construct a pipeline over ancestral lands with sacred burial sites. The protests at Standing Rock attracted national attention, and pointed out, yet again, the need for the United States to address American Indian land rights. It also calls into question the effectiveness of grass-roots protests to address these problems.

The international focus on indigenous land rights continued with the issue of the collective rights of indigenous peoples considered during the Permanent Forum session in 2018. Indigenous interests in land are often collective, rather

---

110. Concluding Observations on the Combined Sixteenth to Twenty-Third Periodic Report of the Holy See, Committee on the Elimination of Racial Discrimination, January 11, 2016, CERD/C/VAT/CO/16-23. https://documents-dds-ny.un.org/doc/UNDOC/GEN/G16/003/38/PDF/G1600338.pdf?OpenElement.
111. Ibid., para. 17.
112. Ibid., para. 17.

than individual (although individual claims also can exist), which is often contrary to the state system for land rights. The Permanent Forum recognized the important of land to indigenous peoples, calling for increased support for these rights through increased domestic enforcement, across all three branches of government.[113]

Three key observations in that discussion point to the problems that culminated in the Standing Rock protests. One was the occurrence of resource extraction on and near indigenous lands:

> [t]he challenges faced by indigenous peoples in exercising and enjoying both individual and collective rights to lands, territories and resources are due to a range of factors related to conflicts, extractive industries, infrastructure and development projects, commercial logging, population and socioeconomic pressures.[114]

The second observation is on the failure of states to provide sufficient protection to indigenous land rights, including the vulnerability of these rights to superior state interests:

> Some States do acknowledge that indigenous peoples have legal collective entitlements to lands, territories, or resources, with specific legal concepts such as aboriginal title or ancestral domain. However, such rights are often subject to State power to extinguish such title, in contrast to the legal protection in most countries for lands and properties of non-indigenous citizens and corporations.[115]

Such is the situation with the interest given to American Indian land rights, as has been discussed in this chapter. Despite the international attention to indigenous rights from the UNPFII as to both the Doctrine of Discovery and the need to improve protection and recognition of collective rights to land, nothing has changed in the United States legal framework. The protests at Standing Rock exemplify this.

The third observation points out the dangers that the defenders of indigenous human rights face. This was eerily prescient of the events that unfolded in 2016-2017, at Standing Rock Reservation, in South Dakota, United States:

> The Permanent Forum draws attention to the number of reports, from around the world, of acts of intimidation and reprisal, including restrictions on the ability of representatives to attend the Forum's

---

113. UNFPII, E/C.19/2018/S, Permanent Forum on Indigenous Issues, Seventeenth Session, April 2017, para 16.
114. Ibid., para 17.
115. Ibid., para. 18.

sessions. Indigenous leaders and human rights defenders face disproportionately high rates of intimidation and reprisal, as shown by various studies, including by the Special Rapporteur on the situation of human rights defenders.[116]

At the heart of the issues at Standing Rock were plans by the United States government to run a pipeline near indigenous lands. The original path of the pipeline underneath Bismarck, South Dakota was altered when the risk of a pipeline rupture and contamination of city water sources was deemed too high.[117] As a result, the path of the pipeline was altered to cross ancestral lands of the indigenous peoples of Standing Rock.[118] This pipeline is known as the Dakota Access Pipeline.[119]

The pipeline was to run across land that while not within the boundaries of the Standing Rock Reservation was nevertheless traditional ancestral land, and held sacred burial sites.[120] The plans to dig up the sacred lands as well as the risk that the pipeline would pose to groundwater and the health of those living in the nearby Standing Rock reservation were met with protests.[121]

Protest camps were set up, "which mobilized assemblies of indigenous peoples from over 90 tribes from across the United States and Canada."[122] In the end the protests ended, with the camps broken up, and the pipeline laid, after outbreaks of violence and the activists arrested.[123]

While the Standing Rock protests did not succeed in stopping the digging up of sacred burial grounds or the laying of the pipeline, they do point to the potential effectiveness of these measures. International pressure and measures do not seem to sway the United States, which has made no move to alter its reliance upon the Doctrine of Discovery. While there are calls for the use of grassroots protests to address American Indian land rights,[124] the question remains if these are any more effective than the calls for reform at the international level. There

116. United Nations Permanent Forum on Indigenous Issues (Report on the Seventeenth session) E/2018/43*-E/C.19/201811*, para 13.

117. E Steinman, "Why was Standing Rock and the #NODAPL Campaign so Historic? Factors Affecting American Indian Participation in Social Movement Collaborations and Coalitions" (2018) 10 *Ethnic and Racial Studies* 1,12.

118. M L Cappelli, "Standing With Standing Rock: Affective Alignment and Artful Resistance at the Native Nations Rise March (July-September 2018)" *Sage OPEN* 1, 1.

119. Steinman, n.117, 12.

120. Cappelli, n. 118, 1.

121. Ibid., 1

122. Ibid., 1.

123. See for instance, S Levin, "He's a Political Prisoner: Standing Rock Activists Face Years in Jail", *The Guardian*, June 22, 2018.

124. J Heath, "The Doctrine of Christian Discovery: Its Fundamental Performance in the United States Indian Law and the Need for its Repudiation and Removal" (2017) 10 *Albany Government Law Review* 112, 156.

are some who remain hopeful that the UNDRIP itself provides an effective platform for these grassroots protests.[125]

Steinman frames the questions:

> Will Standing Rock provide a template through which others can make sense of, validate and contribute to similar campaigns? ...Or will it enter into popular and movement consciousness as a valiant but failed effort that satisfies and exhausts receptiveness and critical attention to American Indian concerns?[126]

But at the present, these remain without answer, and the land rights of American Indians no more protected or recognized.

125. Cappelli, n. 118, 5.
126. Steinman, n. 117, 18.

SUBVERTING OR AFFIRMING INDIGENOUS RIGHTS - THE AUSTRALIAN PROBLEM WRIT LARGE

Jocelynne A. Scutt

INTRODUCTION

Indigenous Australian rights have a complicated history, often brutal, at times paternalistic, not infrequently patronising, and sometimes positively affirming. Australia's history is replete with breaches of Aboriginal Australians' rights. At the same time there are occasions when the country comes together solidly in support of Indigenous Australia. Just where Australia stands on the United Nations Declaration on the Rights of Indigenous Peoples cannot be understood without reference to this history. Almost 250 years of colonisation, settlement or invasion cannot be undone simply, if at all. Whether the Declaration will have any positive effect must be seen against the backdrop of government relations with Aboriginal Australia and the position of political parties in their policy making. The future prospects for the Declaration lie in the dominant community and their parliamentary representatives endeavouring to comprehend how Indigenous Australians have experienced and continue to experience their loss of sovereignty. Whether this is possible remains in question. A recitation of the history may provide an insight into whether the Declaration can or will make a difference.

Thursday 30 September 2007 saw the Declaration adopted by the General Assembly with four votes against: the United States (a not infrequent voter against

UN treaties and resolutions),[1] Canada, Aotearoa/New Zealand and Australia. The Australian Minister for Indigenous Affairs, Mal Brough, justified the repudiation of the Declaration in his assertion that there should be "only one law for all Australians and we should not enshrine in law practices that are not acceptable in the modern world."[2] Earlier, the government's position was articulated in the Senate, with greater elaboration, by Liberal Senator Marise Payne. Speaking in a debate on a Motion proposing that the Australian government "should support the adoption of the proposed United Nations Declaration on the Rights of Indigenous Peoples when it is put to the vote in the current session of the UN General Assembly,"[3] Senator Payne said the government identified "six key concerns … with the text as it currently stands."[4] She pinpointed "the references to self-determination and the potential for misconstruing them", observing that not only her state of New South Wales had those concerns.[5] She went on to state two further aspects, namely:

> On the question of land and resources, we are concerned that the provisions on those areas in the text ignore the contemporary realities of many countries which have Indigenous populations. They seem … to require the recognition of Indigenous rights to lands which are now lawfully owned by other citizens, both Indigenous and non-Indigenous, and therefore to have some quite significant potential to impact on the rights of third parties.
>
> Intellectual property is the third point we would raise. We believe that, as our laws here currently stand, we protect our Indigenous cultural heritage, traditional knowledge and traditional cultural expression to an extent that is consistent with both Australian and international intellectual property law and we are not prepared to go as far as the provisions in the text of the draft declaration currently do on that matter.[6]

---

1. For example, the Convention on the Rights of the Child: S Mehta, "There's Only One Country That Hasn't Ratified the Convention on Children's Rights: US", *ACLU*, 11/20/2015 (accessed 04/19/2019), and refusal to join the International Criminal Court: Global Policy Forum: "US Opposition to the International Criminal Court", https://www.globalpolicy.org/international-justice/the-international-criminal-court/us-opposition-to-the-icc.html (accessed 04/19/2019); D Schneider, "A love-hate affair: the United Nations and the United States have long been ambivalent about each other. But as the UN marks its 60th anniversary, the relationship is more complicated than ever", *The New York Times Upfront/The Free Library*, 09/19/2005, https://www.thefreelibrary.com/A+love-hate+affair%3a+the+United+Nations+and+the+United+States+have...-a0137860021 (accessed 04/19/2019).
2. Quoted "Indigenous rights outlined by the UN," BBC News, 13 September 2007 (accessed 11/30/2018).
3. "Matters of Urgency: United Nations Declaration on the Rights of Indigenous People," Deputy President, Motion from Senator Bartlett (Queensland), *Senate Hansard*, 10 September 2007, Australian Parliament, 50-51, https://parlinfo.aph.gov.au/parlInfo/download/chamber/hansards/2007-09-10/toc_pdf/5648-4.pdf;fileType=application%2Fpdf#search=%222000s%22 (accessed 11/30/2018).
4. Senator Marise Payne, *Senate Hansard*, 09/10/2007, ibid, 53.
5. Ibid.
6. Ibid.

Her fourth concern was "the inclusion in the text of an unqualified right of free, prior and informed consent for Indigenous peoples on matters affecting them …"[7] This, she said, "implies to some readers that [Indigenous peoples] may then be able to exercise a right of veto over all matters of state", including "national laws and other administrative measures."[8] She added that "any sovereign government" would "obviously" be concerned about that possibility.[9]

As to the Declaration's "seeking to give Indigenous people exclusive rights over intellectual, real and cultural property" her concern was that the draft text "does not acknowledge the rights of third parties—in particular, their rights to access Indigenous land and heritage and cultural objects where appropriate under national law."[10] Albeit acknowledging that this "should not be a big stumbling block," she said this remained "a matter which we wish to see addressed" for:

> The text in its current form fails to consider the different types of ownership and use that can be accorded to Indigenous people and the rights of third parties to property in that regard.[11]

Customary law was Senator Payne's final point of departure, the concern lying with "the way the text is currently drafted … and whether that may place Indigenous customary law in a superior position to national law:"

> We understand in talking about customary law that it is a law based on culture and tradition and is not one which is expected to override national laws and is certainly not one which should be used selectively by certain Indigenous communities where it is possibly convenient to permit the exercise of practices which would not be acceptable across the board.[12]

These concerns drove the Australian government's stand alongside the United States, Canada and Aotearoa/New Zealand to vote against the Declaration. However, all have since changed their position.[13] Australia took this step on 3 April 2009. A new Labor government reversed the previous Liberal-National Party government's objection. In so doing, Jenny Macklin, the Minister for Indigenous Affairs said this would "reset" the relationship between non-Indigenous and Indigenous Australians, "an important step" towards "closing the gap" between

7. Ibid.
8. Ibid.
9. Ibid.
10. Ibid., 53-54.
11. Ibid., 54-55.
12. Ibid., 55.
13. UNDESA, United Nations Declaration on the Rights of Indigenous Peoples, https://www.un.org/development/desa/indigenouspeoples/declaration-on-the-rights-of-indigenous-peoples.html (accessed 09/01/2018).

them and affirming the aspirations of all Indigenous peoples.[14] Acknowledging that "relationships will be tested and will evolve" the Minister focused on health and education in particular as potentially "taking time" to improve, adding that the "declaration gives us new impetus to work together in trust and good faith."[15] Adopting the Declaration, she said, meant Australia "takes another step to make sure the flawed policies of the past will never be revisited."[16] Meanwhile, Indigenous Australian Professor Mick Dodson emphasized that setting standards, albeit a positive move, was insufficient. The value of human rights lay not simply in their existence, he said, but "in their implementation."[17] On the other hand, the Liberal and National parties, now in opposition, maintained their position that the Declaration was a "flawed document."[18] Adverting to their original dissent and objections, the Liberal-National party opposition declared the decision by the Labor government to adopt the Declaration to be "a grave error."[19]

THE POLITICS OF DENIAL AND AFFIRMATION OF INDIGENOUS AUSTRALIAN RIGHTS

This political split between Australia's major political parties, along with the stress placed by Indigenous Australia on making the Declaration effective in practice, highlights the division within the Australian community as a whole as to what support there is for Indigenous Australian rights. History following adoption of the Declaration, particularly the "second invasion" as the federal government intervention into Indigenous communities in the Northern Territory is known,[20] also raises questions as to the commitment to the Declaration reflected in the decision to withdraw the original objection.

For Indigenous Australians, answers come against a backdrop of denial. The litany of denial begins with the proposition that Australia was *terra nullius* or not an occupied land when settled or invaded by Britain.[21] Both contiguous with

---

14. The Hon. Jenny Macklin, Minister for Indigenous Affairs, quoted Emma Rogers, online parliamentary correspondent, "Australia adopts UN Indigenous declaration," ABC News, 04/03/2009, http://www.abc.net.au/news/2009-04-03/aust-adopts-un-indigenous-declaration/1640444 (accessed 09/01/2018).
15. Ibid.
16. Ibid.
17. Ibid.
18. Ibid.
19. Ibid.
20. See Dr G Venturini, "The New Invasion of the Northern Territory" (Pt 1), *The AIM Network*, https://theaimn.com/new-invasion-northern-territory-part-1/ (accessed September 1, 2018); Dr George Venturini, "The New Invasion of the Northern Territory" (Pt2), *The AIM Network*, https://theaimn.com/new-invasion-northern-territory-part-2/ (accessed 09/01/2018); Dr G Venturini, "The New Invasion of the Northern Territory" (Pt 3), *The AIM Network*, https://theaimn.com/new-invasion-northern-territory-part-3/ (accessed 09/01/2018).
21. See E Scott, "Taking Possession of Australia– The Doctrine of Terra Nullius," *Journal of the Royal Australian Historical Society,* Vol. XXVI, 1941, pp. 3-20; R Edwards, "Terra Nullius," *Australian Society for the Study of Labour History,* 2018 National Conference, http://www.labourhistory.org.au/hummer/vol-2-no-4/terra-nullius/ (accessed 11/29/2018). The British did know that Australia was occupied; however, the doctrine was used to assert that the Indigenous occupiers had no sovereignty over the land. See *Mabo*

this and as a part of a proposition that Indigenous Australians were not killed in any numbers, if at all, by the settlers, colonisers or invaders, is the denial that wars were fought by Indigenous Australians against this settlement or invasion.[22] Simultaneously comes the denial that Indigenous Australians were subjected to genocide or attempted genocide – by various means of death and removal of children from their families. Death included killing by guns in the wars "that never happened," and poisoning by the most often used method – fatal substances released into waterholes near Aboriginal camps and ceremonial places. Removal of children to missions and schools was aimed at "civilizing" those who were fair-skinned and obviously the product of inter-racial relations (whether consensual or by rape).[23]

Denial continues with a refusal to admit that racism is embedded within the dominant culture and that eliminating it requires, first, resolute acknowledgement and, secondly, determined commitment to ending it by affirming Indigenous Australian rights – both personal and collective. This refusal is articulated well by a former Australian Prime Minister, John Howard, in his repudiation of the Human Rights and Equal Opportunity Commission's report on "the stolen generations." Despite former High Court Justice Ronald Wilson's conclusion (together with his fellow Commissioners) that removal of Aboriginal children from their parents constituted genocide in its aim of separating them not only from their families but from their culture and social roots, Howard asserted there was no genocide and that racism, if it ever existed, was of the past. He, along with his contemporaries, had no responsibility, he averred.[24]

Indigenous Australians' intimate relationship with and to the land has been denied, or denied the status of "ownership" whether or not understood in the way English common law recognises property, and Aboriginal conceptions of

and Anor v Queensland and Anor (No 1) [1988] HCA 69; (1988) 166 CLR 186, http://www.austlii.edu.au/au/cases/cth/HCA/1988/69.html (accessed 09/01/2018); *Mabo and Ors v Queensland (No 2)* [1992] HCA 23; (1992) 175 CLR 1, http://www.austlii.edu.au/au/cases/cth/HCA/1992/23.html (accessed 09/01/2018); *The Wik Peoples v State of Queensland & Ors; The Thayorre People v State of Queensland & Ors* [1996] HCA 40, (1996) 187 CLR 1, http://www.austlii.edu.au/au/cases/cth/HCA/1996/40.html (accessed 09/01/2018) and discussion later this chapter.

22. See A Grassby and M Hill, *Six Australian Battlefields*, Allen & Unwin, St Leonards, Australia, 1988; N A Loos, *Invasion and Resistance: Aboriginal-European Relations on the North Queensland Frontier 1861-1897*, (Canberra, ACT, Australia: ANU Press, 1982); H Reynolds, *Forgotten War*, (Sydney, Australia: NewSouth Books, 2013); P Stanley, *The Remote Garrison: The British Army in Australia 1788-1870*, (Kangaroo Press, Kenthurst, Australia, 1986); R Foster, R Hostling and A Nettleback, *Fatal Collisions: The South Australian Frontier and the Violence of Memory,* (Wakefield Press, Adelaide, Australia, 2001).

23. See, for example, A Jalata, "The Impacts of English Colonial Terrorism and Genocide on Indigenous/Black Australians," *Sage Open*, August 7, 2013, https://journals.sagepub.com/doi/full/10.1177/2158244013499143 (accessed 11/28/2013); J A. Scutt, "The Stolen Generations: Stealing children, stealing culture, stealing lives" in J A Scutt, *The Incredible Woman – Power and Sexual Politics*, vol. 2, chapter 31 (Artemis Publishing, Melbourne, Victoria) 215-230; and further this chapter.

24. A Bonnell and M Crotty, "Australian's History under Howard, 1996-2007", *Sage Open*, 05/01/2008, https://journals.sagepub.com/doi/pdf/10.1177/0002716207310818 (accessed 11/28/2018); H Davidson, "John Howard: there was no genocide against Indigenous Australians," *The Guardian*, 09/22/2014, http://www.theguardian.com/world/2014/sep/22/john-howard-there-was-no-genocide-against-indigenous-australians (accessed 11/28/2018).

"ownership" constituted by the land "owning" them are given short shrift.[25] In 1988 the High Court in *Mabo* at last affirmed that *terra nullius* was never applicable in or to Australia, yet failed to grasp the nature or strength of this continuing bond.[26] Further, the repudiation of this concept of land ownership goes hand in hand with the denial of Indigenous Australians' sophisticated socio-political structure, family and group relationships and language.[27]

Yet now for the contradictions giving rise to the complexities. Advances in the affirmation of Indigenous Australian rights testify to a forward and back approach. Positive steps to uphold Indigenous Australian rights are propelled by Indigenous Australian voices (accompanied by supporters of Indigenous rights). Generally, the Australian Labor Party responds affirmatively.[28] When in government, progressive action is taken. The 1962 federal voting rights and the landmark 1967 referendum[29] to eliminate racist provisions of the Australian Constitution[30] took place under a Liberal-Country Party[31] government. However, this is not indicative of the general picture. Backward steps are a consequence

---

25. See, for example, L Watson, "Sister, Black is the Colour of My Soul" in JA Scutt, *Different Lives – Reflections on the Women's Movement and Visions of Its Future*, (Penguin Books Australia, Ringwood, Australia, 1987) 44-53; G Smallwood, "Demanding More than a Great Vocabulary" in JA Scutt, *Breaking Through – Women, Work and Careers* (Artemis Publishing, Melbourne, Australia, 1992) 71-80.
26. *Mabo and Anor v Queensland and Anor (No 1)* [1988] HCA 69; (1988) 166 CLR 186, http://www.austlii.edu.au/au/cases/cth/HCA/1988/69.html (accessed September 1, 2018); *Mabo and Ors v Queensland (No 2)* [1992] HCA 23; (1992) 175 CLR 1, http://www.austlii.edu.au/au/cases/cth/HCA/1992/23.html (accessed 09/01/2018); *The Wik Peoples v State of Queensland & Ors; The Thayorre People v State of Queensland & Ors* [1996] HCA 40, (1996) 187 CLR 1, http://www.austlii.edu.au/au/cases/cth/HCA/1996/40.html (accessed 09/01/2018). See later this chapter.
27. Ngaanyatjarra Pitjantjatjara Women's Council Aboriginal Corporation, *Traditional Healers of Central Australia: Ngangkari* (Magabala Books, Broome, Australia, 2013); Centre for Australian Indigenous Studies, *Australian Game, Australian Identity: (Post)Colonial Identity in Football*, Monash University, 2007; AS Malaspinas, A C Westaway and Others, "A Genomic History of Aboriginal Australia," *Nature*, vol. 538, 207-213, *Nature online*, September 21 2016, https://www.nature.com/articles/nature18299 (accessed November 28, 2018); H Devlin, *Indigenous Australians most ancient civilisation on earth DNA study finds*, https://www.theguardian.com/australia-news/2016/sep/21/indigenous-australians-most-ancient-civilisation-on-earth-dna-study-confirms (accessed 11/28/2018).
28. Although Indigenous Australians are critical of both sides of politics, a natural response since few hold positions within either of the major political parties, or in the minor parties, and varying efforts have been made to ensure Aboriginal representation through "all Indigenous" bodies such as ATSIC (the Australian and Torres Strait Islander Commission). ATSIC (1990-2005) comprised of Indigenous Australian members elected by Indigenous Australians from around the country and was established up by the Hawke Labor government under the *Australian and Torres Strait Islander Commission Act* 1989 (Cth). Chaired by Lowitja O'Donoghue (1990-1996), Gatjil Djerrkura (1996-2000), Geoff Clark (2000-2004) and Lionel Quartermaine (2003-2004), appointed by government, ATSIC was abolished by the Howard Liberal-National Party government in 2005.
29. National Museum of Australia, *Collaborating for Indigenous Rights: the 1967 Referendum: history and archival resources on the 1967 Referendum*, NMA (Canberra, ACT, Australia, 2007); G Whitlam, *The Whitlam Government 1972-1975*, Viking, Ringwood, Victoria, Australia, 1985; F Bandler, "A Good Innings" in JA Scutt, *As a Woman – Writing Women's Lives*, Artemis Publishing, Melbourne, Australia, 1992, 166-176.
30. *Constitutional Alteration (Aboriginals) Act 1967* (Cth), amending the *Australian Constitution Act* 1901 by abolishing s. 127 and removing from s. 51 (xxvi) the words "other than the aboriginal race in any state" so that Indigenous Australians would be counted in the Census and the federal government would be able to enact laws relating to them. Responsibility for provision of services and rights of Indigenous Australians moved from the states to the Commonwealth.
31. Renamed the National Country Party in 1975 and the National Party in 1982: see *The Nationals for Regional Australia*, http://nationals.org.au/ (accessed 11/30/2018).

of reactionary forces most often supported by the conservative side of politics. Generally, regressive policies are effected through Liberal-National Party governments.

Recognising the "forward and back" contradictions, it is nonetheless instructive that advances have come ahead of the Declaration. This has its own significance and provides hope for a potential for greater forward movement under the Declaration.

Advances include the extension of voting rights to Indigenous Australians where previously denied. Initially in the 1850s (and finally in 1896 for Tasmania) on a colony-by-colony basis all male British citizens over 21 years gained voting rights, including Indigenous Australian men – except in Queensland and Western Australia.[32] Aboriginal women gained the vote in South Australia in 1894 along with non-Indigenous Australian women.[33] Yet practice was another matter: laws restricted Aborigines to reserves, curbing their freedom of movement, and the ballot box was remote from the reserves, so inaccessible except to Aborigines who had gained freedom from the reserves. With federation in 1901 and the introduction of the White Australia Policy[34] Indigenous voting rights were denied through a refusal to register Indigenous Australians on the electoral roll and variable acceptance by electoral officials of them as "legitimate" voters. The *Immigration Restriction Act* 1901 (Cth) was used to deny the right to vote to Indigenous Australians who had not registered to vote before 1901. It was not until 1962 that the Menzies Liberal-Country Party government righted the wrong, ensuring Indigenous Australian women and men could vote in federal elections.[35] Western Australia (1962) and Queensland (1965) affirmed this right at the respective state levels.[36]

Advances that anticipated the Declaration, introduced before it was drafted or came into effect, include land rights legislation which provided substantive rights and procedural avenues for Indigenous Australians to pursue land claims. Tribunals were established to hear claims, and an appeals process meant rejected claims could be further litigated. Funding for housing and education (scholarships and educational institutions) also predated the Declaration. So, too, did establishment of medical and legal centres for advice and aid – including the Aboriginal Medical Service and Aboriginal Legal Aid.[37] The *Racial Discrimination Act* 1975 (Cth), an initiative of Attorney-General Lionel Murphy (later High Court Justice), was the first legislation at state or federal level to provide a comprehensive regime

32. "Voting Rights for Aboriginal People," *Creative Spirits*, https://www.creativespirits.info/aboriginalculture/selfdetermination/voting-rights-for-aboriginal-people#top (accessed 11/28/2018); J Korff, *Aboriginal Cultural Essentials*, National Library of Australia, Canberra, ACT, 2018.
33. Ibid.
34. M Willard, *History of the White Australia Policy to 1920* (Melbourne University Press, Melbourne, Australia, 1923); J Jupp and M Kabala, *The Politics of Australian Immigration* (AGPS, Canberra, ACT, Australia, 1993); G Tavan, *The Long, Slow Death of White Australia* (Scribe, Canberra, ACT, Australia, 2005).
35. *Commonwealth Electoral Act* 1962 (Cth).
36. Aborigines and Torres Strait Islander Legal Service, *Beyond the Act* (Foundation for Aboriginal and Islander Research Action, Brisbane, Qld, Australia, 1979).
37. See Whitlam, *The Whitlam Government*, n.29.

for discrimination claims by Indigenous Australians (and Australians of minority ethnic origin or nationality).[38]

Additionally, two major Inquiries were established in the 1980s under the Hawke Labor government: the Royal Commission into Aboriginal Deaths in Custody;[39] and the Human Rights Commission Inquiry into removal of Indigenous Australian children from their families and its recognition as genocide.[40]

Against this backdrop of denials and affirmations of Indigenous Australians' humanity, existence and rights, then, where does Australia stand insofar as the Declaration is concerned? How have elements of the Declaration been anticipated, how have elements been subverted even before it came into existence or was agreed to by Australia, and what hope may it anticipate for the future? What is the prospect for Indigenous Australians and what for the Australian community in its entirety, insofar as the benefits of acknowledging Indigenous Australian rights consistent with the Declaration? This chapter considers these issues.

DENIAL OF DECLARATION RIGHTS

Article 7 – Genocide, Article 8 – Forced Assimilation, Article 10 – Forcible Removal from Lands & Territories

Genocide has ancient and contemporary patterns. The United Nations Convention on the Prevention and Punishment of Genocide provides that "genocide" means "any of the following acts committed with intent to destroy, in whole or in part, a national, ethnical, racial or religious group" including:

(a) Killing members of the group;
(b) Causing serious bodily or mental harm to members of the group;
(c) Deliberately inflicting on the group conditions of life calculated to bring about its physical destruction in whole or in part;
(d) Imposing measures intended to prevent births within the group;
(e) Forcibly transferring children of the group to another group.[41]

---

38. JA Scutt, *Lionel Murphy – A Radical Judge* (McCulloch Publishing, Melbourne, Australia, 1987).
39. National Archives of Australia, *Royal Commission into Aboriginal Deaths in Custody – Fact Sheet*, http://www.naa.gov.au/collection/fact-sheets/fs112.aspx; Indigenous Law Resources, *Royal Commission into Aboriginal Deaths in Custody - Reports into Aboriginal Deaths in Custody, http://www.austlii.edu.au/au/other/IndigLRes/rciadic/* (accessed 11/28/2018); Australian Human Rights Commission, *Indigenous Deaths in Custody: Report Summary*, https://www.humanrights.gov.au/publications/indigenous-deaths-custody-report-summary (accessed 11/28/2018).
40. Australian Human Rights Commission, *Bringing Them Home: The Stolen Children Report*, AHRC, Canberra, ACT, Australia, 1997, https://www.humanrights.gov.au/our-work/aboriginal-and-torres-strait-islander-social-justice/publications/bringing-them-home-stolen (accessed November 28, 2018); Colin Tatz, "Genocide in Australia," *Journal of Genocide Research*, vol. 1, no. 3, 1999, 315-352, https://www.tandfonline.com/doi/abs/10.1080/14623529908413964?src=recsys (accessed 11/28/2018).
41. United Nations Human Rights, Office of the High Commissioner, *Article II, UN Convention on the Prevention and Punishment of Genocide*, https://www.ohchr.org/EN/ProfessionalInterest/Pages/CrimeOfGenocide.aspx (accessed 11/28/2018).

Four groups come under the Convention's protection: a national group (identity defined by a common country or nationality or national origin), an ethnical group (identity defined by common cultural traditions), a racial group (identity defined by physical characteristics) and a religious group (identity defined by common religious creeds, beliefs, doctrines, practices or rituals).[42]

Indigenous Australians can come within at least the ethnical group definition, the racial group definition and the religious group definition. There are many different Indigenous Australian groups, with hundreds of different languages now being recovered throughout Australia,[43] and the groups have some distinctive traditions as well as spiritual values and rituals.[44] Yet whether as a whole or in terms of each individual group (Tasmanian Aborigines, and various populations including the Bardi people from Broome in Western Australia, the Pitjatjantjara, Ngarrindjeri and Nunga from South Australia, Nyunga from Western Australia, Queensland Murris, Victorian Kooris, New South Wales Gurris and others), Indigenous Australians come within the terms of the Convention.

Indigenous Australians have been subjected to at least two versions of genocide: outright killing and the practice of endeavouring to assimilate Indigenous Australian children into the dominant culture and away from their familial setting. This breaches Article 7 of the Declaration, which provides:

1. Indigenous individuals have the rights to life, physical and mental integrity, liberty and security of person.
2. Indigenous peoples have the collective right to live in freedom, peace and security as distinct peoples and shall not be subjected to any act of genocide or any other act of violence, including forcibly removing children of the group to another group.[45]

As the provision has been violated from the time of settlement or invasion by Captain Philip at Sydney Cove in 1788, this can stand only as an exhortation for future conduct, as do Articles 8, 9 and 10, being prohibitions against assimilation and destruction of Indigenous Australian culture, and forcible removal from lands and territories. Assimilation policies and destruction of culture as well as

---

42. Ibid. Australia was the third country to sign and ratify the Convention by the *Genocide Convention Act 1949* (Cth).
43. Australian Institute of Aboriginal and Torres Strait Islanders, *Balgabalga – Indigenous Australian Languages*, https://aiatsis.gov.au/explore/articles/indigenous-australian-languages (accessed 11/28/2018); OZBIB, *A Linguistic Bibliography of Aboriginal and Torres Strait Islander Languages*, http://ozbib.aiatsis.gov.au/ozbibDisclaimer.php (accessed 11/28/2018).
44. R Villaneuva Siascoco, "Aboriginal Australia – History and Culture of Australia's Indigenous Peoples," *Sandbox Networks*, https://www.infoplease.com/aboriginal-australia (accessed 11/28/2018); M Andrews, *Journey into Dreamtime* (Magabala Books, Broome, Australia, 2019); *Journey into Dreamtime with Aunty Munya Andrews*, https://www.youtube.com/watch?v=IuzqofEBhM8, accessed 11/28/2018); J Boyce, *Van Diemen's Land* (Black Inc./Schwarz Media, Melbourne, Australia, 2009).
45. United Nations Human Rights, Office of the High Commissioner, *UN Declaration on the Rights of Indigenous Peoples*, https://www.ohchr.org/EN/Issues/IPeoples/Pages/Declaration.aspx (accessed 11/28/2018).

forcible removal from lands and territories are part of Australia's history and part of the history imposed upon Indigenous Australians by colonial governments and their successors. This is well illustrated by reference to past and newly emerging work published by Lyndall Ryan, Henry Reynolds and others as recounted briefly here.

Thus, in her ground-breaking work relating the history of Tasmania's Indigenous Australians, Lyndall Ryan recounted the deliberate killing, including the notorious "black line" where non-Aboriginal Australians trawled the island, forming a line to "catch" every Indigenous Australian so as to rid the colony of them,[46] and the isolation of Aboriginal (Palawa) people on Flinders Island and Oyster Cove consistent with the practice of genocide.[47] She followed with research into massacres of Indigenous Australians in Central and Eastern Australia from 1788-1930, including killings of non-Indigenous Australians (far fewer in number and place) by Indigenous Australians in battles.[48] Henry Reynolds' extensive research similarly confirms the deliberate killing of Aboriginal people in Central Australia, on the East Coast and in Tasmania which took place during massacres, by methods such as poisoning waterholes or food sources, banishment to isolated areas, or battles.[49] An effort to discount this historical reality was waged in what became known as "the history wars" where an historian, Keith Windschuttle, effectively joined forces with the John Howard Liberal-National Party government, asserting that claims of genocide were misplaced, that the numbers of Aboriginal people massacred were exaggerated, and that non-Indigenous Australians suffered disproportionally at the hands of Indigenous Australians. Ryan, Reynolds and Robert Manne, amongst others, responded with further confirmatory research of genocide and death during battles fought by Aboriginal Australians against invasion.[50]

---

46. L Ryan, "The Black Line in Van Diemen's Land (Tasmania), 1830" (2013) 37(1) *Journal of Australian Studies* 3-18. History is silent as to what happened to the elderly woman and young boy who were the only Indigenous Australians captured in this notorious trawl.

47. L Ryan, *The Aboriginal Tasmanians*, University of Queensland Press, Brisbane, 1981; L Ryan, *The Aboriginal Australians*, 2nd edn (Allen & Unwin, Sydney, 1995); L Ryan, *Tasmanian Aborigines: A History Since 1803* (Allen & Unwin, Sydney, 2012).

48. L Ryan, J Richards, J Debenham, R J. Anders, W Pascoe, M Brown, D Price (Stage 1 Research Team); L Ryan, W Pascoe, J Debenham, M Brown, R Smith, D Price, J Newley (Stage 2 Research Team), *Map – Colonial Frontier Massacres in Central and Eastern Australia 1788-1930*, University of Newcastle/Australian Research Council, Newcastle/Canberra, ACT, https://c21ch.newcastle.edu.au/colonialmassacres/ (accessed 09/01/2018); https://c21ch.newcastle.edu.au/colonialmassacres/map.php (accessed 09/01/2018).

49. H Reynolds (ed.) *Aborigines and Settlers: the Australian Experience, 1788-1939* (Cassell Australia, Nth Melbourne, 1972); H Reynolds, *The Other side of the Frontier: Aboriginal Resistance to the European Invasion of Australia* (UNSW Press, Sydney, 1981); H Reynolds, *Frontier: Aborigines, Settlers and Land* (Allen & Unwin, Sydney, 2000); H Reynolds, *Dispossession: Black Australia and White Invaders* (Allen & Unwin, Sydney, 1989), 2nd edn 1996; H Reynolds, *This Whispering in Our Hearts* (Allen & Unwin, Sydney, 1998); H Reynolds, *An Indelible Stain? The question of genocide in Australia's History* (NewSouth Books, Sydney, 2001); H Reynolds, *A History of Tasmania* (Cambridge University Press, Cambridge, 2011); H Reynolds, *Forgotten War* (New South Books, Sydney, 2013).

50. K Windschuttle, *The Fabrication of Aboriginal, Volume One: Van Diemen's Land 1803-1847* (Macleay Press, Sydney, 2002); L Ryan, "Who is the Fabricator?" in Robert Manne (ed.), *Whitewash: On Keith Windschuttle's Fabrication of Aboriginal History* (Black Inc. Agenda, Sydney, 2003); H Reynolds,

The "history wars" were fought out unrelentingly during the years of the Howard Liberal-National Party government.[51] The impact went beyond academic disagreement and publications, erupting into the mainstream media, with television panel programmes, interviews and documentaries, and radio programmes featuring the exaggerated posturing of those radio personalities known as "shock jocks."[52] Tabloid newspapers also ran stories generally favouring those who derided academic work that confirmed the systematic killing of Indigenous Australians during and after invasion, albeit some took a more critical stance.[53] At its height, Indigenous Australians turned their backs on the Prime Minister at a major convention in Melbourne, earning his ire and generating both sympathy and antagonism from the Australian public.[54] Generated by the "history wars" and feeding into them, the Howard government proposed major changes to the school curriculum, so as to eliminate reference to Indigenous Australian history and culture.[55] The director of the newly established National Museum in Canberra, an Indigenous Australian appointed by the Labour government, was criticised for "bias" in her focus on ensuring that the Museum recognised Indigenous Australian culture alongside the non-Indigenous elements, so as to showcase the "real" Australia. This direction was challenged by the Howard government and "history wars" commentators.[56] Even now, those committed to opposing historical accuracy of the killings of Indigenous Australians continue their attacks.[57]

Why Weren't We Told? (Penguin Books, Melbourne, 2000); R Manne, *Whitewash: On Keith Windschuttle's Fabrication of Aboriginal History* (Black Inc. Agenda, Sydney, 2003).
51. M McKenna, *Different Perspectives on Black-Armband history*, Research Paper No. 5, 1997-1998, Parliament of Australia, Parliamentary Library, Canberra, ACT, Australia, https://www.aph.gov.au/About_Parliament/Parliamentary_Departments/Parliamentary_Library/pubs/rp/RP9798/98RP05 (accessed 11/28/2018); Convict Creations, *The History Wars in Australia*, http://www.convictcreations.com/history/historywars.html (accessed 11/28/2018).
52. Television programmes such as the ABC's *7.30 Report* and *Q & A*, for example, Race wars written out of Australian history: historian http://www.abc.net.au/7.30/stories/s28233.htm (accessed 11/28/2018); radio personalities such as Alan Jones and John Laws: see, for example, D Salter, "Who's for breakfast, Alan Jones?" *The Monthly*, May 2006, https://www.themonthly.com.au/monthly-essays-david-salter-whos-breakfast-mr-jones-sydney039s-talkback-titan-and-his-mythical-power (accessed 11/28/2018); C Masters, *Jones Town: The Power and the Myth of Alan Jones* (Allen & Unwin, Sydney, Australia, 2007).
53. For example, C Graham, "Australian university accused of 'rewriting history' over British invasion language," *The Telegraph*, 03/30/2016 30, https://www.telegraph.co.uk/news/2016/03/30/australian-university-accused-of-rewriting-history-over-british/ (accessed 11/28/2018); J Smyth, "Return of Australia's 'history wars,'" *Financial Times*, April 1, 2016, https://www.ft.com/content/d0a0e7c2-f7b9-11e5-803c-d27c7117d132 (accessed 11/28/2018).
54. N Thorpe, "7 Legacies of John Howard's government," *NITV*, 03/03/2016, https://www.sbs.com.au/nitv/the-point-with-stan-grant/article/2016/03/03/7-legacies-john-howards-government (accessed 11/28/2018).
55. See, for example, T Taylor, "Australia's 'history wars' reignite, *The Conversation*, 03/31/2016, http://theconversation.com/australias-history-wars-reignite-57065 (accessed 11/28/2018).
56. See, for example, K Windschuttle, "How not to run a museum – People's history at the postmodern museum," *Quadrant*, September 2001, https://web.archive.org/web/20060820050424/http://www.sydney-line.com/National%20Museum.htm (accessed November 28, 2018).
57. See, for example, J Baird, "Bloody week in history wars as Alan Jones takes aim at opening ceremony and Abbott group seizes on Australian hero," *Sydney Morning Herald*, April 6, 2018, https://www.smh.com.au/politics/federal/bloody-week-in-history-wars-as-alan-jones-takes-aim-at-opening-ceremony-and-abbott-group-seizes-on-australian-hero-20180406-p4z86l.html (accessed 11/28/2018).

Removal of Aboriginal and Torres Strait children from their families and displacement into non-Indigenous families was carried out systematically with an admitted aim of converting the children to "white" culture and the accompanying hope that Aboriginal Australia would "die out."[58] In South Australia Daisy Bates notoriously "helped" Indigenous Australians whilst seeing her role as placing "a hand on a fevered brow" and burying the dead whom she believed represented "the race" in its final stages of existence.[59] The Western Australian approach (consistent with that carried out throughout the Australian colonies) is documented cinematically in *The Rabbit-Proof Fence*.[60] Based on Doris Pilkington Garimara's biography *Follow the Rabbit-Proof Fence*, the book and film recount her mother Molly's story of running away with two other captured girls from Moore River Native Settlement north of Perth to return to their families 1500 miles (2400km) away.[61] The Aboriginal Protection Act 1886 gave the "Protector" (inspectors of police, magistrates, gaol wardens, justices of the peace and sometimes ministers of religion appointed by a five member board, itself appointed by the Governor) power to initiate legal proceedings to remove children "at risk." Not infrequently the terms of the Act were honoured in the breach, Protectors capturing children and forcibly removing them, followed by a perfunctory legal process. Some ten years later the Aborigines Act 1897 abolished the Aboriginal Protection Board and established the Aborigines Department with a Chief Protector of Aborigines. Indicative of the way in which "protection" was applied, removal of Aboriginal children continued then and with the transfer of the role from the 1897 Act to the Department of Aborigines and Fisheries by the Aborigines Act 1905. Such forced removal is an act of genocide under the Geneva Convention and the Declaration.[62]

Indigenous Australians spoke out against the dominant culture's efforts to subdue and disrupt Aboriginal and Torres Strait Islander culture; they dissented, presented submissions and published books.[63] Research and activist bodies recognised the

58. *Working with Indigenous Australians*, "Colonisation 1788-1890," http://www.workingwithindigenousaustralians.info/content/History_3_Colonisation.html (accessed 11/28/2018); Australians Together, *A White Australia*, https://www.australianstogether.org.au/discover/australian-history/a-white-australia/ (accessed 11/28/2018).
59. D Bates, *The Passing of the Aborigines – A Lifetime spent among the Natives of Australia*, University of Adelaide, https://ebooks.adelaide.edu.au/b/bates/daisy/passing/index.html (accessed 09/01/2018), originally published 1938.
60. Phillip Noyce (Director), IMDb, 2002, https://www.imdb.com/title/tt0252444/ (accessed 09/01/2018).
61. Queensland University Press, St Lucia, 1996.
62. Geneva Convention, https://www.ohchr.org/EN/ProfessionalInterest/Pages/CrimeOfGenocide.aspx (accessed 11/28/2018).
63. See, for example, G Ward, "Wandering Girl" (Magabala Books, Broome, 1987); L Bellear, "Keep Fighting, Keep Speaking Out" in JA Scutt (ed.), *Breaking Through – Women, Work and Careers* (Artemis Publishing, Melbourne, 1992), 57-63; E Johnson, "A Question of Difference" in JA Scutt (ed.), *Taking a Stand – Women in Politics and Society* (Artemis Publishing, Melbourne, 1994) 251-262; J Dowling, "Taking Control of Your Future" in JA Scutt (ed.), *Singular Women – Reclaiming Spinsterhood* (Artemis Publishing, Melbourne, 1995) 151-161; M Andrews "For My People" in JA Scutt (ed.) *As a Woman – Writing Women's Lives*, JA Scutt (ed.), (Artemis Publishing, Melbourne, 1992) 81-92; G Baldini, "A Whole World of Difference" in JA Scutt (ed.), *City Women, Country Women* (Artemis Publishing, Melbourne,1995), 116-128; Interview of Deborah Hocking and Lisa Brown in *A Greenshell Necklace*

institutionalised racism inherent in state government practices, producing reports and engaging in protest;[64] however, their genocidal nature was finally acknowledged officially by the Australian Human Rights Commission in its 1997 report *Bringing Them Home – The "Stolen Children"* report.[65] The Commission limited its scope to the period up to the 1970s, however, the practices continued in more outwardly subtle ways, although the impact on its recipients was not subtle. Into the 1990s children were removed by religious organisations by placing them in private schools in capital cities away from their families: this was projected as "help" and "valuable" for the children, however, it served to separate them not only from family but from culture, consistent with the previous more brutal practice.[66] The "Aboriginal child placement principle," adopted nationally and by the states in the 1980s, is designed to address this in the context of adoption.[67] However, Indigenous Australian children remain at risk as exemplified by reports of rising numbers being removed from their families.[68]

Article 10 – Forcible Removal from Lands or Territories, Articles 25 & 26 – Rights to Lands and Territories & to Maintain and Strengthen Spiritual Relationship with Lands and Territories

Land rights loom large in relations between Indigenous and non-Indigenous Australians, and state, territory and federal governments. For Aboriginal and Torres Strait Islander people, Land Rights have been an issue from the time of settlement or invasion. Non-Indigenous denial of ownership, of assertion of rights, or even existence of a people to assert rights or ownership of land have underpinned "white" resistance to Indigenous claims. Forcible removal was a standard pattern not only for Tasmanian Aborigines as aforenoted,[69] but for Indigenous Australians around the country. Before even contemplating the impact of Articles 10, 25 and 26 of the Declaration, it is essential to understand the depth of denial of land rights at the most basic level. The history must come

---

(film), K Buczynkski-Lee and J A Scutt, *The Incredible Woman Productions*, Hobart, 2004.
64. See, for example, Aborigines and Torres Strait Islanders Legal Service (Qld), *Beyond the Act* (Foundation for Aboriginal and Islander Research, Brisbane, 1979).
65. Human Rights Commission, *Bringing Them Home: National Inquiry into the Separation of Aboriginal and Torres Strait Islander Children from Their Families*, https://www.humanrights.gov.au/our-work/aboriginal-and-torres-strait-islander-social-justice/publications/bringing-them-home-stolen (accessed 09/01/2018).
66. M Thorpe, "A Fair and Equitable Settlement," in JA Scutt (ed.), *City Women, Country Women – Crossing the Boundaries* (Artemis Publishing, Melbourne, 1995), 26 -38; L Hunter, "Desert Over Concrete Any Day," in *City Women, Country Women* (Artemis Publishing, Melbourne 1995), 193-199; J Scutt, "The Stolen Generations," n. 23 (and see reference to further Indigenous Australian contributions therein).
67. Find & Connect, *Aboriginal Child Placement Principle* (1987), https://www.findandconnect.gov.au/guide/nsw/NE00952 (accessed 11/28/2018).
68. N Evershed and L Allam, "Indigenous children's removal on the rise 21 years after Bringing Them Home," *The Guardian*, May 25, 2018, https://www.theguardian.com/australia-news/2018/may/25/australia-fails-to-curb-childrens-removal-from-indigenous-families-figures-show (accessed 11/28/2018).
69. Indigenous Australians removed to Flinders Island and Oyster Cove. See sources n. 47 and Interview with D Hocking and L Brown in *A Greenshell Necklace* (film), K Buczynski-Lee and J A. Scutt, 'The Incredible Woman Productions,' Hobart, 2004.

first as it constitutes the lived experience of Indigenous Australians and underpins any appreciation of what might be able to be achieved by the Declaration.

As to Article 26 and its exhortation to "rights to lands," in one of the most blatant state assertions of "no land entitlement," the Bjelke-Petersen Queensland government denied Indigenous Australians equal rights to land ownership. The Bjelke-Peterson government refused to acknowledge John Koowarta's right to purchase the Archer River Pastoral Holding by way of lease. This denial was purely upon the basis of Koowarta's seeking to do so on behalf of himself and fellow members of the Winychanam Group, Indigenous Australians resident at Aurukun and elsewhere in Queensland. Negotiations had the backing of the Aboriginal Land Fund Commission, established under the Aboriginal Land Fund Act 1974 (Cth).[70] A contract was entered into. However, the provisions of the Land Act 1962 (Qld) required any sale or transfer of the lease to have approval or permission of the Queensland Minister for Land. The letter notifying refusal of consent or permission said that the proposed acquisition of Archer River Pastoral Holding came within government policy set out by a September 1972 cabinet decision which stated that the government did not "view favourably proposals to acquire large areas of additional freehold or leasehold land for development by Aborigines or Aboriginal groups in isolation." The letter went on to say that accordingly "as it is considered that sufficient land in Queensland is already reserved and available for use and benefit of Aborigines, no consent [would] be given to the transfer of Archer River Pastoral Holding No. 4785 to the Aboriginal Land Fund Commission."[71]

The cabinet policy was the reason, or the dominant reason, for the cabinet's decision to refuse consent to transfer of the lease to the Commission and why the Minister for Lands refused consent or permission for the transfer.

The case was brought by John Koowarta, claiming that in its refusal the Queensland government breached the *Racial Discrimination Act* 1975 (Cth), by reason of his or other members of the Winychanam Group's Aboriginal race, colour or ethnic origin as associate or associates of the Commission. A claim was included for loss, and loss of dignity, injury to feelings and humiliation. The Queensland government in turn claimed that the Racial Discrimination

---

70. An Act passed under the Whitlam Labor government, advancing Indigenous Australian rights consistent with, although well prior to, the Declaration. During the Whitlam government (1972-1975) substantive steps were taken to advance and support Aboriginal and Torres Strait Islander status and claims including housing – Tangentyre Council, https://www.tangentyere.org.au/ (accessed 09/01/2018) and Alice Springs Housing Associations, https://www.otl.gov.au/other-leasing-aboriginal-land/alice-springs-town-camps# (accessed September 1, 2018) as part of a major Indigenous Australian housing programme – substantially changed since the NT Intervention – see later; educational programmes including scholarships and support for Indigenous Australian educational institutions; the Aboriginal Legal Service and Aboriginal Legal Aid, and Aboriginal Medical Service and associated initiatives, including the transformation of the Office of Aboriginal Affairs (OAA, created by the Holt Liberal government after the 1967 referendum gave the Commonwealth government new powers under the Australian Constitution) and Department of the Environment, Aborigines and the Arts (established by the McMahon Liberal government) into the Department of Aboriginal Affairs in 1972.
71. Quoted *Koowarta v. Bjelke-Petersen* [1982] HCA 27; (1982) 153 CLR 168 (11 May 1982), Gibbs, CJ, 2, para 2.

Act ("the Act"), passed under the Commonwealth's external affairs power by reference to the United Nations International Convention on the Elimination of All Forms of Racial Discrimination, was not within the Commonwealth's power.[72] Effectively, the Queensland government challenged sections 9 and 12 of the Act.

Section 9 holds racial discrimination to be unlawful where an act involves "a distinction, exclusion, restriction or preference based on race, colour, descent or national or ethnic origin" having "the purpose or effect of nullifying or impairing the recognition, enjoyment or exercise, on an equal footing, of any human right or fundamental freedom in the political, economic, social, cultural or any other field of public life." Further, a person requiring another "to comply with a term, condition or requirement which is not reasonable having regard to the circumstances of the case," acts unlawfully where the other person does not or cannot comply, and the requirement to comply "has the purpose or effect of nullifying or impairing the recognition, enjoyment or exercise, on an equal footing, by persons of the same race, colour, descent or national or ethnic origin as the other person, of any human right or fundamental freedom in the political, economic, social, cultural or any other field of public life." This is unlawful as "an act involving a distinction based on, or an act done by reason of, the other person's race, colour, descent or national or ethnic origin." References in section 9 to "a human right or fundamental freedom in the political, economic, social, cultural or any other field of public life" includes any right of a kind referred to in Article 5 of the Convention.[73]

Section 12 relates to land, housing and other accommodation. It makes it unlawful for a person, as principal or agent, to engage in a number of activities, most relevantly here to refuse or fail to "dispose of any estate or interest in land, or any residential or business accommodation, to a second person;" or refuse to allow the second person to occupy any land or any residential or business accommodation; by reason of the race, colour or national or ethnic origin of that second person or of any relative or associate of that second person.

In passing the Act, insofar as relevant here, the Commonwealth relied upon articles 2(1) and 5 of the Convention.[74] Ultimately, Koowarta and the

---

72. UN Convention on the Elimination of All Forms of Racial Discrimination, http://legal.un.org/avl/ha/cerd/cerd.html (accessed 1 September 2018); *Racial Discrimination Act* 1975 (Cth), https://www.legislation.gov.au/Details/C2014C00014 (accessed 09/01/2018).

73. The provisions of the Act relating to work and employment were invoked because the purpose of seeking the lease (held by an absentee American investor) was to provide employment for members of the Winychanam Group).

74. First, that States parties "condemn racial discrimination and undertake to pursue all appropriate means and without delay a policy of eliminating racial discrimination in all its forms and promoting understanding among all races." Further, "to this end" prohibiting and bringing to an end, "by all appropriate means, including legislation as required by circumstances, racial discrimination by any persons, group or organisation:" Art 2(1). "Secondly, undertaking to "prohibit and eliminate racial discrimination in all its forms and to guarantee the right of everyone, without distinction as to race, colour, or national or ethnic origin, to equality before the law, notably in the enjoyment of … rights … including … (d) other civil rights, in particular: … (v) the right to own property alone as well as in association with others; … [and] (ix) the right to freedom of peaceful assembly and association. Further as to (e) economic, social and cultural rights, in

101

Winychanam Group succeeded in the High Court,[75] but were subverted by the Bjelke-Petersen government. In 1982 by a four-three majority the High Court held the Racial Discrimination Act fell within the external affairs power. The Queensland Supreme Court then held that in denying transfer of the lease, the Bjelke-Petersen government had breached the Racial Discrimination Act. Immediately before the transfer was to take place, the Bjelke-Petersen government (generally not an upholder of public parks or environmental concerns) declared the property to be the Archer Bend National Park (now Oyala Thumotang National Park). That meant private ownership or leasehold was impossible.[76]

Nonetheless, the High Court's upholding of the validity of the Racial Discrimination Act was a crucial step in the advancement of recognition of the rights of Aboriginal and Torres Strait Islanders. It meant that the Whitlam government's efforts to outlaw racial discrimination, enabling access to courts and legal processes for Indigenous Australians to assert their rights were affirmed. However, just as Australia's approach to Indigenous Australian rights takes forward and backward steps, as noted earlier, the Northern Territory intervention or "second invasion" incorporated a renunciation of the Racial Discrimination Act.[77]

Despite Koowarta and the Winychanam Group not securing their sought-after lease, the case did confirm that Indigenous Australians have the same rights to purchase and lease land as non-Indigenous Australians. Indeed, any other decision would have been aberrant. Nonetheless, this outcome did not address Land Rights in the spirit intended by the Declaration. Determination of Indigenous Australian's Land Rights in this sense awaited the *Mabo* and *Wik* cases – landmarks coming before the High Court in the late 1980s and 1990s.[78]

Article 26 of the Declaration provides that Indigenous peoples:

particular: (i) the rights to work, to free choice of employment, to just and favourable conditions of work, to protection against unemployment, to equal pay for equal work, to just and favourable remuneration; [and] ... (iii) the right to housing; ... :" Art 5.

75. *Koowarta v Bjelke-Petersen* [1982] HCA 27; (1982) 153 CLR 168 (11 May 1982), and see commentary, for example, C Howard (1982), "Case Note – *Koowarta v. Bjelke-Petersen and Ors; Queensland v. Commonwealth of Australia* – External Affairs Power," *Melbourne University Law Review*, vol. 13(4), 635-642; [1982] MelbULawRw 22, http://www.austlii.edu.au/au/journals/MelbULawRw/1982/22.pdf (accessed 09/01/2018).

76. Much later, the incoming Bligh Labor government sought to redress this in somewise, with a freehold transfer of some 75,000 hectares (750km squared) of the park to Wik-Mungkana peoples (John Koowarta's people): P Berry, "Indigenous land return ends shame," *Sydney Morning Herald/The Age*, http://news.theage.com.au/breaking-news-national/qld-land-return-ends-shame-20101006-166yd.html (accessed 09/01/2018).

77. See later in this chapter.

78. *Mabo and Anor v Queensland and Anor (No 1)* [1988] HCA 69; (1988) 166 CLR 186, http://www.austlii.edu.au/au/cases/cth/HCA/1988/69.html (accessed September 1, 2018); *Mabo and Ors v Queensland (No 2)* [1992] HCA 23; (1992) 175 CLR 1, http://www.austlii.edu.au/au/cases/cth/HCA/1992/23.html (accessed September 1, 2018); *The Wik Peoples v State of Queensland & Ors; The Thayorre People v State of Queensland & Ors* [1996] HCA 40, (1996) 187 CLR 1, http://www.austlii.edu.au/au/cases/cth/HCA/1996/40.html (accessed 09/01/2018).

1. … have the right to the lands, territories and resources which they have traditionally owned, occupied or otherwise used or acquired.
2. … have the right to own, use, develop and control the lands, territories, and resources that they possess by reason of traditional ownership or other traditional occupation or use, as well as those which they have otherwise acquired.

Further, states are required to "give legal recognition and protection" to such lands, territories and resources, with that recognition being conducted "with due respect to the customs, traditions and land tenure systems of the indigenous peoples concerned".[79]

Attention by non-Indigenous Australia to the rights now articulated in the Declaration is most strongly located decades earlier, in the 1960s. The Yolngu people of Yirrkala in north-east Arnhem Land (in the Northern Territory) protested against acquisition of part of their land for a bauxite mine. Without consultation and, indeed, ignoring absolutely the existence of the Yolngu people and their occupation of the land, the Menzies Liberal-Country Party government acted unilaterally. In 1963 the Yolngu people presented a bark petition to the federal parliament incorporating a demand that their Land Rights be honoured. Despite a government inquiry and subsequent court action initiated by the Yolngu people, bauxite mining by private mining interests took preference, a struggle which continues.[80] Three years later, in 1966 the Gurindji people went on strike. Working at the Vestey Wave Hill cattle station, they demanded wages-for-work and the return of some of their traditional lands. Camping at their country, Daguragu, they acted consistently with their traditional laws that see the land as their country, and their country as a part of them. Their culture is recognised as existing for more than 40,000 years, they speak some 13 Indigenous languages, and sacred art used in traditional ceremonies associated with the land is drawn on bark. Their petition for return of their country to them was delivered to the federal Parliament on bark.[81] Despite rejection of their demands, the Yolngu petition and people impressed Indigenous and non-Indigenous Australians around Australia. When the Labor government came to power in 1972, Prime Minister Gough Whitlam honoured his election campaign commitment to "legislate to give Aboriginal Land Rights because all of us as Australians are diminished while the Aborigines are denied their rightful place in this nation."[82] Justice Woodward was appointed to head an inquiry into the recognition of Land Rights in the Northern Territory – this approach was adopted because the federal government had powers in relation

---

79. Art 26 (3).
80. Central Land Council (CLC), "History of the Land Rights Act," *The Aboriginal Land Rights Act*, https://www.clc.org.au/index.php?/articles/info/history-of-the-land-rights-act/ (accessed 09/01/2018); see *Milirrpum v Nabalco Pty Ltd* (1971) 17 FLR 141 (04/27/1971).
81. "A history of the Yolngu," *The Yolngu*, http://www.yolnguboy.com/directory/htm/the-yolngu/index-yolngu.htm (accessed 11/30/2018).
82. Quoted Central Land Council (CLC), n. 80.

to the Northern Territory which meant a precedent could be established without "state's rights" arguments and assertions clouding the issue. Once established, it was believed, it would be easier to found arguments for an Australia-wide Commonwealth Land Rights law recognising Indigenous Australian rights to assert ownership of their traditional lands.[83]

Woodward's report effectively affirmed the Labor government's stand that Land Rights were essential to extend "the doing of simple justice" to "a people who have been deprived of their land without their consent and without compensation."[84] The government also saw this as vital for the wider Australian community in promoting "social harmony and stability" by addressing Indigenous Australians' "legitimate causes of complaint" rightly held by a significant minority.[85] Woodward addressed the question of mining rights versus Land Rights by stating that this and other developments should be determined by consent of Indigenous Australian landowners. Without it, mining or development would be denied unless, on the basis of "national interest," the government determined it should do so "as a matter of necessity."[86] The Labor government's Land Rights Bill incorporated a process for claims being made to land and for conditions of communal tenure (that being consistent with Indigenous Australians' principle and philosophy) on the basis of inalienable freehold. In the upshot, Labor's Bill never became law, at least not as it was intended. Dismissal of the Whitlam government in 1975 gave control to the new Fraser Liberal-Country Party government.[87] Concessions were made to mining and pastoral industry groups, consistent with conservative politicians' concerns. A new Bill was drafted, excluding many of the Whitlam Bill's provisions. Amongst other changes, the Fraser government's Aboriginal Land Rights (Northern Territory) Act 1976 gave the Northern Territory Legislative Assembly (seen as "pro" development, mining and big business),[88] power to fashion "complementary" legislation addressing protection of sacred sites, closure of seas, and permits for access to Aboriginal land. The Act was passed with bipartisan support, coming into force

83. E Woodward, *Australian Aboriginal Land Rights Report*, AGPS, Canberra, ACT, 1973, http://apo.org.au/node/36136 (accessed September 1, 2018); Natalie Cromb, "Woodward Commission Anniversary - Looking back at Land Rights," *NITV*, https://www.sbs.com.au/nitv/article/2017/02/08/woodward-commission-anniversary-looking-back-land-rightshistory (accessed 09/01/2018).
84. Quoted Central Land Council (CLC), n. 80.
85. Quoted Central Land Council (CLC), n. 80.
86. Quoted Central Land Council (CLC), n. 80.
87. J Hocking, *The Dismissal Dossier – The Palace Connection* (Melbourne University Press, Melbourne, 2017); J Hocking, *Gough Whitlam – His Time* (The Miegunyah Press, Melbourne, 2013); D Markwell, *Constitutional Conventions and the Headship of State: Australian Experience* (Connor Court Publishing, Redland, Qld, 2016).
88. See, for example, J Hocking, *His Time*, ibid., fn 87; D Markwell, *Constitutional Conventions and the Headship of State*, n. 87; Territory Government, *Submission to the Productivity Commission – Draft Report on Horizontal Fiscal Equalisation* (NT Government, Darwin, 2017); Jane Bardon, "CLP MLA Kezia Purick threatens to use her vote to stop leaked Government plan to urbanise Holtze," *ABC News*, 03/13/2015, https://www.abc.net.au/news/2015-03-13/kezia-purick-threatens-to-use-vote-stop-plan-urbanise-holtze/6314734.

on 26 January 1977;[89] however, significant amendments have further undermined provisions preserved from the Woodward Inquiry.[90]

Nevertheless, before the dismissal, the Whitlam government did resolve the Gurindji's long outstanding claim: in 1975 the title to the land claimed at Wattie Creek was vested in the Gurindji people and during a ceremony granting the title on 16 August 1975 Gough Whitlam poured sand into elder Vincent Lingiarie's hand.[91] This was a symbolic recognition of the Gurindji people's attachment to the land as a living, breathing part of themselves: the land is a part of them, just as they are a part of the land. Indigenous Australians do not exist without the land, their spiritual presence is bound to the land, and the passing of the sand from the "white" Prime Minister's hand to the hand of the principal representative of the Gurindji people meant that at last the land was coming home to them, as they were coming home to the land. It resonated around Australia, becoming the subject of a nationally celebrated song. "From Little Things Big Things Grow" memorialised the symbolic and factual return of the land to the Gurindji people.[92] It represented hope, too, for better Indigenous and non-Indigenous relations.[93]This affirmation of the Declaration decades before it came into being remains an important symbol for Indigenous and non-Indigenous Australians. Yet consistent with the forward and back trajectory of Indigenous Australian rights, struggles to effect full (or often even partial) realisation of Land Rights continued to the end of the twentieth century and into the twenty-first. The next steps antedating the Declaration occurred in the 1980s and 1990s, with Article 26 being anticipated to some degree through the High Court decisions in *Mabo* and *Wik*.[94] However, Article 25 remains problematic and *Mabo* in particular, although seen as a breakthrough, highlights the lack of consideration given to the scope of Article 25:

> Indigenous peoples have the right to maintain and strengthen their
> distinctive spiritual relationship with their traditionally owned or

89. Ironically, this date – Australia Day – is now termed "Invasion Day" by many Indigenous and non-Indigenous Australians, recognising it celebrates the taking over of the country at Sydney Cove by Captain Phillip and, hence, the denial of Indigenous Australians' ownership, occupation and connection as the original peoples.

90. See "the second invasion," later this chapter.

91. Whitlam Dismissal, "Gurindji Land Ceremony," http://whitlamdismissal.com/1975/08/16/gurindji-land-ceremony.html (accessed 09/01/2018).

92. Written by Kev Carmody (Kevin Daniel Carmody) and Paul Maurice Kelly, *From Little Things, Big Things Grow* was played at Gough Whitlam's funeral as itself a potent recognition of Whitlam and his government's commitment to Indigenous Australian rights and the efforts of his government. Introducing the song, Kev Carmody (with his brother, one of the stolen generations) said, "We always felt he was a comrade in our camp ...." As the song played, with funeral attendees joining in, the screens over the stage were filled with the image of Whitlam pouring the sand into Lingiari's hand. People wept, https://www.bing.com/search?q=rom+little+things+big+things+grow&qs=AS&pq=rom+little+things+&sc=2-18&cvid=057A866DC781458B8ABC03367C55860E&FORM=QBRE&sp=1 (accessed 11/28/2018).

93. The regression embodied in the Northern Territory intervention or "second invasion" is notable here. See later in this chapter.

94. *Mabo (No 1)* [1988], n. 79; *Mabo (No 2)* [1992], n. 26; *The Wik Peoples* [1996], n. 26.

otherwise occupied and used lands, territories, waters and coastal seas and other resources and to uphold their responsibilities to future generations in this regard.

It is the spiritual relationship with traditionally owned lands that fails to be met through Australian legislation and court decisions so far.[95] Thus, despite Whitlam's recognition of this dimension, in *Milirrpum v Nabalco Pty Ltd*[96] the Northern Territory Supreme Court refused to acknowledge the Yolngu people's claim in regard to the Commonwealth government's assent to bauxite mining on their land. Justice Blackburn rejected the proposition that Indigenous Australians held title to the land, determining that British colonial law applied at the time of settlement or invasion; that the Crown had power to extinguish Aboriginal title (if it existed); that "desert and uncultivated" land included land occupied by "uncivilized inhabitants in a primitive state of society;" and that this applied to the Yolngu land.[97] Two decades on, the question was addressed by the High Court in *Mabo and Ors v Queensland (No 2)*.[98]

Eddie Mabo and the people of the Torres Strait Mer Islands, annexed to Queensland in 1879, sought High Court recognition of a "just and legal" claim to their lands on Mer, embodied in their status as Indigenous Australians. To put an end to any such claim, the Queensland government had passed the Queensland Coast Islands Declaratory Act 1985. That Act purported to deny any right or claim to compensation for the land being taken over by Queensland, and stated that to "remove any doubt that may exist ... upon [the islands] becoming a part of Queensland:"

(a) The islands were vested in the crown in right of Queensland freed from all other rights, interests and claims of any kind whatsoever and

95. The issue remains problematic for Indigenous and non-Indigenous populations not only in Australia, but for Canada, South Africa, Aotearoa/New Zealand and South America. For Canada, see *Rethinking the relationship between spirituality and reconciliation – A Symposium*, University of Victoria, March 8-9, 2018, http://www.reconciliation-and-spirituality.ca/program/ (accessed 11/30/2018). For South Africa, see "Land and Spirituality in Africa," *Connections*, http://www.wcc-coe.org/wcc/what/jpc/echoes-16-05.html (accessed November 30, 2018). For Aotearoa/New Zealand, see C Charters, "An Imbalance of Powers: Maori land Claims and an Unchecked Parliament," *Cultural Survival Quarterly Magazine*, March 2006, https://www.culturalsurvival.org/publications/cultural-survival-quarterly/imbalance-powers-maori-land-claims-and-unchecked (accessed November 30, 2018). For South America, see R Roldan Ortega, *Models for Recognizing Indigenous Land Rights in Latin America*, Biodiversity Series, Paper No 99, October 2006, http://siteresources.worldbank.org/BOLIVIA/Resources/Roque_Roldan.pdf (accessed 11/30/2018). For views on the spiritual connection and its meaning to Australia's Indigenous peoples, see for example, M van der Velden, "Indigenous Philosophies," (2018) 127 *Philosophy Now*, https://philosophynow.org/issues/127/Indigenous_Philosophies (accessed 11/28/2018); J Atkinson, "The Importance of Land," *Sharing Culture*, http://sharingculture.info/the-importance-of-land.html (accessed 11/28/2018), Robbie Thorpe, "Relationship to the Land," *Treaty Republic*, http://www.treatyrepublic.net/Indigenous-Relationship-to-Land-Robbie-Thorpe-Australia (accessed 11/28/2018).
96. (1971) 17 FLR 141 (NT) (04/27/1971).
97. (1971) 17 FLR 141, 143 (NT)(04/27/1971).
98. [1992] HCA 23; (1992) 175 CLR 1, http://www.austlii.edu.au/au/cases/cth/HCA/1992/23.html (accessed 09/01/2018).

became waste lands of the Crown in Queensland for the purposes ... of the Constitution [of Queensland] Act;

(b) The laws to which the islands became subject included the Crown lands legislation then and from time to time in force;

(c) The islands could thereafter be dealt with as crown lands for the purposes of Crown lands legislation then and from time to time in force in Queensland.[99]

Applying the Racial Discrimination Act, the High Court held that this attempted retrospective abolition of Land Rights (or "native title rights") was invalid. This set the scene for consideration of the claim in *Mabo (No 2)*. The majority (with one dissent) agreed on all counts. First, the High Court repudiated Justice Blackburn's finding in *Milirrpum* that native title did not exist, holding that at common law there is a concept of native title. Furthermore, the notion that Australia was terra *nullius* upon arrival of Captain Phillip and the colonisation or settlement of the country was undertaken in the absence of any claim to sovereignty or express or implicit relinquishment of sovereignty, was false. There was, said the Court, an Indigenous Australian population existing under an established system of law. That system of law would, accordingly, remain in force except when modified or extinguished by specific legislative or executive action. There was no immediate vesting in the Crown of absolute beneficial ownership. Rather, Crown title would exist subject to native title rights where there was no valid extinguishment of those native title rights. Common law tenure could co-exist with native title rights, though the latter would be extinguished by a valid Crown grant of fee simple. Yet any contention that native title was extinguished must be manifest by a clear and plain intention.

Insofar as native title was to be established, the nub of the matter was that the source of native title was the traditional connection to or occupation of the land, determined by the character of the connection or occupation under traditional laws or customs. However, that connection or occupation had necessarily to be a continuing one without legal or practical interruption. This aspect of the decision at least in its interpretation of a "continuing" connection or occupation, reflects the Anglo-centric bonds of the High Court and remains particularly problematic for Aborigines, a matter for further reflection after consideration of the High Court in *Wik*, where leases came into question.[100]

The *Wik case* was based on two areas of northern Queensland in relation to which leases had been granted for pastoral purposes under the *Land Act* 1910 (Qld) (the Holroyd River Holding and the Mitchellton Lease,[101] and leases

---

99. *Queensland Coast Islands Declaratory Act* 1985 (Qld), s. 3. https://www.legislation.qld.gov.au/view/html/asmade/act-1985-027 (accessed 09/01/2018).

100. *Wik Peoples v Queensland ("Pastoral Leases case")* [1996] HCA 40; (1996) 187 CLR 1; (1996) 141 ALR 129; (1996) 71 ALJR 173 (12/23/1996) http://www.austlii.edu.au/cgi-bin/viewdoc/au/cases/cth/HCA/1996/40.html (accessed 11/28/2018).

101. Being a lease not limited to pastoral purposes under the *Land Act* 1962-1974 (Qld)(the Holroyd River Holding).

for bauxite mining under the *Commonwealth Aluminum Corporation Pty Ltd Agreement Act* 1957 (Qld), *Aurukun Associates Agreement Act* 1975 (Qld) (Holroyd River Holding). The Holroyd River Holding was subject to claims by the Wik people. The Mitchellton Lease was subject to claims by both the Wik people and the Thayorre people. In the latter case, a 1915 lease had been forfeited for non-payment of rent (neither had any entry into possession occurred), a lease granted in 1919 had not been taken up by the leaseholder (not having gone into possession) and was surrendered in 1921, with the land being reserved for Indigenous Australians' benefit from that time. None of the leases contained any express reservation in favour of Aboriginal people.

The original Federal Court decision made no determination as to whether or not native title rights had existed at any time, but did determine that the grant of leases extinguished any native title rights. This meant that exclusive possession lay with the lessees and neither the Wik nor the Thayorre people had any valid claim.[102] The High Court held otherwise. All seven judges focused on the leases and the purposes for which they were granted. By a four/three majority the High Court determined that native title rights do exist, so that the grant of a lease does not extinguish any remaining native title rights. Further, rights and obligations are dependent upon the nature and terms of a lease. In any case, pastoral leases do not necessarily confer exclusive rights of possession on the leaseholder. Further, where rights of the lease conflict with native title rights, the rights under the lease prevail to the extent of any inconsistency.[103]

The *Mabo* and *Wik* decisions provoked enormous political controversy, stirred mainly by the conservative side of politics and so-called "shock jocks" – radio commentators engaging in provocative remarks, initiating phone-ins and stirring talk-back from listeners taking often frankly racist positions. In 1992 when *Mabo* was decided, Labor was in power. The Keating Labor government enacted the *Native Title Act* 1993 (Cth) by which the National Native Title Tribunal (NTTA) was established as the first step in and for native title claims, its decisions appealable to the Federal Court of Australia and thence the High Court. With *Wik*, the Liberal-National Party held government. The government's response to the High Court's judgment was to promote fear that householders' backyards were "at risk" of being taken over by Indigenous Australians making native title claims.[104] The Native Title Act was extensively amended, the government

102. *The Wik Peoples Who Include the Persons Mentioned In the Schedule, Each of Whom Brings This Proceeding On Their Own Behalf, and On Behalf of the Wik Peoples v Queensland, Commonwealth of Australia, Aboriginal and Islander Affairs Corporation*, [1996] FCA 1205 (01/29/1996), http://www.austlii.edu.au/cgi-bin/viewdoc/au/cases/cth/FCA/1996/1205.html (accessed 09/02/2018).
103. Ibid., at paras [75]-[86]. and see F Brennan, "The Wik Judgment: Parliament's Opportunity to Restore Certainty and to Rectify a Significant Moral Shortcoming in Australian Land Laws – The Case for Non-Extinguishment, Non-Discrimination and Negotiation", *UNIYA Occasional Paper* No 97 (March 1997), https://aiatsis.gov.au/sites/default/files/products/research_outputs_statistics_and_summaries/wik-coexistance-pastrol-leases-mining-nati-vetitle-ten-point-plan_0.pdf (accessed 11/30/2018).
104. K McNeil (1997), "Co-Existence of Indigenous and Non-Indigenous Land Rights: Australia and Canada Compared in Light of the Wik Decision," IndigLawB 77; *Indigenous Law Bulletin*, vol 4(5), 4, http://www.austlii.edu.au/au/journals/ILB/1997/77.html (accessed 09/02/2018, 2018); K McNeil, "Racial

making it clear that Indigenous Australians should not envisage a new era of rights affirmation.

As it was, albeit these High Court decisions did provide a modicum of hope for Indigenous rights, they also illustrated a failure to appreciate the difference in cultural and social organisation of Torres Strait Islanders and Australian Aborigines. The former could generally conform to the requirement of continuing occupation of land: their islands and the northern part of Queensland were far less likely to have been invaded or settled by "outsiders," whilst those parts of the country originally inhabited by the latter were highly unlikely not to have been imposed upon by non-Indigenous Australians. Settlements from the time of colonisation were bound to be concentrated in and upon traditional Aboriginal lands: people, whether Indigenous or non-Indigenous will gather around waterholes and arable land. Whether or not they grow crops, arable land will be their focus because it will generate means of survival – namely food whether crops or edible native plants and fauna. Australia's capital cities and other major population centres will inevitably be located where Australian Aborigines had their homes and traditional connections. That they might be absent at times from those locations did not mean that they relinquished connection: rather, the peripatetic nature of their traditional way of life meant that connections remained in their absence. Hence, to require Aboriginal Australians to limit their claims to areas where they had "continuing occupation" does not accord with their cultural and social organisation, nor with the reality of their being swept from their home-bases by colonisation, settlement or invasion. They fought to retain their occupancy – the battles attested to through oral history and academic research confirms this.[105]

As to the requirement of "traditional connection" again this is more readily fulfilled by Torres Strait Islanders because of the lower likelihood of occupation, settlement and invasion. The way in which "traditional connection" is interpreted or translated has an impact too. That Australia's capital cities are built-up, concrete, tar and bitumen covering the land with footpaths, pavements, roads and highways does not mean that Indigenous Australians' connections disappear. Dreaming, dreamtime and song lines persist – but invoking them in terms that would satisfy the requirements of *Mabo* and (effectively) *Wik* is unlikely. These decisions were attacked by the conservative side of politics as giving "too much," and accepted by the small "l" liberal side as landmark recognitions of native

Discrimination and Unilateral Extinguishment of Native Title" (1996) 1 *Australian Indigenous Law Reporter* 181-186.
105. See, for example, H Reynolds, *Forgotten* War (NewSouth Books, Sydney, 2013); H Reynolds, *The Other Side of the Frontier: Aboriginal Resistance to the European Invasion of Australia* (UNSW Press, Sydney, 1981) and maps produced by L Ryan, J Richards, J Debenham, R J. Anders, W Pascoe, M Brown, D Price (Stage 1 Research Team); L Ryan, W Pascoe, J Debenham, M Brown, R Smith, D Price, J Newley (Stage 2 Research Team), *Map – Colonial Frontier Massacres in Central and Eastern Australia 1788-1930* (University of Newcastle/Australian Research Council, Newcastle/Canberra, ACT), https://c21ch.newcastle.edu.au/colonialmassacres/ (accessed 09/01/2018); https://c21ch.newcastle.edu.au/colonialmassacres/map.php (accessed 09/01/2018).

title and Indigenous Australian rights. However, they go only part way toward the Article 26 provision of affirming "traditional ownership." They say little or nothing as to Article 25 in its affirmation of the "right to maintain and strengthen their distinctive spiritual relationship with their traditional owned ... lands ..."

The problem hits at the very heart of the Declaration, for as Indigenous peoples explain, their connection with the land is spiritual.[106] "Traditional ownership" is not governed by the notion promoted by the High Court in *Mabo*,[107] that of living continuously on the land of their people to maintain a connection with it. That concrete and clay, building, streets, roads and highways interpose themselves so as to cover the land does not negate Indigenous Australians' connection with the land. The country remains Indigenous Australians' country spiritually, whether non-Indigenous people purchase it, live on it, establish Torrens Title[108] over it, or assume that because they are no longer "there," Indigenous Australians no longer see the land as their country, their mother's country, their mother's mother's country[109] and so back into the mists of time, long before invasion, settlement or colonisation. How this will be recognised by Western governments remains a question. Australia having signed and ratified the Declaration, however, it will have to be grappled with and cannot simply be shunted to one side.

THE DECLARATION AND THE FUTURE

When he made the 1971 *Milirrpum* decision denying native title existence as a concept, Justice Blackburn wrote a confidential memorandum to government and opposition stating his view that Indigenous Australian land rights were "morally right and socially expedient." Publicly, at the conclusion of his judgment, he evinced sympathy with the title claimants' position, saying he was "especially conscious that for [them] it is a matter in which their personal feelings are involved."[110] Although the claimants had far more than "personal feelings" involved, Blackburn represented a strain within Australian society which acknowledges the importance of principles embodied in the Declaration.

This was reflected too in Justice Woodward's Report, published during the term of the Whitlam Labor government [1972-1975]. Woodward acknowledged the essential nature of "land holdings" as having a spiritual dimension. For Woodward, the preservation, "where possible," of "... the spiritual link with his own land which gives each Aboriginal his sense of identity and which lies at the heart of his spiritual beliefs," could be best achieved by "preserving and strengthening all Aboriginal interests in land and rights over land which exist

---

106. elden, n. 95; Atkinson, n. 95; Thorpe, n. 95.
107. *Mabo*, n. 98.
108. The system of land title invented and employed in Australia rather than Old System Title (of the Old System Title that existed, most if not all has converted to Torrens Title) – *The Free Dictionary*, https://legal-dictionary.thefreedictionary.com/Torrens+Title+System (accessed 11/28/2018).
109. See Watson, n. 25.
110. *Milirrpum v Nabalco Pty Ltd* (1971) 17 FLR 141 (NT) (04/27/1971).

today, particularly all those having spiritual importance."[111] He further advocated steps to ensure "that none of these interests or rights are further whittled away without consent, except ... where the national interest positively demands it – and then only on terms of just compensation."[112] He was mindful of the position of "those Aborigines who have been irrevocably deprived of the rights and interests which they would otherwise have inherited from their ancestors, and who have obtained no sufficient compensating benefits from white society."

This strain is further demonstrated by the apology which was one of the first acts of the Labor government when it came to power in 2007. On 13 February 2008 Prime Minister Kevin Rudd introduced the motion with the words:

> Mr Speaker, there comes a time in the history of nations when their peoples must become fully reconciled to their past if they are to go forward with confidence to embrace their future. Our nation, Australia, has reached such a time. That is why the parliament is today here assembled: to deal with this unfinished business of the nation, to remove a great stain from the nation's soul and, in a true spirit of reconciliation, to open a new chapter in the history of this great land, Australia ...[113]

The motion stated:

> That today we honour the Indigenous peoples of this land, the oldest continuing cultures in human history. We reflect on their past mistreatment. We reflect in particular on the mistreatment of those who were Stolen Generations—this blemished chapter in our nation's history. The time has now come for the nation to turn a new page in Australia's history by righting the wrongs of the past and so moving forward with confidence to the future.
>
> We apologise for the laws and policies of successive Parliaments and governments that have inflicted profound grief, suffering and loss on these our fellow Australians. We apologise especially for the removal of Aboriginal and Torres Strait Islander children from their families, their communities and their country. For the pain, suffering and hurt of these Stolen Generations, their descendants and for their families left behind, we say sorry. To the mothers and the fathers, the brothers and the sisters, for the breaking up of families and communities, we

---

111. Central Land Council (CLC), n. 80; Woodward, n. 83; and see sources relating to Canada, South Africa, Aotearoa/New Zealand and South American, n. 95.
112. On this aspect ("just compensation"), see as to the Northern Territory "intervention" later this chapter, in relation to the Howard government's *Northern Territory National Emergency Response Act* 2007 (Cth).
113. Kevin Rudd, "Apology to Australia's Indigenous People," *Hansard*, February 13, 2008, http://parlinfo.aph.gov.au/parlInfo/search/display/display.w3p;query=Id%3A%22chamber%2Fhan-sardr%2F2008-02-13%2F0003%22 (accessed 09/05/2018)

say sorry. And for the indignity and degradation thus inflicted on a proud people and a proud culture, we say sorry.

We the Parliament of Australia respectfully request that this apology be received in the spirit in which it is offered as part of the healing of the nation. For the future we take heart; resolving that this new page in the history of our great continent can now be written. We today take this first step by acknowledging the past and laying claim to a future that embraces all Australians.

Northern Territory National Emergency Response Act 2007 (Cth

A future where this Parliament resolves that the injustices of the past must never, never happen again. A future where we harness the determination of all Australians, Indigenous and non-Indigenous, to close the gap that lies between us in life expectancy, educational achievement and economic opportunity. A future where we embrace the possibility of new solutions to enduring problems where old approaches have failed. A future based on mutual respect, mutual resolve and mutual responsibility. A future where all Australians, whatever their origins, are truly equal partners, with equal opportunities and with an equal stake in shaping the next chapter in the history of this great country, Australia.[114]

The apology, supported by both sides of Parliament (apart from a few outspoken dissenters),[115] received general acclaim from Indigenous and non-Indigenous Australia. Nonetheless, deficiencies starkly remain in Australia's commitment to the principles of the Declaration. This is nowhere better reflected than in the approach taken – again by both sides of politics – to the Howard government's *Northern Territory National Emergency Response Act* 2007 (Cth), passed not long before his government was replaced by the Rudd Labor government. This Act, some 300 pages long, went through Parliament overnight. Any contention that members could have read it, much less reviewed and digest it, cannot be sustained. The tenor was that Indigenous children were being systematically subjected to family and community sexual abuse, and that their protection was at the heart of this intervention.[116]

---

114. Ibid.
115. Dissenters included Wilson Tuckey, MP Western Australia and Peter Dutton, MP amongst others, of whom Dutton alone remains in the Australian Parliament. See Lynette Russell, "Kevin Rudd's Indigenous apology - Sorry, but not much has changed," Monash Indigenous Studies Centre, Monash University, February12 2018, https://lens.monash.edu/2018/02/11/1313817/kevin-rudds-indigenous-apology-sorry-but-not-much-has-changed-in-10-years (accessed 11/30/2018). For Indigenous Australians' response, see "Kevin Rudd's Apology," *Creative Spirits*, https://www.creativespirits.info/aboriginalculture/politics/sorry-apology-to-stolen-generations#toc3 (accessed 11/30/2018).
116. J A Scutt, "Dealing in Hypocrisy – The Art of Doing Violence whilst preaching against it," *OnLine Opinion*, 26 June 2007, http://onlineopinion.com.au/view.asp?article=6032 (accessed 09/03/2018); J A Scutt, "Black or White – A Man's Home is his Castle," *OnLine Opinion*, 07/13/2007, http://onlineopinion.

Child sexual abuse and neglect are present within Indigenous Australian communities, just as they are present in non-Indigenous Australian communities and, indeed, communities the world over. Yet the Act and the intervention staged under it was rough-shod, ignorant and abusive in itself. It trampled on Indigenous Australians' rights in the Northern Territory, overlooked the work being done and the expertise developed within Indigenous communities – including the Aboriginal Medical Service, Aboriginal Legal Service, Land Councils, Housing Associations, and local programmes aimed at addressing alcohol and drug abuse, criminal assault at home and other forms of domestic violence (including the exploitation and abuse of children) – and (as was later exposed) was a consequence of a cynical political move by a government fighting to retain power.[117]

The basis upon which the intervention was framed was exposed as supported by false "evidence." The Minister, Mal Brough, claimed that "paedophile rings" existed within Northern Territory's Indigenous communities. Upon criticism and challenge to this claim, the Australian Broadcasting Corporation (ABC) aired "explosive allegations" by an interviewee promoted as a "youth worker" claiming all claims were true, including that there was a paedophile ring in a NT Aboriginal community where children were "traded as sex slaves." It was later revealed that the interviewee was not a youth worker, had not lived in Mutitjulu (the community about which the sex slaves claim was made) for nine months as he asserted, not having lived there at all, had a reputation for manufacturing false claims about life in Mutitjulu – and held a position in the Minister's office.[118] The Australian Crime Commission (ACC) was given extensive powers to investigate the paedophile ring claims – finding they had no substance.[119]

The army – with no experience of Indigenous Australians' housing needs or interaction with Indigenous Australians – was brought in to construct houses, despite organisations such as Tangentyere Council having decades of working with experienced architects living in the Northern Territory as a commitment to the building programme.[120] Medical practitioners lacking any history of working with Indigenous Australians were flown in, despite years of experience and expertise within the Aboriginal Medical Service. A report *Little Children Are Sacred* found that young teenage girls from Indigenous communities were being sexually exploited by non-Indigenous men from mining communities and that

com.au/view.asp?article=6085&page=2 (accessed 09/03/2018).

117. The 2007 Australian federal election saw the Prime Minister John Howard lose his seat of Bennelong, a long-held safe Liberal Party seat, as the second Australian Prime Minister to do so since federation in 1901 (after Stanley Bruce (1929). AustralianPolitics.com, "Prime Minister John Howard (1996-2007)", http://australianpolitics.com/executive/pm/howard (accessed 09/03/2018).

118. M Brull, "A Decade On - The Fraud of the NT Intervention Exposed," *New Matilda*, https://new-matilda.com/2017/06/28/a-decade-on-the-fraud-of-the-nt-intervention-is-exposed/ (accessed 09/03/2018).

119. J McMullen, "Influencing the Public Discourse: Racism, Sunrise, Alan Jones, *et al.*," *Independent Australia*, 04/11/2018, https://independentaustralia.net/business/business-display/influencing-the-public-discourse-racism-sunrise-alan-jones-et-al,11385 (accessed 09/03/2018).

120. Tangentyere Council, "Tangentyere Services at a Glance," https://www.tangentyere.org.au/(accesed 09/03/2018).

child and sexual abuse within families and communities did exist and should be addressed, but that this was no different from non-Indigenous communities whether in the Northern Territory or elsewhere in Australia.[121] Ultimately none of the recommendations of the report were followed, despite its being written by Patricia Anderson, an Indigenous female worker with considerable expertise in the field, and Rex Wilde, QC, a non-Indigenous lawyer with long-standing working experience with the communities.[122] Monetary benefits were replaced by debit cards that could be used for the purchase of particular goods from designated stores which were often difficult for Indigenous Australians living in remote communities to access. Despite dissent from lawyers and others working in the discrimination field, the Act ousted the Racial Discrimination Act from operation in the Northern Territories Indigenous communities.

Nonetheless, the intervention continued. When the government changed in 2007, it commissioned a review of the programme. Yet the original report drafted in the context of this review was revealed to have been rewritten to lessen the severely critical stance taken,[123] and the Labor government continued its support under the command of its Minister for Aboriginal Affairs who had required the "toning down" of the commissioned report; this despite substantive criticism from community workers and others with long-standing experience in the Northern Territory, particularly Indigenous Australians themselves. Some Indigenous voices expressed support, but the most powerful of these were not from the Northern Territory and thus in accordance with Indigenous Australian cultural norms were not entitled to speak for Northern Territory Indigenous Australians.[124]

The "second invasion" took place in 2007, two years before Australia withdrew its vote against the Declaration in 2009. Had the Declaration been adopted in 2007, every aspect of the NT "intervention" would have run the risk of being a breach. Financial controls over Indigenous Australians' benefits (social security) denied them autonomous control of their lives at the very basics of grocery shopping.[125] Land devolved to Indigenous Australians under the Land Rights

---

121. Patricia Anderson and Rex Wilde, QC, *Report of the Northern Territory Board of Inquiry into the Protection of Aboriginal Children from Sexual Abuse, Ampe Akelyernemane Meke Mekarle "Little Children are Sacred" – In our law children are very sacred because they carry the two spring wells of water from our country within them*, April 30, 2007, http://www.inquirysaac.nt.gov.au/pdf/bipacsa_final_report.pdf (accessed 09/03/2018).
122. M Brull, "A Decade On - The Fraud of the NT Intervention Exposed," *New Matilda*, https://new-matilda.com/2017/06/28/a-decade-on-the-fraud-of-the-nt-intervention-is-exposed/ (accessed 09/03/2018).
123. P Toohey, "Rewrite takes sting out of NT report," *The Australian*, October 14, 2008, https://www.theaustralian.com.au/archive/news/rewrite-takes-sting-out-of-nt-report/news-story/614a0ce5d4c4d832baf-5361dc3e74d5a (accessed 09/03/2018).
124. F Brennan, "Eyeballing Injustice," *Eureka Street*, May 1, 2011, http://www.eurekastreet.com.au/article.aspx?aeid=26042 (accessed 09/03/2018; "Pearson finally distinguishes his NQ Intervention from the NT Intervention," *Treaty Republic*, 05/01/2011, http://www.treatyrepublic.net/content/pearson-final-ly-distinguishes-his-nq-intervention-nt-intervention (accessed 09/03/2018).
125. P Gibson, "10 impacts of the NT intervention," *NITV*, June 21, 2017, https://www.sbs.com.au/nitv/article/2017/06/21/10-impacts-nt-intervention (accessed November 30, 2018); Australian Human Rights Commission, *Social Justice Report 2007*, Chapter 3, "The Northern Territory 'Emergency Response' intervention," https://www.humanrights.gov.au/publications/social-justice-report-2007-chapter-3-northern-terri-

Act of 1976 passed back into the government's hands through the creation of ninety-nine year leases, ignoring Articles 25 and 26 of the Declaration. As Ian Viner, formerly Minister for Aboriginal Affairs in a Liberal-National government said, "These leases turn traditional ownership upside down:"

> ... they put the Commonwealth back into ownership and control of traditional Aboriginal land [as] it was before the Land Rights Act was passed ... . No one can really imagine that in 99 years' time the Commonwealth will, or could, return to the people absolute ownership of traditional land ... alienated by these 99-year leases. A Commonwealth Head Lease is a device by the Commonwealth to take control of Aboriginal land away from traditional owners.[126]

Aboriginal traditional owners had freehold title over this land. Changing it to leasehold immediately undercut Articles 25 and 26.

Additionally, Viner considered there was "good reason" to surmise the Commonwealth government "devised 99-year leases ... as a way to avoid having to compensate Aboriginal people on just terms under the Constitution for taking control of their traditional lands".[127] This direct discrimination against Indigenous Australians was reflected in the suspension of the Racial Discrimination Act 1975 so as to deny its application to the Territory's Indigenous Australians. This was a sweeping renunciation of the Convention on the Elimination of Racial Discrimination. It would have directly breached the Declaration.

The election of the Rudd Labor government in 2007 did not reverse this. The signing and ratification of the Declaration in 2009 went ahead despite these provisions, which continued.[128] Ironically, Australia did better in honouring the Declaration *before* it came into effect. This includes advances under the Whitlam government, the 1962 recognition of Indigenous Australians' voting rights, the 1967 Referendum, the Hawke-Keating government's support of *Mabo* and *Wik* through legislative recognition, and Prime Minister Rudd's "Apology".[129]

---

tory-emergency-response-intervention (accessed 11/28/2018).

126. I Viner, "The plan to undermine the Land Rights Act," *Respect and Listen – The NT Intervention*, http://www.respectandlisten.org/nt-intervention/land-rights/land-rights-under-attack/ian-viner.html (accessed November 30, 2018); also published NLC Land Rights News, http://www.concernedaustralians.com.au/media/Ian_Viner_Plan_to_undermine_Land_Rights_Act.pdf (accessed 11/30/2018).

127. Section 51(xxxi) of the Australian Constitution provides for the Commonwealth to make laws with respect to "the acquisition of property on just terms from any State or person for any purpose in respect of which the Parliament has power to make laws." It guarantees just compensation for compulsory acquisition or purchase of land.

128. The incoming Minister, Jenny Macklin, continued the intervention: Lisa Martin, "Macklin defends NT intervention," *News.com.au*, August 2, 2012, https://www.news.com.au/national/breaking-news/macklin-defends-nt-intervention/news-story/d74d0225a00e4b815d1ec7f35f7ea210 (accessed 11/28/2018).

129. National Archives of Australia, "Bob Hawke – In Office," *Australia's Prime Ministers*, http://primeministers.naa.gov.au/primeministers/hawke/in-office.aspx (accessed November 30, 2018); National Archives of Australia, "Paul Keating – In Office," *Australia's Prime Ministers, http://primeministers.naa.gov.au/primeministers/keating/* (accessed 11/28/2018); Akari Thorpe, "Paul Keating's Redfern Speech, 25 Years On," *NITV*, December 11, 2017, https://www.sbs.com.au/nitv/nitv-news/article/2017/12/10/paul-keatings-redfern-speech-25-years (accessed November 28, 2018); Australian Government, "Apology to Australia's

CONCLUSION – AUSTRALIA, INDIGENOUS RIGHTS AND THE DECLARATION

Returning, then, to the Declaration: one of the most significant impacts of the Northern Territory intervention has been the effective reversion of land held by Indigenous Australian communities and organisations to federal government control. Although dressed up in words purporting to implement programmes directed at protection, support and advancement to Indigenous Australians' benefit, the intervention not only was based on a false premise but reverted to the welfarist approach that, back in the 1970s, the Whitlam Labor government had sought to transcend.

It would be wrong to suggest that the Declaration is honoured in the breach. Positive advances continue to be made, particularly on a local level. For example, considerable work is being devoted to recovering Indigenous Australian languages and this has now been supported at state level. In 2017 the New South Wales government introduced the first Australian law to revive Indigenous languages.[130] Nevertheless, true to the "forward and back" history that characterises Australia's approach to Indigenous Australian rights and the historical regard and lack of regard to the Declaration or its principles, the then Minister for Foreign Affairs in the Liberal government was cited as calling for a ban on teaching Indigenous culture in schools.[131]

Contrarily, for years the Northern Territory has had its own Indigenous Australian radio station and television station, and media run by Indigenous organisations exists in other parts of the country.[132] The Northern Territory has been a leader in "two-way" or "both ways" education. Often in defiance of the Northern Territory government, this has been an Indigenous Australian initiative.[133] Indigenous Australians recognise the importance of ensuring their children have access to "European" schooling. They also know that learning will not be possible, at least not to an optimal degree, without a good, solid grounding for the children in their own Indigenous culture. Both Indigenous and non-Indigenous children are advantaged by this educational approach.[134]

Indigenous Australians exist within a dominant culture that too often ignores Indigenous Australians or discriminates against them. The politics of addressing

---

Indigenous People's," *Australia.gov.au*, https://www.australia.gov.au/about-australia/our-country/our-people/apology-to-australias-indigenous-peoples (accessed 11/30/2018).

130. ABC, "Should learning an Indigenous language be compulsory?" *Triple JJJ Hack*, http://www.abc.net.au/triplej/programs/hack/should-learning-an-indigenous-languages-be-compulsory-at-school/10238848 (accessed 09/01/2018).

131. "Julie Bishop and the plan to ban teaching Aboriginal culture in schools," *Welcome to Country*, 11/06/2017, https://www.welcometocountry.org/julie-bishop-ban-aboriginal-culture-in-schools/ (accessed 09/03/2018).

132. CAAMA and Indigenous Broadcasting, http://dl.nfsa.gov.au/module/1548/ (accessed 09/03/2018).

133. "About 'Both-Ways' Education," *Living Knowledge*, http://livingknowledge.anu.edu.au/html/educators/07_bothways.htm (accessed 11/30/2018).

134. B Wilson, "A Share in the Future – Review of Indigenous Education in the Northern Territory," NT Government, Darwin, 07/31/2013 (accessed 09/03/2018).

the Declaration are ever-present. In May 2017 Indigenous Australians gathered over days at Uluru, producing their Uluru Statement from the Heart. The Uluru Statement demands recognition of Australia's First Peoples in the Australian Constitution.[135] This would be significant for the Declaration. Yet when the Labor opposition leader announced that a Labor government would revisit the question of Australia's becoming a republic,[136] initially no reference to Indigenous Australians, the Uluru Statement, or inclusion of Indigenous Australians in the Constitution appeared. At the insistence of Indigenous Australians, this was quickly righted.[137] Although some consider the Constitution itself breaches Indigenous Australian sovereignty,[138] a significant number of Aboriginal Australians want constitutional recognition. That their voice could not be ignored is significant and enhances the prospects for implementing the Declaration.[139]

Upon accepting his nomination as Australian of the Year back in 1978, Galarrwuy Yunupingu said: "We are at last being recognised as the Indigenous people of this country who must share in its future." Some forty years have since passed, and a decade or so since Australia's objection to the Declaration was withdrawn in 2009. This confirms that there is no cause to be sanguine about Australia's commitment to the terms of the Declaration, and it can be expected that the forward and back approach will continue at least for the predictable future. Some, of course, hope otherwise.

---

135. Australian Human Rights Commission, "Uluru Statement calls for First Nations voice in the Constitution," *News*, May 26 2017, https://www.humanrights.gov.au/news/stories/uluru-statement-calls-first-nations-voice-constitution (accessed 11/30/2018).
136. A referendum held in 1999 was lost: "An Australian republic?" *Australian.politics.com*, http://australianpolitics.com/topics/republic (accessed 11/30/2018).
137. AAP, "Bill Shorten wants Australia to vote on Indigenous treaty and republic together," *The Guardian Australia*, 10 June 2018, https://www.theguardian.com/australia-news/2018/jun/10/bill-shorten-wants-australia-to-vote-on-indigenous-treaty-and-republic-together (accessed 11/30/2018).
138. "Recognising the Con in the Australian Constitution," *Green Left Weekly*, 01/15/2016, https://www.greenleft.org.au/content/Recognising-CON-Constitutional-Re (accessed 11/30/2018).
139. P Dodson and G Perrett, "Road Rules for Our Country – Australia's Constitution and Australia's First Peoples" (2019) 30 (2) *Denning Law Journal* (Special Issue: Constitutional Law) 179-87.

SOUTHERN AFRICA'S GARDEN OF EDEN AND ITS BOUNTY OF TRADITIONAL KNOWLEDGE

Jo Samanta

INTRODUCTION

Contemporary discourse on indigenous rights has tended to focus on matters of land tenure and beneficial ownership of natural resources. This is not unexpected in view of the profound and far-reaching implications of rights-based violations such as these. A somewhat lesser explored area concerns indigenous, or traditional, knowledge-based claims and relationships between indigenous peoples and third parties who seek to commodify that knowledge. This chapter explores ownership of intellectual property rights in traditional knowledge in the context of the United Nations Declaration on the Rights of Indigenous Peoples (UNDRIP) and opportunities for the commercial exploitation of medicinal plants of Southern Africa. This region is a uniquely biodiverse area which supports myriad plants that possess pharmacologically active compounds, many of which have been recognised and used by traditional healers of the region for centuries. Knowledge-sharing relationships with indigenous communities and multinational pharmaceutical giants present considerable opportunities to confer reciprocal benefits on both parties. Non-exploitative benefit sharing schemes between traditional knowledge holders and the research and development arms of pharmaceutical companies can offer mutually beneficial partnerships, at least in theory. This is clearly an important issue in that United Nations estimates suggest that developing nations lose around US $ five billion in royalties each year to multinational companies that use the traditional knowledge of indigenous peoples.[1]

---

1. K McLeod, *Owning Culture: Authorship, Ownership and Intellectual Property Law* (New York: Peter

Recognition of ownership rights over intellectual property, such as traditional knowledge, underpins fair and equitable benefit sharing agreements and is a fundamental factor to be considered before negotiation of terms can take place. Such recognition is not without its challenges primarily due to problems such as ascertaining the identity of the primary knowledge holders concerned. Customary practices such as word of mouth transmission and notions of collective, rather than individual, ownership makes this area ripe for unjust exploitation, whether this is intended or not. Further root cause challenges exist when trying to apply conventional and mainly Western constructs of intellectual property laws to this area.

This chapter begins by outlining the demographics of modern South Africa against a backdrop of centuries of mass migration and colonisation. The region's rich political history can make it difficult to ascertain the identity of indigenous peoples, which is imperative to properly ascribe rights and determine ownership of traditional knowledge. Against this background the interrelationship of international human rights instruments such as the UNDRIP, the Nagoya Protocol, and the Convention on Biological Diversity (CBD) are considered alongside their actual, or theoretical, value as a means of protecting traditional knowledge rights, as a form of intellectual property, over medicinal plants and their usage. Although the chapter focuses primarily on Southern Africa, the analysis has synergies with traditional knowledge-based claims of indigenous peoples of other jurisdictions, and other contexts, such as South Asia and South America.

SOUTH AFRICA'S INDIGENOUS POPULATIONS

South Africa's current population stands at around 50 million people with estimates suggesting that indigenous populations comprise around one percent.[2] Despite their significant number these populations are not distinguished at national policy level, which means that these groups are effectively unrepresented in governance.[3] In South Africa, accurate accounts of indigenous populations have been difficult to ascertain albeit mainly due to political reasons. For example, the 2011 population census relied upon previous 'apartheid-style' categories of Black, White, Coloured, Indian/Asian and Other. This meant, for example, that the indigenous Khoe-San peoples had to self-identify using categories of 'Coloured' or 'Other' which lead to reluctance to engage and calls for a re-census using categories such as San, Khoekhoe or Khoe-San.

Lang Publishing, 2001).

2. IWGIA 12 September 2011 https://www.iwgia.org/en/south-africa/722-indigenous-peoples-in-south-africa.

3. R Chennells, "Traditional knowledge and benefit sharing after the Nagoya Protocol: Three cases from South Africa" (2013) *Law, Environment and Development Journal* p163 available at http://www.lead-journal.org/13163.pdf.

Indigenous peoples are classified usually as being persons outside of a state's mainstream system.[4] The Martinez Cobo Study offers a working definition of indigenous peoples. These are categorised as peoples that emanate from a background of pre-invasion and a pre-colonial society that developed on their territory. Importantly, they consider themselves distinct from other societies that inhabit those territories, or parts thereof. As peoples they typically form non-dominant sectors of society and seek to preserve, develop and transmit their ethnic identity in accordance with their own culture, social institutions and governance systems.[5] There is no definition of 'indigenous' in the UNDRIP and the principle of 'self-identification' is used instead to determine who is indigenous. For Corntassel and Hopkins Primeau it is quite understandable that indigenous peoples insist on the right of self-identification given the enduring violence that has been inflicted upon them historically.[6] Yet lack of a clear definition can be problematic for the purposes of recognising and protecting indigenous rights.[7] For the purposes of this chapter, the notion of indigeneity will be ring-fenced to encapsulate the considerable diversity and dynamism of cultural practices among the peoples who characterise themselves as indigenous.[8]

Indigenous peoples, as bearers of rights, played a central role in the protracted negotiations over the content of the UNDRIP.[9] Throughout this process, indigenous persons themselves strongly opposed the inclusion of an official definition of indigeneity on the basis that categorisation such as this had defined indigenous people's lives since their very first contact with colonising powers.[10] Instead, preferred criteria include self-identification, historical continuity with pre-settler societies, special relationships with ancestral lands, non-dominance and perpetuation.[11] According to the International Law Association's Interim Report on the Rights of Indigenous Peoples,[12] not all of these criteria have to be met and a flexible approach ought to be used to reflect the inherent diversity of indigenous populations living across the world. Nevertheless, although the principle of self-identification is centrally important this can at times be problematic, as seen with the African nation-led block of a scheduled vote on the UNDRIP in 2006.[13]

---

4. Ibid.
5. Martinez Cobo Study *Study of the problem of discrimination against indigenous populations* (E/1982/34).E/CN.4/Sub.2/1986/7/Add.4, para. 379.
6. J Corntassel and T Hopkins Primeau, "Indigenous 'Sovereignty' and International Law: Revised Strategies for Pursuing 'Self-Determination'" (1005) 17(2) *Human Rights Quarterly* 364.
7. Contassel and Hopkins Primeau n. 6 at 365.
8. M Marschke, D Szablowski and P Vandergeest, 'Engaging Indigeneity in Development Policy' (2008) 26 *Development Policy Review* 483.
9. See, for example, A Organick, *Listening to Indigenous Voices: What the UN Declaration on the Rights of Indigenous Peoples Means for U.S. Tribes* (2009) https://works.bepress.com/aliza-organick/1/.
10. E Pulitano, *Indigenous rights in the age of the UN Declaration* (2012) Cambridge University Press at 11.
11. UN Permanent Forum on Indigenous Issues Factsheet of 21 October 2007.
12. C Magallanes, *International Law Association Interim Report on a Commentary on the Declaration of the Rights of Indigenous Peoples* (2010) at http://ssrn.com/abstract=2175897.
13. https://www.tandfonline.com/doi/full/10.1080/13642987.2011.529687

Without some conceptualisation of the term 'indigenous,' however, states might well argue that the UNDRIP does not apply to their own particular country and unique circumstances.[14] Sapignoli and Hitchcock, for example, maintain that the South African government's position has, at times, been that all of the country's populations are indigenous,[15] a stance that could effectively deprive indigenous groups of their rights under the UNDRIP, as well as more widely.

The ability to identify indigenous peoples is a basic requisite for effective application of international rights. Prior to adopting the UNDRIP several nations expressed concern about the lack of a clear definition of 'indigenous.' Nevertheless, the San people, also known as Bushmen, were the first peoples to have inhabited the African subcontinent some 20,000 years ago.[16] Two thousand years later the Khoikhoi, a nomadic pastoralist people, also settled throughout the country. Furthermore, and perhaps more importantly, both tribes self-identify as indigenous peoples. Nowadays the Khoikhoi and the San peoples are recognised by the South African Government by the composite term 'Khoisan' as being the representative body of both tribes.[17]

During negotiation of the UNDRIP it was decided that differentiation between indigenous and non-indigenous peoples was a matter to be addressed by each country at national level.[18] This is not, however, a simple matter for a country such as Southern Africa due to its history and continued waves of migration, colonisation and miscegenation.[19]

ETHNOBOTANY IN CONTEXT

Southern Africa is an exceptionally biodiverse region with one of the highest botanical species densities in the world. Its rich temperate flora is characterised by two floristic kingdoms, the Palaeotropical and the Cape Floristic.[20] A range of unique plants that inhabit the region have recognised medicinal qualities that have been used for centuries by traditional healers, as well as more widely, for primary healthcare.[21] For this reason, Southern Africa has long been explored by bio-

---

14. Contassel and Hopkins Primeau n. 6 at 365.
15. M Sapignoli and R Hitchcock (2013) "Indigenous Peoples in Southern Africa", *The Round Table: The Commonwealth Journal of International Affairs,* 102:4, 355-365, DOI:10.1080/00358533.2013.795013.
16. Chennells n. 3.
17. N Crawhall, "Still invisible: San and Khoe in the New South Africa" *13/3 Southern Africa Report 26* (1998).
18. R Sommer, *Indigenous Peoples Rights Declaration U.N.* Part 1 Video (2017) SommerFilms at https://www.youtube.com/watch?v=C6ZjjZJO9Os.
19. H Kuper, "The Colonial Situation in Southern Africa" (1964) *The Journal of Modern African Studies* 2(2) 149-164.
20. R Klopper, M Hamer, Y Steenkamp, G Smith, N Crouch, "Richest of the rich: South Africa's biodiversity treasure trove" (2010) *Quest 6* (3) 20-23.
21. A Gurib-Fakim, T Brendler, L Philips, J Eloff, *Green Gold Success Stories Using Southern African*

prospectors, who seek plant species from which to extract active pharmacological compounds for medicinal drugs, augmented by the first-hand knowledge and experience of local communities.

The last decade has witnessed a major resurgence of international and local efforts to explore South Africa's biodiversity in respect of pharmacologically active substances in native flora.[22] Researchers have successfully identified the chemical profiles and compositions of myriad medicinal plants and have isolated their bioactive compounds for a range of aliments. Conditions such as human immunodeficiency virus, cancer, and diabetes, are now all targets for plant-based drugs. Less positively, intensive harvesting of indigenous medicinal plants has sometimes resulted in overexploitation and poses a potential threat to the biodiversity of regions such as the Cape Province.[23] The latter, in particular, is a unique biosphere that supports a range of plants found nowhere else on earth. Some moves to commercial cultivation, mainly resourced by 'Big Pharma', have contributed to a growing economy and niche job creation, although these initiatives need to be managed carefully to protect the unique and fragile ecosystems involved.

Three medicinal plants that have shown promise for commercial use, or are already being used, are *Hoodia gordonii*, *Sceletium*, and the African potato. The extent to which stewardship of traditional knowledge has effectively protected the rights of the peoples concerned, has been mixed. In a thoughtfully considered treatise, Roger Chennells[24] believes that the benefit-sharing agreement negotiated carefully between the Khoisan and the corporations concerned has considerable potential as a model for regulating future bio-prospecting initiatives that could be used more widely.[25]

a) Bushman's hat
The medicinal plant at the heart of the Hoodia controversy has the botanical name of *Hoodia gordonii* (also known as Xhoba or Bushman's hat). It is a leafless spiny succulent plant characterised by thick finger-like stems that branch near the ground. It grows to around a meter high and bears flowers that smell of rotting meat. This pungent odour attracts flies which aid pollination. The indigenous San peoples who reside in the harsh, desert environments of the Karoo, Namibia and Cape Province use the plant, which

Medicinal Plant Species (AAMPS Publishing, 2010).
22. E Rybicki, R Chikwamba, M Koch, J Rhodes, J Groenewald, "Plant-made therapeutics: an emerging platform in South Africa" (2012) *Biotechnology Advances* 30(2) 449–459.
23. K Wiersum, A Dold, M Husselman, M Cocks, "Cultivation of medicinal plants as a tool for biodiversity conservation and poverty alleviation in the Amatola region, South Africa in *Medicinal and Aromatic Plants*, (2006, Springer) R Bogers, L Craker, D Lange (eds.) 43–57.
24. R Chennells was the lawyer who represented the San people in the Hoodia case.
25. Chennells n. 3.

is eaten like a cucumber. The San shepherds and hunters, in particular, have relied on Hoodia for its appetite and thirst suppressant qualities for millennia.

In the 1960's this practice came to the attention of the South African Council for Scientific and Industrial Research (CSIR) which undertook primary research and isolated the pharmacologically active appetite suppressant substance known as 'P57'.[26] Although the CSIR was charged initially with exploitation of the San peoples' knowledge about the plant's qualities without appropriate recognition and compensation, after protracted negotiations the San peoples' contribution was acknowledged in a memorandum of understanding.[27] A subsequent patent application over P57 was registered in 1996, followed by international patent registration.[28] It was also patented in the United States.[29]

International interest in the plant was significant due to the market potential for a natural appetite suppressant that had relatively few side effects. However, the CSIR, as a semi-public research institute, could not fully exploit the marketing and commercial opportunities that it offered.

A subsequent benefit-sharing agreement between the American pharmaceutical company, Pfizer, and representatives of the San people in 2003 recognised the San peoples' contribution with a 6% share of all future royalties. Subsequently, in anticipation of commercial success, the San Hoodia Benefit Sharing Trust was created to ensure that any royalties received could be used for general improvements and the development of the San community. Its objects extended to the purchase of land as well as investment in medicine and education. Pfizer, however, later withdrew from the initiative on account of the technical challenges involved in the synthesis of P57.[30] By this time Hoodia preparations,[31] manufactured outside of the benefit-sharing scheme, were beginning to be sold following the sale of plants by local farmers to international nutritional supplement companies. In 2004, Phytopharm and Unilever collaborated to look for a new range of weight loss products, although Unilever subsequently withdrew its involvement following the results of initial clinical research. A relatively damning study, carried out under the aegis of the two companies, concluded that at best the drug was ineffective and that the compound was also accompanied by a range of potentially harmful effects.[32] Notwithstanding these

---

26. Hoodia Case Study: WIPO January 2008. Available at: https://www.wipo.int/export/sites/www/academy/en/about/global_network/educational_materials/cs1_hoodia.pdf.
27. MJ Finger, P Schuler, *Poor people's knowledge: Promoting Intellectual Property in developing countries* (2003, Washington, World Bank).
28. Through the Patent Cooperation Treaty (PCT) (WO98/46243) filed on April 15, 1998 which covered more than 100 countries.
29. Patent: US6376657.
30. Hoodia Case Study: WIPO January 2008. Available at: https://www.wipo.int/export/sites/www/academy/en/about/global_network/educational_materials/cs1_hoodia.pdf.
31. Based on the plant (which is unprotected) rather than the patented pharmacologically extract 'P57'.
32. W Blom, S Abrahamse, R Bradford et al., "Effects of 15-d repeated consumption of Hoodia gordonii

adverse findings and negative publicity a considerable range of Hoodia plant based products are still freely available, albeit these are marketed on traditional, rather than evidence-based, medicinal use.

b) African potato

The African wild potato (*Hypoxis hemerocallidea*) was used for centuries by traditional healers across Southern Africa.[33] As a medicinal plant it has been used as a remedy for cardiac disease, impotence, infertility, cancer, and also as an immune enhancer.[34] For the latter in particular, if its efficacy can be proven in an age of widespread concern regarding antibiotic resistance, it offers significant commercial potential. Some clinical research has already proven its efficacy as a remedy for benign prostatic hypertrophy.[35] Phytosterols are the bioactive compounds thought to be responsible for its pharmacological activity.

A key limitation against its adoption and use is that efficient cultivation and propagation would be necessary to meet potential demand. Although the plant grows freely in its natural habitat, it is difficult to propagate in sufficiently large quantities for commercial use. In fact, its use as a traditional medicine is already placing considerable demands on existing native populations of the species, which could come under threat. Research using tissue culture and innovative seed germination techniques have so far been without sufficient success to ensure an economically viable supply.

The African wild potato's pharmacological qualities have been recognised for centuries. Van Wyk, for example, catalogued the plant's historical origins,[36] and the fact that sangomas and traditional healers have always regarded this as a 'wonder drug.' Notwithstanding this widespread recognition, some recent accounts reported that the drug was 'discovered' by westerners, thereby disputing traditional knowledge claims. For example, according to Mukuka,[37] an editorial in the South African Retail Chemist journal[38] claimed that the African wild potato was 'discovered' by a businessman, RW Liebenberg, following his

purified extract on safety, ad libitum energy intake, and body weight in healthy, overweight women: a randomized controlled trial" (2011) *American Journal of Clinical Nutrition 94(5)* 1171–1181 available at: https://academic.oup.com/ajcn/article/94/5/1171/4597808?papetoc.

33. Y Singh, "Hypoxis: Yellow stars of horticulture, folk remedies and conventional medicine," (1999) 85 *Veld and Flora* 123–125.

34. S Drewes, E Elliot, F Khan, J Dhlamini, M Gcumisa, "Hypoxis hemerocallidea- Not merely a cure for benign prostate hyperplasia," (2008) 119(3) *Journal of Ethnopharmacology* 593 – 598.

35. C Ulbricht, *Natural Standard Herb & Supplement Guide: An Evidence-Based Reference* (2010, Mosby, Elsevier).

36. B Van Wyk, N Gericke, *People's plants: A guide to useful plants of Southern Africa* (2000, Pretoria, Briza) 146.

37. G Mukuka, *Indigenous Knowledge Systems and Intellectual Property Laws in South Africa* (2010) available at https://core.ac.uk/download/pdf/39667211.pdf.

38. South African Retail Chemist 1 August 1997, cited in G Mukuka n. 37.

relative's miraculous recovery from prostate cancer. The so-called discovery had been based on information from a neighbour whose knowledge had been acquired from local indigenous communities. Liebenberg subsequently founded a pharmaceutical company that now holds patent rights to a product containing the biologically active sterols extracted from the plant. Unfortunately, to date, no attempts have been made to recompense, or even acknowledge, the indigenous primary knowledge holder's purported interests.

Somewhat ironically, the supplements extracted from the African wild potato are now being sold back to the indigenous communities under Liebenberg's patent. The root cause of this situation is because the sangomas and traditional healers, as primary knowledge holders, were not in a position to protect their rights using Western constructs of intellectual property. Instead, their knowledge had been handed down across generations and protected by oral rituals and performances based on primal community mores, all of which are unrecognised by contemporary laws and regulation.

c) Sceletium tortuosum

Sceletium tortuosum, also known as Kanna, or Kougoed, is a succulent plant that is indigenous to South Africa. Once again, the San peoples discovered this in prehistoric times and used the plant for its medicinal qualities. With the passage of time, the plant's mood and energy enhancing effects became known across the Northern Cape. A Dutch settler, Jan van Reibeeck, recorded the first written accounts of its properties in 1662.[39] A patent over the 'invention' of its biologically active components[40] was registered in 2000 following the assistance of traditional healers in the Northern Cape.[41] The patent holder, HGH Pharmaceuticals, recognised the San peoples as the 'primary knowledge holders' and entered into a benefit-sharing agreement for royalties to be paid in the event of commercial success. In an attempt to reconcile the fact that two indigenous communities had contributed, in addition to the primary knowledge holders, the San agreement provided for a fifty per cent share of the royalties received to be divided between the two communities. An advance in lieu of royalties has been paid annually since 2008.[42]

The foregoing examples of medicinal plants provide very limited examples of the considerable potential of many of the endemic medicinal plants of the region. Nevertheless, in light of these illustrations, it appears that the extent to which primary knowledge holders are recognised depends more on the benevolence of patent holders, rather than recognition and exercise of any fundamental rights.

---

39. M Smith, N Crouch, N Gericke, M Hirst, "Psychoactive constituents of the genus sceletium and other mesembryanthemaceae: a review" (1996) 50(3) *Journal of Ethnopharmacology*, 119–130.
40. Mesembrine and related compounds that act as serotonin reuptake inhibitors.
41. https://patents.google.com/patent/US6288104.
42. The patented Sceletium product, marketed as 'Elev8,' claims to elevate moods and alleviate stress.

ETHNOBOTANICAL TRADITIONAL KNOWLEDGE

According to Gray, the contribution of traditional knowledge to modern pharmacy and healthcare has been immense. In fact, three quarters of the plants that provide pharmacologically active ingredients were brought to the attention of researchers due to their pre-existing use in traditional medicine.[43]

Although the substance of this chapter concerns the potential misuse and exploitation of a specific aspect of 'traditional knowledge,' this concept is not without tensions due to differences in cross-cultural appreciation and understandings which can impact upon knowledge exchange. Berkes suggests that traditional knowledge holders do not always conceptualise knowledge as a 'noun phrase,' or 'object' in the way of western understandings.[44] By comparison, traditional knowledge holders tend to view knowledge as a dynamic contextual process that interfaces with evolving relationships perhaps best understood as "ways of knowing."[45]

As an aid to recognising traditional knowledge, several characteristic distinguishing features have been proposed: its oral transmission, its intuitive (rather than scientific) basis and being rooted in the traditional and spiritual.[46] Traditional knowledge is not restricted to ethereal considerations, however, but instead focuses on relationships and activities that constitute ways of life, particularly where there is potential for exploitation and misuse.[47]

The UNDRIP itself has steered clear of defining traditional knowledge even though it is recognised as being centrally important and worthy of protection.[48] For the World Intellectual Property Organisation (WIPO) traditional knowledge represents a body of understanding that has been developed, sustained and passed down within communities from generation to generation, and often forms part of a community's cultural or spiritual identity.[49] The adjective 'traditional' refers to the vital relationship with the community from which it emanates, rather than to any ancient or inert characteristics. Clear differences may exist in the way that indigenous peoples conceive of their knowledge as being an intangible right that is based on relationships. By comparison, Western constructs and the scientific method aim to produce validated and transferable knowledge that is universally

---

43. A Gray, *Between the Spice of Life and the Melting Pot: Biodiversity Conservation and its Impact on Indigenous Peoples*, International Working Group for Indigenous Affairs (IWGIA) (1991), Doc. 70.
44. F Berkes,*Indigenous ways of knowing and the study of environmental change*, (2009)39 *J R Soc NZ* 151-156.
45. Berkes n. 44.
46. M Johnson, "Research on Traditional Environmental Knowledge: Its Development and its Role" in M Johnson ed, *Lore: Capturing Traditional Environmental Knowledge* 3, 7 (Ottawa: International Development Research Centre, 1992).
47. F Berkes, *Sacred ecology* (2012, Routledge, London).
48. Article 31(1).
49. WIPO at https://www.wipo.int/tk/en/.

true and objective independent of extraneous factors such as ethnicity, religion and cultural background. The scientific ethos characteristic of Western cultures tends to be geared towards publication, rights of ownership and shared access. By comparison, indigenous ways of knowing tend to be localized geographically, possibly with manifest constraints upon its use.[50] In fact, indigenous peoples may believe that their knowledge has supernatural origins and can be used to communicate with the dead.[51]

Helfer's belief, however, that traditional knowledge is typically 'un-owned' by peoples that lack conceptions of property ownership[52] is not borne out by empiricism. Several studies demonstrate that recognition of traditional knowledge is a broad church and includes spectrums of beliefs, norms and ownership that encompass mainstream property concepts.[53] Thom and Bain,[54] for example, describe several ways by which aboriginal people in Canada are the holders, custodians and owners of rights, powers, property and responsibilities. Recognisable proprietary interests are vested in their rituals, traditional knowledge, songs, stories, dances, shamanic knowledge, and other aspects of tribal life.[55] In similar vein, although some knowledge regarding medicinal plants is likely to be commonplace and shared across communities, the specialist shamanic knowledge of traditional healers is acquired only through extended apprenticeship. Such knowledge is often guarded jealously because of its capacity as a means of earning a living as well as conferring respect and recognition from the community. For the purposes of this chapter the concept of traditional knowledge regarding botanicals for medicinal use represents a body of understanding that is entirely distinct from the allopathic biomedical model of Western constructs of pharmacology.

Traditional knowledge may be regulated by customary norms embedded in networks of relationships that control ownership, usage, and the rituals, words or practices that accompany its use.[56] Knowledge holders typically evaluate the credentials of those seeking to use that knowledge to ensure that recipients have the appropriate attitudes, maturity and responsibility.[57] Despite these

50. N Kipuri, Culture in UNDSP (ed.) "State of the world's indigenous peoples." *United Nations division for social policy and development—Secretariat of the Permanent Forum on Indigenous Issues* (2009) New York pp. 52–81.
51. Kipuri n. 50.
52. LR Helfer, GW Austin, *Human rights and intellectual property: Mapping the global interface* (2011, Cambridge University Press, New York).
53. KA Carpenter, SK Katyal, AR Riley, "In defense of property," (2009) 118 *Yale Law J* 1022 – 1125.
54. B Thom, D Bain, *Aboriginal intangible property in Canada: An ethnographic review* (2004, Industry Canada - Marketplace Framework Policy Branch, Ottawa).
55. J Timbrook, "Virtuous herbs: plants in Chumash medicine," (1987) 7 *J Ethnobiol* 171–180.
56. Thom and Bain n. 54.
57. B Noble, "Owning as belonging/owning as property: The crisis of power and respect in first nations heritage transactions with Canada," in C Bell, V Napoleon (eds.) *First nations cultural heritage and Law: Case studies, voices, and perspectives* (UBC Press, Vancouver, 2004) 465–488.

robust stewardship mechanisms, however, once traditional knowledge has been published and disseminated to others outside of those primary relationships, then that knowledge becomes subject to foreign norms and laws irrespective of the benevolent intentions of the original custodians and researchers.[58] For this reason, and despite all best efforts as well as compliance with protocols and practice, shared knowledge in the public domain will be subject to intellectual property laws and freedom of expression.

This seemingly inevitable situation should not, however, be seen in a solely negative light. While much of the debate regarding indigenous knowledge has been protectionist and viewed through a prism of discrimination and cultural dispute, Mezey suggests that this traditional approach may be overly possessory and preservationist. She argues for a more grounded attitude that embraces the inherent hybridization and cultural fusion that characterises and positively enhances each and every society including indigenous groups.[59] However, irrespective of the approach one adopts to that of indigenous knowledge and cultural property, tensions are likely to remain. The inherent characteristics of traditional knowledge are likely to create challenges for knowledge sharing schemes between primary holders, outsiders and researchers who often share a commercial interest. Hardison and Bannister suggest that scientists who seek to draw on traditional knowledge tend to emphasize the positive values of partnership by using outcome-based terms. Although well-meaning and possibly in-line with research ethics governance frameworks that promote reciprocity, respect and protocol, approaches such as these often fail to identify and safeguard potential intellectual property rights as well as beneficial ownership.[60]

Traditional knowledge can play a centrally important role in local, national and global markets. It has undoubted value to the biotechnology arena and to the wider economy as well as to the indigenous communities concerned. Although cultural taboos and customary laws are the traditional ways of preserving knowledge and regulating its use,[61] this approach has not always been successful. As history reveals, commercial use outside of its primary traditional context has not always brought the anticipated benefits for the communities concerned, whether by way of compensation or at least by recognition.[62] Traditional knowledge is

---

58. AR Riley, "'Straight stealing': towards an indigenous system of cultural property protection," (2005) 80 *Wash Law Rev* 69 – 165.
59. N Mezey, "The paradoxes of cultural property" (2007) 107 *Colum. L Rev* available at https://scholarship.law.georgetown.edu/facpub/899/.
60. PD Hardison, K Bannister, "Ethics in ethnobiology: History, international law and policy, and contemporary issues" in EN Anderson, D Pearsall, E Hunn, N Turner (eds.) *Ethnobiology* (2011, John Wiley & Sons, Hoboken New Jersey) 27–49.
61. M Ouma, "Traditional knowledge: the challenges facing international lawmakers" *WIPO Magazine,* February 2017. Available at: http://www.wipo.int/wipo_magazine/en/2017/01/article_0003.html
62. S Hansen, J Van Fleet, "Issues and Options for Traditional Knowledge Holders in Protecting their Intellectual Property" in S Hansen, J Van Fleet, *Handbook of Best Practices* (2007) 1523 -1538 at http://www.iphandbook.org/handbook/chPDFs/ch16/ipHandbook-Ch%2016%2006%20Hansen-Van%20 Fleet%20Traditional%20Knowledge%20and%20IP%20Protection.pdf.

therefore vulnerable to misappropriation and misuse by third parties and efforts are required to better regulate and protect its custodians.[63]

INTERNATIONAL LAWS

National and international laws and regulations that pertain to the control and use of traditional knowledge share several overriding objectives. They typically seek to define exactly what is to be protected, who is to benefit and how. Their jurisdiction usually seeks to ensure that control over traditional knowledge vests with indigenous or local communities and that knowledge is preserved and protected against misappropriation and misuse by third parties as well as the promotion of equitable benefit sharing schemes.[64] To date, however, most dominant state laws tend to be grounded in Western epistemology that makes it difficult to reconcile indigenous peoples' rights that originate in customs and traditions.[65] This creates inherent tensions in that indigenous justice systems typically give more emphasis to duties, obligations and responsibilities, compared with recognition and protection of rights.[66]

THE UNDRIP

In 2007 the United Nations General Assembly adopted the UNDRIP which is widely regarded as being the most comprehensive international instrument on the rights of indigenous peoples.[67] South Africa voted in favour of the Declaration, which recognises that "indigenous peoples and individuals are free and equal to all other peoples and individuals and have the right to be free from any kind of discrimination, in the exercise of their rights, in particular that based on their indigenous origin or identity."[68] In fact, South Africa was one of the main protagonists of the African states to promote the UNDRIP.[69] The Declaration asserts that indigenous peoples "have the right to maintain, control, protect and develop their Intellectual Property over such cultural heritage, traditional knowledge and traditional cultural expressions ... including human and genetic resources, seeds, medicines, knowledge of the properties of fauna and flora"

63. Ouma n. 61.
64. Ouma n. 61.
65. E Pulitano, *Indigenous Rights in the age of the UN Declaration* (2012) Cambridge University Press: 12
66. Crawhall n. 17.
67. https://www.un.org/development/desa/indigenouspeoples/declaration-on-the-rights-of-indigenous-peoples.html.
68. Art 2.
69. N Crawhall, "Africa and the UN Declaration on the Rights of Indigenous Peoples," (2011)15(1) *The International Journal of Human Rights* 11 - 36.

and they also have the "right to maintain, control, protect and develop their intellectual property over such ... traditional knowledge."[70]

Although the UNDRIP is not technically legally binding under international law it does, to some extent, repackage existing hard law into an indigenous framework.[71] It is also representative of customary international laws. As a 'Declaration' it reflects normative legal standards for the treatment of indigenous peoples and is a significant tool for eliminating human rights violations to combat marginalisation and discrimination.[72] It provides overarching principles to guide interactions between indigenous peoples, local communities, and parties intending to use traditional knowledge and resources.

Under the UNDRIP, indigenous peoples' traditional knowledge is incorporated into a broader human rights framework. By way of illustration, Article 31 states expressly that:

> [i]ndigenous peoples have the right to maintain, control, protect and develop their cultural heritage, traditional knowledge and traditional cultural expressions, as well as the manifestations of their sciences, technologies and cultures, including human and genetic resources, seeds, medicines, knowledge of the properties of fauna and flora, oral traditions, literatures, designs, sports and traditional games and visual and performing arts. They also have the right to maintain, control, protect and develop their intellectual property over such cultural heritage, traditional knowledge, and traditional cultural expressions.

In sum, therefore, the Declaration identifies explicitly the rights of indigenous peoples to protect, control and develop their traditional knowledge pertaining to botanical resources such as seeds and medicines as well as their own knowledge of the properties of flora in its broadest connotations.

THE CONVENTION ON BIOLOGICAL DIVERSITY AND THE NAGOYA PROTOCOL

A range of other international instruments specifically assert to protect the transfer of traditional knowledge to third parties. The objectives of the Convention on Biological Diversity (CBD), for example, extends to the fair and equitable sharing of benefits that arise from accessing genetic resources while at the same time ensuring its conservation and the sustainable usage of biodiversity.[73]

---

70. UNDRIP Art 31.
71. See International Lawyers Association, Sofia Conference 2012, Rights of Indigenous Peoples Available at: file:///C:/Users/Jo/AppData/Local/Microsoft/Windows/INetCache/IE/ZAE12DLM/Conference%20 Report%20Sofia%202012.pdf.
72. Https://web.archive.org/web/20130413164920/http://www.un.org/esa/socdev/unpfii/documents/ FAQsindigenousdeclaration.pdf.
73. Convention on Biological Diversity, Rio De Janeiro, 5 June 1992, 1760 UNTS 79; 31 ILM 818 (1992)

The CBD has three overriding objectives: conservation of biological diversity; the sustainable use of its components, and fair and equitable benefit sharing regarding the use of genetic resources.[74] The first convention meeting recognised the specific importance of conserving biological resources for economic and socially sustainable development for the benefit of humanity.[75]

The Nagoya Protocol was the first piece of international law to be negotiated following the adoption of the UNDRIP. It aims to provide legal certainty and transparency for users and providers of genetic resources, including those derived from medicinal plants. The Protocol incorporates specific obligations and provides a framework for national legislation or regulatory requirements, such as prior and informed consent and the need for contracts with mutually agreed terms.[76] It seeks to regulate international bioprospecting activities undertaken for commercial and non-commercial purposes, as well as to control privatisation of markets for new medicines underpinned by discoveries from botanical products and traditional knowledge.[77] Compliance with the Protocol and its conditions aims to ensure fair and equitable benefit sharing between indigenous peoples and third parties who seek to access their traditional knowledge, innovations, and practices associated with genetic resources.[78]

In its preamble, the Protocol asserts that its provisions regarding access to traditional knowledge held by indigenous communities will strengthen the ability of those communities to benefit from third party use of their knowledge, innovations and practices.[79] The Protocol is therefore centrally important in the context of bioprospecting due to the inseparable relationship of genetic resources and traditional knowledge. Its provisions include a range of specific requirements such as equitable benefit sharing, and the need for prior and informed consent as well as mutually agreed terms in benefit sharing agreements.

In sum, all three international instruments (the UNDRIP, the CBD and the Nagoya Protocol) emphasise the need for 'free, informed consent' from knowledge holders based upon equitable principles of access and benefit sharing regarding the advantages or profits that result from the traditional knowledge or genetic resources of the indigenous peoples. The central concept of benefit sharing engages with the need to negotiate appropriate terms in contractual or other agreements. Traynor *et al.*, suggests that indigenous peoples can use these principles to develop their own guidelines to engage with

available at http://www.cbd.int/abs/doc/protocol/nagoya-protocol-en.pdf.

74. Article 1, para 1, p 3.

75. Conference of Parties, 1994 http://legal.un.org/avl/ha/cpbcbd/cpbcbd.html.

76. Secretariat of the Convention on Biological Diversity, 2011.

77. Secretariat of the Convention on Biological Diversity, 2011 n. 76.

78. Secretariat of the Convention on Biological Diversity, 2011 n. 76.

79. Nagoya Protocol on Access to Genetic Resources and the Fair and Equitable Sharing of Benefits Arising from their Utilisation to the Convention on Biological Diversity.

parties interested in accessing their knowledge or resources.[80] Nevertheless, it is easy to anticipate power imbalances in these relationships that could skew the outcome.

As declared by the United Nations in a press release, the UNDRIP confers rights to "full and effective participation in all matters that concern [indigenous peoples] and their right to remain distinct and to pursue their own visions of economic and social development"[81] and yet several manifest obstacles remain against achieving this goal.

FREE, PRIOR INFORMED CONSENT

Free, prior informed consent (FPIC) is a foundational principle of the UNDRIP (as well as for international human rights discourse more generally) for protecting the rights of indigenous peoples. It aims to complement two overarching rights: that of self-determination and the right of indigenous communities to participate in decisions that affect them. The concept underpins all three aforementioned United Nations instruments as a means of creating procedural safeguards for decision-making by indigenous peoples. Although there is some suggestion that its aim is to ensure that when indigenous communities are approached for access to their knowledge they are first given sufficient information to reach an informed decision,[82] this meaning has been contested. In the context of the UNDRIP, as well as more widely, much of the debate centres around whether FPIC represents a substantive right to veto a proposal, or whether it instead demands compliance with a process – namely that of proposing a method for consulting with the group concerned.[83] As was made clear at the Sofia Conference, for example,[84] FPIC refers to procedural formalities, such as *bona fide* consultation processes rather than requiring actual informed consent in the medical sense. Nevertheless, FPIC is a centrally important issue that engages directly with the relationships between interested parties namely the commercial entity, the indigenous peoples and the state's right to develop its natural resources. In effect, the interpretation

---

80. C Traynor, Y Kisuule, G De Wet, R Le Fleur, T Schonwetter, L Foster, A Williamson, "Protecting and Promoting Indigenous Peoples Rights in Academic Research Processes: A Guide for Communities in South Africa" (2018) *Natural Justice* at http://ip-unit.org/wp-content/uploads/2018/06/Protecting-Promoting-Indigenous-Peoples-Rights-English.pdf.

81. United Nations Adopts Declaration 2007, para. 5.

82. FSC, *FSC Guidelines for the Implementation of the Right to Free, Prior and Informed Consent (FPIC)* (2018) Version 1. Forest Stewardship Council, Bonn.

83. S Sargent, "What's in a name? The contested meaning of free, prior and informed consent in international financial law and indigenous rights" in V Vadi, B de Witte (eds.), *Culture and International Economic Law* (2015, London: Routledge) 87-103.

84. International Law Association, *The Hague Conference, Rights of Indigenous Peoples, Interim Report* (2010); reaffirmed in International Law Association, *Sofia Conference, Rights of Indigenous Peoples, Final Report* (2012).

given to FPIC will determine whether, in practice, FPIC offers more than the 'illusion of inclusion.'[85]

Leaving aside these fundamental normative tensions, compliance with the need for FPIC may be accompanied by more prosaic considerations and challenges. For the purposes of obtaining consent, for example, or for conducting appropriate consultation exercises regarding the use of traditional knowledge, it might be difficult to ascertain the relevant body with sufficient decision-making authority due to diversity of organisational structure. Whereas Tribes and First Nations in the United States and Canada tend to be organised into governments with manifest decision-making authority, arrangements such as these will not necessarily apply to other groups. Difficulties may arise due to actual or perceived conflicts of interest or lack of trust between political authorities and primary knowledge holders.

Potential conflicts of interest may also exist within indigenous groups themselves, which are unlikely to be homogenous. For example, in the context of traditional ethnobotanical knowledge held by indigenous peoples in Southern Africa, the economic interests of the majority could be juxtaposed against those of the sangomas, or traditional healers, who might well rely upon more nuanced interpretations of traditional knowledge for the purposes of pursuing their own occupations.

INTELLECTUAL PROPERTY

But how can indigenous knowledge, as a form of cultural heritage or perhaps intellectual property, best be protected? Fundamental debates concern whether application of the law would be the most equitable and effective way of protecting indigenous knowledge, or whether some alternative framework would be more appropriate. For example, the mainly western construct of 'intellectual property' is used to describe 'creations of the mind' and as such incorporates inventions, designs, works of art, performances, plant varieties, and names, signs and symbols.[86] A key mechanism used traditionally to safeguard such rights is that of patent protection. At its most basic, a patent will give its owner a recognised and enforceable right to prevent others from making, using, selling and importing the subject of protection for a limited period of time.[87] In return, public disclosure and registration of the subject of the patent is required. Patent protection can only be given over something that can be used or made, if this is new and inventive. By definition, therefore, plant varieties cannot be patented which explains the commercial imperative to identify and extract a specific pharmacologically

85. J Corntassel, "Towards sustainable self-determination: Rethinking the contemporary indigenous rights discourse" (2008) 33 *Alternatives* 105-132 at 111.
86. *Intellectual Property and Genetic Resources, Traditional Knowledge and Traditional Cultural Expressions* (2015) WIPO available at http://www.wipo.int/edocs/pubdocs/en/tk/933/wipo_pub_933.pdf.
87. Typically of 20 years duration.

active component. Some central concepts of intellectual property laws, such as the novelty requirement for patent laws, the limited duration of protection and the preference for applications from single or small groups of inventors, can make it difficult to apply patent protection to the unique circumstances of traditional knowledge.

Intellectual property laws are often of labyrinthine complexity and complicated further when purported rights span several jurisdictions and ownership is based on knowledge transmitted by word of mouth across the millennia. As discussed previously, hoodia was discovered first by the shepherds of the San people. Even though this historical fact is unchallenged and acknowledged, that knowledge will have been developed and shared with others across generations without thought to protection of intellectual property rights, which are primarily an individualistic concept that runs counter to collectivist values. Over time and generations, the ability to point accurately to the original source of knowledge and demonstrate categorically how particular knowledge has developed will be impossible to define. This means that at the point at which an interested commercial entity, or researcher, seeks to capitalise on that knowledge it will be difficult, if not impossible, to identify ownership sufficiently to give appropriate credit and recompense.

In recent years indigenous peoples (usually those living in developing nations), have demanded intellectual property protection for their traditional knowledge. A central challenge is that under conventional approaches, such knowledge is regarded usually as being in the public domain, and therefore outside of the regulatory compass. The WIPO suggests that indigenous peoples' rejection of 'public domain' arguments makes them vulnerable to misappropriation and misuse.[88] It suggests that in these circumstances appropriate compensation ought to be given to the primary knowledge holders. For these purposes, misappropriation includes acquisition, appropriation or use of traditional knowledge by unfair or illicit means. It embraces the derivation of commercial benefit from traditional knowledge where the person or organisation knows, or negligently fails to establish, that the knowledge was acquired or appropriated by unfair means or contrary to honest practices.[89]

Bioprospecting, and the search for new medicinal compounds has been debated considerably in recent years to minimize exploitation of South African resources as well as to recognise and recompense traditional knowledge holders. To date, however, these regulatory attempts have often been viewed negatively by commercial entities as bureaucratic hurdles that stymie the promotion

---

88. *Intellectual Property and Genetic Resources, Traditional Knowledge and Traditional Cultural Expressions* (2015) WIPO available at http://www.wipo.int/edocs/pubdocs/en/tk/933/wipo_pub_933.pdf.
89. Art 1(2) WIPO/GRTKF/IC/8/5 2005 b:18.

and development of bioactive compounds and that ultimately fail all parties concerned.[90]

Some non-governmental organisations prefer the term 'biopiracy' to describe the misappropriation of traditional knowledge regarding plants and their uses, followed by acquisition of intellectual property rights (such as patent protection) where this has occurred without recompense and acknowledgement of primary knowledge holders. The basic allegation is that businesses in the developed world have exploited the knowledge of indigenous peoples at their countries' expense. The accompanying narrative suggests that when researchers learn of a traditional plant-based remedy they perform basic laboratory testing to isolate the bioactive compound before establishing patent protection to enable commercialisation.

Biopiracy is not a phenomena confined to South Africa. In India, for example, attempts have been made to register patents on derivatives of turmeric.[91] Similar attempts were made in the United States with pharmacological extracts of the 'may apple', and the American conglomerate, Eli Lilly, over the Madagascan rosy periwinkle. To harness the benefits of their traditional knowledge appropriately, communities need substantial financial and technical support and knowledge.[92]

In the context of traditional knowledge based claims, critics of the patent system suggest that industrialised countries have been too quick to grant patents rights and that they have failed to undertake appropriate due diligence exercises prior to registration. Schuler contends further that the considerable expense and complexity of post-award dispute resolution acts as a major deterrent for indigenous peoples, or developing nations, against bringing otherwise meritorious claims.[93]

APPROACHES FOR PROTECTING TRADITIONAL KNOWLEDGE

What is certainly apparent is that developing a robust and fair international system to protect traditional knowledge is a challenge. In many instances traditional

90. NR Crouch, E Douwes, M Wolfson, GF Smith, TJ Edwards, "South Africa's bioprospecting, access and benefit-sharing legislation: current realities, future complications, and a proposed alternative," (2008) 104(9) *South African Journal of Science* 355–366.
91. N Roht-Arriaza, "Of Seeds and Shamans: The Appropriation of the Scientific and Technical Knowledge of Indigenous and Local Communities" (1996) 17 *Mich. J. International Law* 919 at Http://repository.uchastings.edu/faculty_scholarship/683.
92. R P Wynberg, SA Laird, S Shackleton *et al.*, "Marula policy brief: marula commercialisation for sustainable and equitable livelihoods," (2003) 13(3) *Forests Trees and Livelihoods* 203–215.
93. P Schuler, "Biopiracy and commercialisation of ethnobotanical knowledge" in Finger and Schuler *Poor people's knowledge: promoting intellectual property,* 159 at https://www.innovationpolicyplatform.org/sites/default/files/rdf_imported_documents/poor_knowledge_2003.pdf.

knowledge does not fit neatly into established systems for intellectual property. Misuse of patents to legitimise misappropriation of indigenous knowledge,[94] has led to distrust of western intellectual property regimes and calls have been made for urgent revision of the conceptual framework.[95] South Africa, as a state that approved the UNDRIP and CBD, has fundamental obligations to honour these instruments by incorporating their norms and obligations into its national laws and policy. As far as the general protection and commercialisation of indigenous knowledge is concerned, current debate focuses on whether traditional knowledge is best protected by intellectual property regimes, or whether instead by a more customised and separate *sui generis* approach.

THE INDIGENOUS KNOWLEDGE SYSTEMS POLICY

In 2004, South Africa adopted the Indigenous Knowledge Systems Policy which was the country's first attempt at recognizing and protecting traditional knowledge. Following several years of parliamentary debate the Intellectual Property Laws Amendment Act 2013 was enacted which aimed to permit indigenous communities to protect their knowledge using conventional intellectual property devices, such as patents. This approach has been criticised because traditional knowledge does not typically meet the fundamental requirements of intellectual property protection such as the requirement to show 'novelty'. Other perceived constraints include the limited duration of protection and the preference for individual, rather than the collective ownership that commonly accords to indigenous knowledge.[96]

One of the main advantages of establishing an international legal framework is that these arrangements provide for minimum acceptable standards of protection and thereby create greater legal certainty by offering some degree of harmonization of national laws. In effect, this should make it easier for rights holders, including custodians of traditional knowledge, to manage and trade their assets.[97]

Against this backdrop the South African Department of Science and Technology introduced a Bill aimed at protecting indigenous knowledge in a unique way.[98] In line with the Nagoya Protocol the Bill requires that use of traditional knowledge, whether for commercial purposes or not, requires the prior informed consent of the primary knowledge holder concerned. According to the

---

94. C Oguamanam, "Patents and Traditional Medicine: Digital Capture, Creative Legal Interventions, and the Dialectics of Knowledge Transformation" (2008) *Indiana J Global Legal Studies* 489-528.
95. Ouma n. 61.
96. C Traynor, Y Kisuule, G De Wet, R Le Fleur, T Schonwetter, L Foster, Andrew W, "Protecting and promoting indigenous peoples rights in academic research processes" (2018) *Natural Justice: Lawyers for Communities and the Environment*. Available at: http://ip-unit.org/wp-content/uploads/2018/06/Protect-ing-Promoting-Indigenous-Peoples-Rights-English.pdf.
97. M Ouma n. 61.
98. A first version of the Bill was introduced in 2015, a revised Bill was tabled in 2016, and version B6B-2016 was passed by Parliament on 14th November 2017. Thereafter the Bill was sent to the National Council of Provinces for concurrence, and the final stage will be signing by the President.

non-governmental organisation 'Natural Justice,' the draft legislation offers an alternative route for protecting traditional knowledge which includes recording and documenting exercises, as well as *sui generis* protection for taking into account the moral and economic rights of the knowledge holders concerned.[99] Instead of being time limited, in accordance with conventional intellectual property protection, this approach uniquely offers collective ownership in perpetuity, or at least for as long as the protected knowledge continues to meet the eligibility criteria. Ouma suggests that a system such as this requires policymakers to build on existing legal frameworks, rather than starting *de novo*. For example, she refers to Article 8(j) of the CBD, which requires parties "to respect, preserve and maintain knowledge, innovations and practices of indigenous and local communities embodying traditional lifestyles relevant for the conservation and sustainable use of biological diversity." In similar vein, the Nagoya Protocol deals with traditional knowledge associated with genetic resources, and addresses issues like prior and informed consent, equitable remuneration and maintenance of community laws and procedures as well as customary use and exchange.[100]

During the Bill's passage through parliament a range of concerns focused on its practical application. Alongside the pre-existing Intellectual Property Laws Amendment Act of 2013 (which it does not seek to replace), it remains to be seen how the two legislative approaches can co-exist, although the Bill appears to assume a subsidiary role in respect of other intellectual property legislation.[101] Alternatively, Traynor *et al.*, suggests that knowledge holders themselves might choose between the different options for protection as provided for in the legislation.[102] At present, the final mandate of the Protection, Promotion, Development and Management of Indigenous Knowledge Bill (B6B-2016) has been passed to both Houses and has been sent to the President for assent.[103] Karjiker suggests that despite its earlier promise, one limitation is that the proposed legislation incorporates traditional cultural expression into its definition of traditional knowledge. Perhaps of even greater concern is the Bill's national jurisdictional reach, which means that only South Africans will be curtailed from using traditional knowledge and that outsiders may use such knowledge with impunity.[104]

The Bill of Rights in the South African Constitution already incorporates several specific rights that are fundamentally important for the region's indigenous

---

99. C Traynor et al., n. 96.

100. M Ouma n. 61.

101. Section 32(1) of the latest version of the Indigenous Knowledge Bill states that: "This Act does not alter or detract from any right in respect of any statute or the common law."

102. C Traynor et al., n. 96.

103. The Bill was sent to the President on the 12th September 2018. See South African Parliamentary Monitoring Group at https://pmg.org.za/bill/635/.

104. S Karjiker, *The Protection, Promotion, Development and Management of Indigenous Knowledge Systems Bill, 2016: Has the DST lost its resolve?* (2016) available at: http://blogs.sun.ac.za/iplaw/2016/04/18/the-protection-promotion-development-and-management-of-indigenous-knowledge-systems-bill-2016-has-the-dst-lost-its-resolve/.

peoples. These include a right to the environment;[105] a right to language and culture;[106] a right to belong, and practise, as a member of a cultural community[107] and rights to access information[108] and the courts.[109] To some extent the National Environmental Management: Biodiversity Act 10 of 2004 also provides some protection for traditional knowledge under its provisions relating to bioprospecting with regard to indigenous biological resources for commercial or industrial use and benefit sharing agreements.[110]

The economic significance of this issue should not be underestimated. Almost twenty years ago, Ten Kate and Laird hypothesised that the annual value of products derived from genetic and biological resources amounted to between 500 and 800 billion US dollars.[111] If only ten per cent of that total had been derived from traditional knowledge then that would still amount to between 50 and 80 billion dollars per annum. They suggest that even if indigenous peoples received a modest ten per cent of this total then that would certainly go some way to meeting their basic needs.[112]

CONCLUSION

A considerable range of botanically extracted compounds play an important role in the development of new drugs, and traditional knowledge has made significant contributions to pharmaceutical research and the development of a range of modern medicines for catastrophic diseases such as cancer.[113]

As a soft law instrument the UNDRIP cannot eliminate and resolve the seemingly ubiquitous problems of biopiracy and the potential for exploitation of traditional knowledge holders and indigenous medicinal plants. Nevertheless, the UNDRIP represents a globally significant achievement for indigenous people, taken in conjunction with other international safeguards such as the CDP and the Nagoya Protocol and together with other innovative domestic approaches herald significant promise for better outcomes.

---

105. Section 24.
106. Section 30.
107. Section 32.
108. Ibid.
109. Section 34.
110. See section 82 National Environmental Management: Biodiversity Act 10 of 2004 https://www.sanbi.org/documents/national-environmental-management-biodiversity-act-no-10-of-2004/.
111. K Ten Kate, S Laird, *The commercial use of biodiversity* (1999) London: Taylor & Francis Inc.
112. M Y Teran, The Nagoya Protocol and Indigenous Peoples (2016) 7 (2) *The International Indigenous Policy Journal* 2-34 Available at: https://www.researchgate.net/publication/305716853_The_Nagoya_Protocol_and_Indigenous_Peoples.
113. S Laird, R Wynberg (eds.), *Access and Benefit Sharing in Practice: Trends in Partnerships Across Sectors* 12, Convention on Biological Diversity Secretariat, Montreal: Technical Series, No. 38 (2008).

It is doubtful whether contemporary western constructs of intellectual property law can protect the interests of traditional knowledge holders and their communities adequately. One way forward would be to adopt a *sui generis* approach. A suitably bespoke and flexible framework of protection, based on innovative intellectual property principles, might make it possible to accommodate the inherent and unique characteristics of traditional knowledge and ensure that the stewards of that knowledge are able to manage and beneficially exploit it in line with customary practice. Such a system would need to provide ways of preventing third parties from the nefarious acquisition of intellectual property rights over traditional knowledge. If fact, some jurisdictions have achieved this to some extent already by using, for example, a bespoke and searchable traditional knowledge database that has reduced the number of invalid patent registrations derived from indigenous knowledge.

A *sui generis* system also has potential to empower communities to promote their knowledge positively, to control its use and to benefit from future commercial success. An underlying and persistent challenge is that of jurisdictional reach: by definition, the reach of national legislation means that it is unlikely to be effective for dealing with international transgressions. Nevertheless, early evidence suggests that innovative new ways to approach this challenging issue are being explored and developed outside of traditional Western constructs of intellectual property laws.

"AFRICAN LEGAL ORDER" OR "AFRICAN LEGAL ORDERING?": THE EMERGENCE OF TRANSNATIONAL CUSTOMARY AFRICAN LAW IN THE TRANSBOUNDARY MANAGEMENT OF NATURAL RESOURCES

Hephzibah Egede

INTRODUCTION

Sub-Saharan Africa is richly endowed with natural resources. To some degree, natural resource exploitation has been beneficial to the continent and has contributed to its economic and social development.[1] At the same time, natural resource exploitation has caused resource related conflicts within the sub-continent. Substantive research[2] has been undertaken on the causes of resource related conflicts in the region and how they can be resolved or

---

1. J Reilaender: "Making the Most of its Natural Resources" *OECD Observer* 2013.
2. See generally, A Alao, *Natural Resources and Conflict in Africa: The Tragedy of Endowment* (29 Rochester Studies in African History and the Diaspora) University of Rochester Press; T Lumumba-Kasongo, *Land Reform and Natural Conflicts in Africa: New Developments Paradigms in the Era of Global Liberalization* (Routledge, 2016); F Botchway, *Natural Resources Investment and Africa's Development* (Edward Elgar, 2011); R Ngomba-Roth, *Multinational Companies and Conflicts in Africa: The Case of the Niger-Delta- Nigeria* (Lit Verlag, 2006).

best managed.[3] Generally, the legal approach to resolving natural resource conflicts in this region is based on received Western law. In some cases, the use of received Western law has proven grossly inadequate in tackling resource disputes, particularly those involving local communities.[4] For this reason, some experts in resource conflict management have canvassed for the adoption of non-Western legal ordering rules to address intractable resource disputes in Sub-Saharan Africa.

The aim of this chapter is to examine the role, if any, that an "African Legal Order" or "African Legal Ordering" can play in the avoidance or resolution of natural resource conflicts in Sub-Saharan Africa. Part one of the chapter provides an overview of the positivist theory of legal order. Part two examines the concept of legal ordering and considers whether there is any distinction between this concept and the established positivist concept of a legal order. Part three explores whether there is an African legal philosophy and deliberates on how this can be utilized to advance a homegrown legal order or legal ordering in the Sub-Saharan continent. Part four evaluates how international regimes on indigenous rights such as the United Nations Declaration on the Rights of Indigenous Peoples (UNDRIP) 2007 can be deployed to promote the use of a homegrown "African Legal ordering" in the transnational management of natural resources in Sub-Saharan Africa. Part five provides the concluding remarks of the chapter.

PART ONE: AN OVERVIEW OF THE CONCEPT OF LEGAL ORDER

This section of the chapter provides a brief introduction to the concept of the legal order especially from the perspective of legal positivism. The intent of this section is to lay a foundational context on the conception of a legal order in Western jurisprudence. It will discuss how the positivist understanding of a legal order has contributed to the delegitimization of non-Western law in developing jurisdictions such as sub-Saharan Africa. Hans Kelsen in his influential text[5] provides a classical positivist definition of this term. He defines a "legal order" as:

---

3. See generally United Nations, *Natural Resources and Conflict: A Guide to Mediation* (United Nations Department of Political Affairs, United Nations, 2017) 101 pp; R Ngomba- Roth, *The Challenges of Conflict: The Case of the Cameroon-Nigerian Border Conflict* (Lit Verlarg, 2008).
4. Tsegai Berhane Ghebretekle, "Traditional Natural Resource Conflict Resolution vis-à-vis Formal Legal Systems in East Africa: The Cases of Ethiopia and Kenya" (2017) 17(1) *African Journal of Conflict Resolution* 29.
5. See generally H Kelsen, *Pure Theory of Law, Translated from the Second (Revised and Enlarged) German Edition by Max Knight* (The LawBook Exchange, 2005, 2009).

An aggregate or a plurality of general and individual norms that govern human behaviour, that prescribe, in other words, how one ought to behave.[6]

He explains that a legal order is an established, formal or organised structure, system or body of norms and rules that regulate a given society. The focus on "structure" and "system" suggests that a legal order is not an informal or "spontaneous social order."[7] Instead law should be regarded as a system of binding rules which regulates or controls the conduct of an identified community within a specified space and for a determinate period of time.[8] Other influential positivists like Hart[9] argue that a legal order must have a rule of recognition. This validating rule will help to determine if there is an established legal system and will serve as "a conclusive affirmative indication that it is a rule of the group to be supported by the social pressure it exerts."[10]

Strict positivism also requires that a legal order should have a sovereign authority with powers to monitor and determine what acceptable behavior is, and to sanction unacceptable behavior in society. A fundamental charge that has been raised against non-Western law is that it does not possess these essential features of a positivist legal order. For this reason, some within the positivist school have questioned whether non-Western law can be considered as law.[11] The impact that legal positivism and its insistence on formalist legal order has played in the delegitimization of non-Western law[12] such as African customary law norms will be further discussed in part three of this chapter.

While legal positivism is still highly relevant in Western legal theory, there are other theoretical schools that provide different perspectives on law and its role in society. One school of thought is the sociology of law, which adopts a sociological approach.[13] Early contributors to this school include Weber, Pound, Ehrlich and Llewellyn. More contemporary writings include Foucalt, Kennedy, Erickson, Delgado and Schwartz.[14] One of its hallmarks is its rejection of extreme formalism in the development of the theory of law and how law is to be conceived. This position is seen in the early writings of Erhlich[15] where he

---

6. Kelsen, n. 5, 84.
7. G Hadfield, B Weingast, "What is Law? A Coordination Model of the Characteristics of Legal Order," (2012) 4(2) *Journal of Legal Analysis* 471.
8. A Frandberg, *The Legal Order: Studies in the Foundation of Juridical Thinking* (Springer, 2018) chapter 2.
9. HLA Hart, *Concept of Law* (Oxford University Press, 2002) 92.
10. Hart, n.9.
11. T Kayaoglu, *Legal Imperialism: Sovereignty and Extraterritoriality in Japan, the Ottoman Empire and China* (Cambridge University Press, 2010) 34.
12. Kayaoglu, n.11.
13. M Deflam, *Sociology of Law: Visions of a Scholarly Tradition* (Cambridge University Press, 2008) 1.
14. A. Javier Trevino, *The Sociology of Law: Classical and Contemporary Perspectives* (Routledge, 2017).
15. E Ehrlich, *Fundamental Principles of the Sociology of Law*. Translated by Walter L. Moll, with an

canvasses for an organic or free movement approach to the conceptualization of law in Western legal thinking.

This is why some view the sociology of law as similar to natural law in its rejection of strict formalism.[16] This is because both schools regard the concept of law as transcending the formal rules set out in legislation and case law. However, unlike the sociology of law, natural law adherents regard law as a higher set of moral rules that prevail over the law of man. In the case of the sociology of law, the development of law is regarded as being driven and shaped by society and not by divine law as canvassed by natural law proponents. To demonstrate the influence that society has over law, Erhlich explains that:

> ...the center of gravity of legal development lies not in legislation, nor in juristic science, nor in judicial decision, but in society itself.[17]

Unlike Hart and other legal positivists, Erhlich and his ilk within the school of sociology believe that the legal order can develop organically without the need to formally incorporate or introduce new rules. They regard the legal order and the development of law as a living organism with "typical power, though latent, to expand and to adapt itself."[18] This approach is described as "a legal ecological approach"[19] to law and is advanced by other influential voices in the school of sociology of law. For example, Roscoe Pound explains that law like any organism evolves in stages. It begins with primitive law and evolves to the stage of strict law which is characterized by rigid formalism. It then translates to the third, fourth and fifth stages of equity, maturity and the socialization of law.[20]

While Pound's ecological perception of the stages of law is insightful, the terminology of primitive law has been used in Western jurisprudence to provide an unhelpful characterization of non-Western rules.[21] Some have argued that this portrayal is better than other imperialist perspectives where non- Western law is not perceived as law.[22] Imperialist anthropological scholarship casts doubts on whether non-Western local communities were capable of forming equitable and effective legal systems of governance. This line of reasoning has been set straight by subsequent scholarship especially early indigenous African legal scholarship in the field of postcolonial legal studies.[23]

---

introduction by Roscoe Pound. (Harvard University Press, 1936).

16. P Selznick, *Sociology and Natural Law* (Natural Law Forum. Paper 61, 1961). http://scholarship.law. nd.edu/nd_naturallaw_forum/61 (accessed November 11, 2018).

17. Ehrlich, n 15, foreword.

18. S Romano, *The Legal Order*. First editions published in 1917 and 1918 (Taylor and Francis, 2017) 6.

19. E V Walter, 'Legal Ecology of Roscoe Pound' (1950) 4 *Miami L.Q* 188.

20. Walter, n.19.

21. See, for example, M.G Smith, "The Sociological Framework of Law" in H Kuper, L Kuper (eds.) *African Law: Adaptation and Development* (University of California Press, 1965) 24.

22. Smith, n. 21.

23. See, for instance, the ground-breaking study of T Elias, *The Nature of African Customary Law* (Man-

This brief overview of Western jurisprudence establishes that there are varying perspectives on the composition of law and what constitutes an enforceable legal order. However, this chapter will focus on the socio-legal discourse that evaluates the role that legal positivism[24] has played and continues to play in the delegitimization on non-Western legal systems. It will consider why to date, it is difficult to point to a transnational African legal order that is based on African customary law alone. Before developing this point, this chapter will provide an analysis of the concept of legal ordering. It will explore how the concept differs from the established model of the legal order as largely advanced by legal positivism.

PART TWO: LEGAL ORDERING: MYTH OR REALITY?

TRANSNATIONAL LAW AND LEGAL ORDERING

The concept of legal ordering is frequently discussed in the field of transnational law. Judge Phillip Jessup[25] in his pivotal Storres lecture defined transnational law as "all law which regulates situations or events that transcend national boundaries."[26] According to Shaffer[27], transnational law can be labelled in two ways. The first way is a "subject focused approach", which is also a functional approach which[28] focuses on transnational events or activities such as cybercrime, money laundering and human trafficking.

According to Shaffer, the subject based approach to transnational law highlights the limitations of the positivist perspective of formalism. He points out that formalist national legal orders are incapable of dealing with new challenges like cybercrime that transcend national borders. In addition, the subject based approach also recognizes that the two systems of international law, public and private, are also inadequate and cannot effectively combat transnational challenges. This is because public international law for the most part deals with relations between states while private international law focuses on conflict of interest between private parties. Transnational law is therefore required to address this gap as it has the flexibility to utilize international treaties where necessary or to apply national law in an extra -territorial manner.[29]

---

chester University Press, 1956).

24. M Garcia Salmones Rovira, *The Project of Positivism in International Law* (Oxford University Press, 2013) 357.

25. P Jessup, *Transnational Law* (Yale University Press, 1956) 8.

26. Ibid., at 1.

27. Gregory Shaffer, *Transnational Legal Ordering and State Change* (Cambridge University Press, 2013) Chapter 1.

28. Shaffer, n27, 5.

29. Shaffer, n27, 6.

In contrast is the second way: the "source-based approach" to transnational law. The objective of this approach to is to identify and evaluate legal norms that are "exported and imported across borders."[30] The source-based approach towards transnational law also focuses on the transnational networks, organisations and institutions that help to shape and transport these laws across national borders. This approach is described by Shaffer as "transnational legal ordering" and is relevant to a socio-legal understanding of the normative nature of transnational law.

The source-based approach to transnational law is more relevant to the question of whether African customary law can serve as a homegrown transnational law for the resolution of resource-based conflicts in the continent. This is because it allows for an appraisal on whether the current institutions and mechanisms for conflict resolution in the continent can effectively regulate disputes involving non-state actors such as local communities. The possible ways in which a socio-legal perspective to transnational law can reinforce the case for African customary law to serve as a homegrown transnational law for the resolution or management of resource-based conflicts is discussed below.

AFRICAN TRANSNATIONAL LEGAL ORDERING: SOCIO-LEGAL PERSPECTIVES

While intra-state disputes over natural resources are well documented, the discourse on disputes of a transboundary nature appears to be more limited in scope.[31] This is why there has been recent high-level African policy engagement on what needs to be done to intensify transboundary natural resource management in the sub-continent.[32] What appears to be missing from this discussion is whether the current framework of national law and public international law is adequate to deal with natural resource disputes of a transboundary nature within the sub-African continent.

The limitations of these systems of laws are apparent when one considers the type of actors that are involved in such disputes. In many cases, they are non-state actors such as international companies, local communities and militant groups. This chapter therefore argues for the adoption of practical homegrown law of transnational reach that can assist in the resolution or management of natural resource disputes in Africa especially when they affect the sustainability of local communities. In the case of the extractive energy sector, some will argue

---

30. Shaffer, n27.
31. UNECA, High Level Conference *on Transboundary Natural Resources Disputes in Africa: Policies, Institutions and Management Experiences* Concept Note, High Level Conference, July 12-13 2018 (United Nations Economic Commission for Africa, Nairobi, Kenya) 1.
32. See for example, UNECA, *Transboundary natural resource disputes in Africa: Policies, institutions and management experience* (United Nations Economic Commission on Africa, 2018).

that Lex Petrolea already carries out this function on behalf of the international oil and gas sector.[33] However, Lex Petrolea has its limitations. To understand its limitations, it is necessary to explain what Lex Petrolea is[34]. Lex Petrolea is "the customary law of the petroleum industry"[35] The earliest arbitral case law reference to Lex Petrolea is found in the case of *Kuwait v Aminoil*[36] where the tribunal rejected that "a net book value"[37] of determining compensation had now acquired the status of a customary rule for the petroleum industry. Because Lex Petrolea is perceived to be a "law for oil merchants", it is questionable whether it was ever designed to protect the interests of local communities where petroleum exploitation is undertaken.[38] This is why this chapter argues that another trajectory of transnational law is required to cater for the needs of local communities who bear the brunt of natural resource exploitation. The type of transnational law envisioned is transnational African customary law.

Understandably, the call for a homegrown African transnational law will raise questions on how its normative value can be ascertained. The source-based approach to transactional law provides some further guidance on how this can be done. This is because it deals with the construction and processing of the norms that extend beyond national borders. But in many national jurisdictions, African customary rules are generally regarded as localized laws.[39] A country example of the localization of customary law can be found in sections 70 and 258 (1) of the *Nigerian Evidence Act 2011*[40]. For instance, section 70 which covers opinions on customary law makes it clear that its territorial application is "indigenous to the locality in which such law or custom applies." Likewise, section 258 of the Act also defines a custom as a "rule which, in a particular district, has, from long usage, obtained the force of law." It is therefore difficult to see how localized African customary law can serve as transnational law that applies beyond national boundaries.

---

33. See, for instance, A Waryrk "Petroleum Regulation in an International Context: The Universality of Petroleum Regulation and the concept of Lex Petrolea" in T Hunter (ed.) *Regulation of the Upstream Petroleum Sector: A Comparative Study of Licensing and Concession Systems* (Edward Elgar, 2015) 6.
34. A full discussion of Lex Petrolea is beyond the scope of this chapter. For further reading: A Waryrk "Petroleum Regulation in an International Context: The Universality of Petroleum Regulation and the concept of Lex Petrolea" in T Hunter (ed.) *Regulation of the Upstream Petroleum Sector: A Comparative Study of Licensing and Concession Systems* (Edward Elgar, 2015)
35. K Talus, "Internationalization of Energy Law" in K Talus (ed.) *Research Handbook on International Energy Law* (Cheltenham: Edward Elgar, 2015) 8-9.
36. See the seminal case of *Aminoil v Kuwait* (1982) 21 ILM 976 where Kuwait argued that: "... in the course of nationalizations of oil concessions that had occurred in the Middle East in the 1970s, this method had acquired 'an international and customary character, specific to the oil industry,' generating a customary rule valid for the oil industry – Lex Petrolia." (para.155).
37. Aminoil v Kuwait, n. 36.
38. A Waryrk *Petroleum Regulation in an International Context: The Universality of Petroleum Regulation and the concept of Lex Petrolea* 13 (n 33 above); See also H Egede, "African Social Ordering: Grund-norms and an African Lex Petrolea" (2016) 28 *Denning Law Journal* 161.
39. Egede, n. 37, 151.
40. In force June 2011.

However, some leading African scholars assert that there are universal African "social ordering grundnorms"[41] that transcend national boundaries. Chief among these grundnorms is the popular norm of Ubuntu (Zulu concept)[42], Omoluabi (Yoruba concept)[43] or Humwe (Shona concept)[44]. These norms are typically defined as "in this together" "good citizenship" or "us all". They symbolise "Afro-communitarianism", a concept which will be discussed further in part three of this chapter. South African courts have granted judicial recognition to the principle of Ubuntu.[45] This principle was also embodied in the South African interim post-apartheid constitution.[46]

Notwithstanding the national recognition that Ubuntu has been given in South Africa, it is still a matter of debate as to whether this customary norm and its equivalents transcend this jurisdiction. To address this question, it is necessary to consider how Afro-communitarianism is regarded in African legal theory or philosophy. The appraisal of this issue begins with an analysis on whether there is an established African legal theory or philosophy that we can draw from to determine the normative nature of African customary law.

PART THREE: AFRICAN LEGAL THEORY AND THE LEGAL IDENTITY OF AFRICAN CUSTOMARY NORMS

THE CONCEPT OF AN AFRICAN LEGAL THEORY

This part of the chapter further develops the socio-legal discourse on the legal identity of African customary norms. First, it is necessary to consider whether there is an African philosophy of law or an African legal theory that explains the normative nature of African customary norms. Bhahba, an influential post-colonial scholar, points out that there is a mistaken assumption that the task of theoretical formulation and development is only meant for the "socially and culturally privileged... within the imperialist or neocolonial West"[47] This is why some works[48] question whether there is an authentic African legal theory

---

41. B Chigara, "The Humwe Principle: A Social Ordering Grundnorm for Zimbabwe and Africa" in R Home (ed.) *Essays in African Land Law* (Pretoria University Press, 2011) 113. The reference to African "Social Ordering" norms is based on Chigara's work.
42. J Y Mokgoro, *Ubuntu and the Law of the South* (A paper delivered at the first Colloquium Constitution and Law held at Potchefstroom on 31 October, 1997).
43. O Amao, *African Union Law: The Emergence of a Sui Generis Legal Order* (Routledge, 2018) 11.
44. Chigara, n. 40, 113.
45. See, for example, *S v Makwanyane* [1995] ZACC 3; *Port Elizabeth Municipality v Various Occupiers* 2005(1) SA 217 (CC); *Union of Refugee Women and Others v Director: Private Security Industry Regulatory Authority and Others* 2007 4 SA 395 (CC) para 145; *Mayelane v Ngwenyama* 2013 (4) SA 415 (CC).
46. See the Constitution of the Republic of South Africa Act 200 of 1993. Repealed 4 February 1997.
47. H Bhabha, *The Location of Culture* (Routledge, 2012) 28.
48. See further discussions on this point in C Silunwge, "On African Legal Theory: A Possibility, An Impossibility or Mere Conundrum" in O Onazi, *African Legal Theory and Constitutional Problems: Critical Essays* (Springer, 2014) 15.

or philosophy that is free from Western influence. In opposition, postcolonial indigenous African scholarship argues that there is an African legal philosophy that considers "the way in which law, legal concepts and institutions embody or reflect the most salient and common attributes of life in Sub-Saharan Africa."[49] This understanding of law is largely based on the social ordering norm of Afro-communitarianism.[50] The eminent African jurist, Taslim Elias, also argues that Africa has a "pre-colonial repetoire of norms"[51] that predate colonial rule.

Some skepticism has been expressed by Western scholars on the existence of this repetoire of pre-colonial indigenous norms. They argue that it would have been impossible for pre-colonial communities to keep written records of such norms if they truly existed. This is because the historic anthropological works establish that the local communities expressed their cultures through the spoken word.[52] They therefore question how the repetoire of norms could have been retained by oral tradition and not by a written account as would be expected of an established legal order.[53] This perspective is characteristic of the prevailing positivist view of law at the time of colonialisation. Colonial governments employed the positivist recognition doctrine to delegitimise local customs. They only validated "those principles which were created and accepted by the sovereigns"[54] and rejected pre-existing customs that they considered as repugnant to natural justice, good conscience and equity.[55]

It is hard to see how pre-colonial communitarian ideals could have been rejected on such grounds. As discussed in earlier parts of this chapter, such social ordering norms as Ubuntu, Omoluwabi and Shona promote laudable values of community well being and cohesion which would normally be in line with the ideals of natural justice and equity as advanced by Western law. But as Eze argues, the overriding objective of colonialism was to depersonalise and cause an alienation of indigenous peoples "from their culture, society and heritage."[56] This is why those of the revisionist ilk of post-scholarship have rejected the idea of a historic continuity of pre-existing African customary norms.[57] They argue that if pre-existing African customs were retained, they would have been fundamentally

---

49. O Onazi, "Introduction" in O Onazi (ed.) *African Legal Theory and Constitutional Problems: Critical Essays* (Springer, 2014) 1.
50. Onazi, n. 49, 7.
51. Silunwge, n. 47, 18.
52. J Vansina, "Once Upon a Time: Oral Traditions as History in Africa" (1971) *Daedelus* 442; J Vansina, "Recording the Oral History of the Bakuba"(1981) 1(1) *Journal of African History* 143.
53. H Gailey, "An Introduction to African Historiography" in J Wilmer (ed.) *Africa: Teaching Perspectives and Approaches* (Geographic and Area Study Publications, 1975) discussed in C Appiah-Thompson, "The Politics of Researching Africa: The Quality of Anthropo-Historical and Linguistic Data in African Studies" (2017) *Journal of Black Studies* 67.
54. I Watson, *Aboriginal Peoples, Colonialism and International Law: Raw Law* (Routledge, 2015) 6, 132
55. B Ibhawoh, *Imperial Justice, Africans in the Empire's Court* (Oxford University Press,2013) See a detailed discussion on the Repugnancy doctrine in chapter three.
56. M Eze, *Intellectual History in Contemporary South Africa* (Springer, 2010) 119.
57. Silunwge, n. 47, 18-19.

revised to serve colonial purposes.[58] They regard current African customary law as a creation of an African elite, educated and versed in Western education. The quest for an African legal theory is therefore seen as a manifestation of post colonial African cultural nationalism.[59]

The denouncement of a pre-existing repetoire of indigenous norms by some sections of Western scholarship explains why cultural nationalism emerged as part of the post colonial experience. Cultural nationalism is a natural reaction to the colonial delegitimisation of indigenous norms and values. It also confronts the misleading claim that theorectical development is only the sole purview of Western jurisprudence. Cultural nationalism in legal scholarship also offers a thought-provoking counter narrative to the revisionist argument that customary law is a post-colonial creation that has no connection to oral traditions that may have existed prior to colonialism. Some African legal scholars[60] have utilised Bhabha's[61] "cultures in between" to explain how indigenous legal theoretical development has taken place. This concept of "cultures in between" and how it reinforces the case for the existence of an African legal theory or philosophy that explains the normative value of African customary law is provided below.

CULTURES IN BETWEEN AND THE CASE FOR AN AFRICAN LEGAL THEORY

In his groundbreaking research, Bhabha accepts that colonialism has had a radical impact on colonised cultures. Yet he argues that despite its strength and dominance, the received Western system has never been able to completely eradicate pre-existing cultures. Instead, Bhahba[62] speaks of a cultural hybridity that arises from the admixture of received Western cultures and surviving local cultures. He explains that a culture in between is created through this hybridity and it presents a third space to "read anew" the symbols and meanings of the competing cultures.[63] In adopting this position, Bhabha provides a more nuanced approach on how pre-existing cultures can interact with the "stranger" concept of received Western culture.[64]

Silungwe applies Bhabha's "cultures in between" to demonstrate how African legal theory has emerged. He argued that the third space provided an opportunity for African legal scholars to read anew pre-colonial customary norms with the understanding of the nature of law that they had gained in received Western law.

58. Silunwge n. 47.
59. M Chanock, *Neo- Traditionalism and the Customary Law in Malawi* (Commission on Legal Pluralism, 1978, v 16) 83. Full text available at
http://commission-on-legal-pluralism.com/volumes/16/chanock-art.pdf.
60. C Silunwge, *On African Legal Theory: A Possibility, An Impossibility or Mere Conundrum* (n 47)17-30.
61. Bhabha, n. 46, 56, 312.
62. Bhabha, n. 46, 55.
63. Bhabha, n. 46, 56.
64. Chanock, n. 58, 83.

This reading anew of both legal cultures has resulted in the formulation of an African legal philosophy that is able to demonstrate theoretically how Africans view the concept of law.[65] In utilising Bhabha's "cultures in between" Silungwe accepts that it is impossible to deny the permanent impact that received Western law has had on African customary law. However, unlike the revisionist approach, Bhabha's "cultures in between" presents a positive outlook on the theoretical development of an African legal philosophy. It argues that post colonial African scholarship has a dual identity. African theorists therefore operate within the two legal cultures of received Western law and African customary law.[66]

Dual exposure to both cultures of law makes it difficult for African theorists to subscribe to a sentimentalist[67] concept of an African customary law that is completely devoid of western influence. Equally, it would be wrong to accept the revisionist claim that African customs have been fundamentally re-engineered and assimilated into received Western law. Instead, the cultural hybridity concept advanced by Bhabha provides African legal theorists with a plausible explanation for why and how African customary law interacts with received Western law and still at the same time retains its distinctive cultural identity.

The cultural hybridity of the African legal framework is connected with the concept of legal pluralism. Like cultural hybridity, the system of legal pluralism seeks to minimise the tension between received Western law and customary law. It does this by permitting the operation of a multiple legal systems within a jurisdictional sphere. While many African states practise legal pluralism, they apply the weak construction of the concept. The weak construction of legal pluralism is founded in legal positivism and is manifested through a hierarchical system of rules that prioritises received Western law over non-Western law.[68]

The regulation of natural resources in the sub-continent is based on this hierarchical pluralist system. Natural resource management is placed under civic state control due to its social and economic importance. It also accords with the international law principle of permanent sovereignty over natural resources which empower states to exercise sovereignty over their natural resources for the benefit of their peoples.[69] Unfortunately, many African states have had a poor record[70] of utilising natural resources for the benefit of their peoples. State

---

65. Silungwe, n. 47, 22.
66. In some African states, the case will be three cultures: received Western law, Islamic law and African customary law. See A Oba, "Islamic Law as Customary Law: The Changing Perspective in Nigeria" (2002) *51(4) International and Comparative Law Quarterly* 817-850.
67. Silunwge, n. 47, 19.
68. J Griffiths, "What is Legal Pluralism?" (1986) *24 Journal of Legal Pluralism and Unofficial Law* 5.
69. Paragraph 1, United Nations General Assembly resolution 1803 (XVII) of 14 December 1962, "Permanent Sovereignty over Natural Resources" available at https://www.ohchr.org/Documents/ProfessionalInterest/resources.pdf (accessed December 6, 2018).
70. Alao, n.2, chapter 7.

mismanagement of natural resources is one of the key causes of natural resources disputes in Sub-Saharan Africa.[71] This is why it is important to consider what role if any that African customary legal ordering can play in the management and utilisation of natural resources within the continent. The next part of this chapter shall give further consideration to this point.

PART FOUR: AFRICAN PERSPECTIVES OF AN INDIGENOUS RIGHTS REGIME IN NATURAL RESOURCE MANAGEMENT AND EXPLOITATION

This part of the chapter considers whether international regimes[72] on indigenous rights can be employed to champion the use of a homegrown "African legal ordering" in natural resource management and exploitation. In embarking on this discourse, some consideration is given to the meaning of "indigeneity" and "indigenous peoples". Birrell explains that there are different ways in which indigeneity is described. As a legal concept, indigeneity[73] focuses on the "historic continuity, distinctiveness, marginalisation, self-identity and self-government"[74] of indigenous peoples. The term "indigenous peoples" also lacks a singular definition but is broadly defined by the authorative 1984 Martinez-Cobo study[75] as:

> …those which having a historical continuity with pre-invasion and pre-colonial societies that developed on their territories, consider themselves distinct from other sectors of societies now prevailing in those territories, or parts of them. They form at present non-dominant sectors of society and are determined to preserve, develop, and

---

71. Alao, n. 2, chapter 7.

72. See the broad-based regime of rights set out in key instruments such as the *Universal Declaration of Human Rights (UNDHR)*, 1948. Adopted and proclaimed by General Assembly resolution 217 A (III) of 10 December *1948*; *Convention on the Prevention and Punishment of the Crime of Genocide* 78 U.N.T.S. 277, entered into force 12 January, 1951; *International Covenant on Civil and Political Rights (ICCPR)*. Adopted and opened for signature, ratification and accession by General Assembly resolution 2200A (XXI) of 16 December 1966, entry into force 23 March 1976, in accordance with Article 49; *International Covenant on Economic, Social and Cultural Rights (ICESCR)*. Adopted and opened for signature, ratification and accession by General Assembly resolution 2200A (XXI) of 16 December 1966, entry into force 3 January 1976, in accordance with article 27; *Convention on the Elimination of all Forms of Racial Discrimination*. Adopted and opened for signature and ratification by General Assembly resolution 2106 (XX) of 21 December 1965, entry into force 4 January 1969, in accordance with Article 19; International Labour Organisation (ILO) *Convention concerning Indigenous and Tribal Peoples in Independent Countries 1989* (169) (Entry into force: 05 Sep 1991); *Declaration on the Rights of Persons belonging to National or Ethnic, Religious and Linguistic Minorities*. Adopted by General Assembly resolution 47/135 of 18 December 1992; *Council Resolution on Indigenous Peoples within the Framework of the Development Cooperation of the Community and Members States* COM/2002/0291 final and United Nations Declaration on the Rights of Indigenous Peoples (A/RES/61/295) 2007.

73. See generally K Birrell *Indigeneity: Before and Beyond the Law* (Routledge, 2016).

74. See the detailed discourse on the definition of indigeneity in chapter one of Birrell's book, ibid.

75. United Nations Study of the *Problem of Discrimination Against Indigenous Populations: Final report* submitted by the Special Rapporteur, Mr. José Martínez Cobo, 30 July 1981 E/CN.4/Sub.2/476.

transmit to future generations their ancestral territories, and their ethnic identity, as the basis of their continued existence as peoples, in accordance with their own cultural patterns, social institutions and legal systems.[76]

A detailed discourse on indigeneity is beyond the scope of this chapter. The chapter confines its discourse on how African states perceive indigeneity and indigenous rights, and how such state perceptions affect the development of an indigenous African legal ordering in the management of natural resources within the continent.

AFRICAN PERCEPTIONS ON INDIGENEITY, INDIGENOUS PEOPLES AND THE RIGHT TO SELF DETERMINATION

African states have expressed some measure of ambivalence towards the concepts of indigeneity and indigenous rights. This ambivalence is well documented in the *Draft* Aide Memoire *(African Group) United Nations Declaration on the Rights of Indigenous Peoples (Draft* Aide Memoire*)*[77]. In the draft aide memoire, African states expressed their reservations on the establishment of a broad based regime on indigenous rights. They expressed concerns about the lack of state consensus on what it means to be indigenous. The states raised other concerns beyond the scope of this chapter.[78] This chapter focuses on the African states' concern about the absence of state consensus on which groups constitute "indigenous peoples."

To a large degree, the absence of a definition of "indigenous peoples" in the UNDRIP is a positive development. This is because it allows for different regions of the world to develop their own understanding on what it means to be indigenous. Without question, the African understanding of indigeneity and indigenous rights is different from other regions of the world such as Australia and Canada where the indigeneity discourse converges on the relationship between first peoples (aboriginality) and foreign settlers. In contrast, all Africans are regarded as being indigenous to the continent regardless of "where they were born or their migration patterns."[79] This perspective of indigeneity was adopted to reduce ethnic and cultural tensions in a continent where indigeneity is generally associated with ethnicity. Over the years, the African perception of indigeneity has become a little

---

76. United Nations, n. 75.
77. *Draft Aide Memoire (African Group) United Nations Declaration on the Rights of Indigenous Peoples*, 9 November 2006, New York.
78. The states objected to the grant of the right of self determination to indigenous peoples which they felt could jeopardise the territorial integrity of sovereign states.The states also opposed the use of the mechanism of free, prior and informed consent (FPIC) as they felt it could inhibit the rights of sovereign states to develop national legislation. The states further objected to indigenous peoples playing any role in state matters such as the negotiation, ratification and domestication of treaties.
79. D Inman, D Cambou, S Smis "Evolving Legal Protection for Indigenous Peoples in Africa: Some Post -UNDRIP Reflections" (2018)26 *African Journal of International and Comparative Law* 344-5.

more nuanced as evinced by the report of the African Commission's Working Group of Experts on Indigenous Populations/Communities (African Working Group)[80] and from regional case law jurisprudence.

According to the African working group, the word "peoples" within the African Charter is wide enough to envision the existence of distinctive groups of indigenous peoples within the African continent. By applying the generic criteria on indigeneity such as distinctiveness, marginalisation, discrimination and domination by other groups; pastoralist and hunter gatherer groups were identified by the African working group as "indigenous peoples". This nuanced characterisation of indigenous peoples has been applied by the Advisory Opinion of the African Commission on Human and Peoples Rights on the United Nations Declaration on the Rights of Peoples[81] and in African Commission case law like the Social and Economic Rights Action Center for Economic and Social Rights v Nigeria (the Ogoni decision)[82] and the Centre for Minority Development and Minority Rights Group International (on behalf of the Endorois Welfare Council) v Kenya.[83] These cases were brought under the framework of the African Charter on Human and People's Rights (the Banjul Charter).[84] The Banjul Charter has raised interesting questions[85] on whether its use of the word "peoples" includes "indigenous peoples." It is argued that the African Commission in the Ogoni decision recognised for the first time "sub-national groups as holders of the substantive people's rights enshrined in the African charter".[86]

Building on the notion that African sub-national groups are recognised as indigenous peoples, this chapter investigates whether this status allows for them to utilise their customary laws and dispute resolution mechanisms in the resolution of natural resource disputes. Apart from the Banjul Charter, other international rights regimes such as the ILO Convention on Indigenous and Tribal Peoples 169 of 1989 (ILO Convention 169) and the United Nations Declaration on the Rights of Indigenous Peoples 2007 provide substantive rights to indigenous peoples.[87]

80. Adopted by *The African Commission on Human and Peoples' Rights* at its 28th ordinary session.
81. Adopted by *The African Commission on Human and Peoples' Rights* at its 41st ordinary session held in May 2007 in Accra, Ghana.
82. 155/96 : Social and Economic Rights Action Center (SERAC) and Center for Economic and Social Rights (CESR) / Nigeria.
83. 276/03 : Centre for Minority Rights Development (Kenya) and Minority Rights Group (on behalf of Endorois Welfare Council) / Kenya.
84. *African (Banjul) Charter on Human and Peoples' Rights* (Adopted 27 June 1981, OAU Doc. CAB/LEG/67/3 rev. 5, 21 I.L.M. 58 (1982), entered into force 21 October 1986).
85. See a further analysis on this point in D Inman, D Cambou, S Smis, "Evolving Legal Protection for Indigenous Peoples in Africa: Some Post -UNDRIP Reflections" (2018)26, *African Journal of International and Comparative Law* 344-5.
86. Inman, n. 85, 344.
87. The ILO Convention revises the previous *ILO Convention 107* which is in force in a few African countries, namely, Egypt, Ghana, Malawi and Angola.

The ILO Convention 169 has very limited application in Africa as it is in force in only one African state, the Central African Republic. Article 8 of the ILO Convention 169 recognises the rights of indigenous and tribal populations to "retain their own customs and institutions." Yet such customs and institutions should not be "incompatible with the fundamental rights defined by the national legal system and with internationally recognised human rights." The article 8 provision is not dissimilar to the positivist repugnancy doctrine adopted in received English law (and retained by post colonial state laws) which requires that customary laws and rules should not be contrary to public policy or repugnant to natural justice and equity.[88]

In the case of the UNDRIP, the rights afforded to indigenous peoples are provided within a soft law framework. As a UN General Assembly resolution, it lacks binding hard law application. But like other predecessor resolutions, it can attain the status of binding customary law at the international law level. The UNDRIP has a suite of rights that are unique to indigenous communities, including the article 40 right on dispute resolution. Article 40 requires that formalist state dispute resolution mechanisms should give "due consideration to the customs, traditions, rules and legal systems of indigenous peoples". Unlike the positivist approach adopted in article 8 of the ILO 169 Convention, there is no apparent repugnancy test or requirement set out in article 40 of the UNDRIP.

Unlike these international instruments, it is remarkable that the regional Banjul charter provides very limited scope for customary law in the adjudication of disputes. However, articles 17 and 18 of the Charter affirm "African traditional values recognised by the community." While article 18 focuses on the protection of the family unit as the custodian of such traditional values, article 17 allows for wider state responsibility with regard to the protection and promotion of such values. In spite of the international and regional law recognition of indigenous or traditional customary norms, African states have been reluctant to utilise customary law or other traditional methods of dispute resolution in the settlement of energy related disputes. The reasons for this position are considered below.

NATURAL RESOURCE DISPUTES IN SUB-SAHARAN AFRICAN OIL PRODUCING COMMUNITIES: THE ROLE OF INDIGENOUS CONFLICT MANAGEMENT METHODS

A vast majority of energy disputes in Africa are adjudicated and resolved within the civic courts of the formal Westphalian state structures.[89] The chapter will use the Niger Delta as a case study in its evaluation on why there is a limited utilisation of traditional or indigenous African dispute mechanisms in the

---

88. Ibhawoh, n. 54.
89. The characterization of Westphalian states focuses on the modern territorial state system. See S Beaulac, *The Westphalian Model in Defining International Law: Challenging the Myth* (2004) 8(2) Austl J Legal Hist 181.

resolution of energy resource disputes. There are a variety of reasons why this is the case.

First, natural resource governance in Sub-Saharan Africa is domanial in nature. The domanial governance framework vests sovereignty over natural resources in the Westphalian state, and not in local indigenous communities. This aligns with the traditional perspective of permanent sovereignty over natural resources where sovereignty lies with the state and not its peoples. However, some scholarship asserts that paragraph one of the UN General Assembly Resolution 1803 on Permanent Sovereignty over Natural Resources (UNGA Res 1803)[90] envisions a sovereignty framework that applies both to states and peoples.[91] The use of the word "peoples" in paragraph 1 of the UNGA Res 1803 is seen as the foundation for the right of indigenous peoples to exercise self determination or limited sovereignty over natural resources.

The *Ogoni and Endorois* cases envision the potential of sub-national groups to enjoy all "peoples' rights" set out within the Banjul Charter. These rights include the right for indigenous peoples to exercise internal self determination over their resources and wealth.[92] The recognition of the right to internal self determination is laudable but decisions of the African Commission are rarely implemented at the national level.

Second, contracting mechanisms play a role on why energy resource disputes are adjudicated by civic courts and not in the indigenous customary institutions. The parties to the host state agreements governing oil and gas exploitation in African states are the host state and international companies. Local communities are generally not regarded as parties to such host state agreements.[93] This again turns on the strategic importance of oil and gas resources in a domanial state structure where energy resources are seen as *res publica* and not *res communis* resources. The leading empirical research undertaken by Frynas on oil and gas litigation in the Niger Delta[94] confirms this position. The Frynas study indicates that the typical venue for oil and gas litigation is normally undertaken in the civic courts and not in customary courts where indigenous norms and customs are utilised. He points out that the only instances where customary norms may

---

90. General Assembly resolution 1803 (XVII) of 14 December 1962, *Permanent sovereignty over natural resources*.

91. In the case of indigenous peoples, such rights of sovereignty are limited to "internal self-determination." See E Enyew, "Application of the Right to Permanent Sovereignty over Natural Resources for Indigenous Peoples: Assessment of Current Legal Developments" (2017) 8, *Arctic Review on Law and Politics* 228.

92. Enyew, n. 91.

93. See a further discourse in H Egede, E Egede, "The Force of Community in the Oil and Gas Rich Region of the Niger Delta: Propositions for New Legal and Contractual Arrangements" (2016) 25 *Tulane Journal of International and Comparative Law* 45-88.

94. J G Frynas, *Oil in Nigeria: Conflict and Litigation Between Oil Companies and Village Communities* (Lit Verlag, 1993) 62.

apply or where oil related cases are resolved in customary courts are those that have to do with disputed facts over customary title to land.[95]

The groundbreaking edited collection on indigenous conflict management in West Africa[96] however paints a far more positive picture of the use of indigenous traditional conflict management methods in resolving disputes between local communities and other stakeholders in energy exploitaiton. For example, Eselebor[97] points to the role that the council of elders and other traditional institutions such as kings and chiefs, age grades and the general assembly of the peoples in the village squares play in the management of disputes within their local communities. Understandably, the use of such traditional institutions are relevant in local disputes; but how relevant are such institutions when the disputes in question are between local communities and "outsiders" such as international oil companies and formal state institutions? The Niger Delta amnesty initiative discussed below is a clear example on the important role that traditional institutions play in resolving disputes between local communities and outsiders.

THE ROLE OF INDIGENOUS ELDERS IN MEDIATION IN THE NIGER DELTA AMNESTY INITIATIVE

The Niger Delta is one of the primary theatres of resource conflicts in Sub-Saharan Africa. Several attempts have been made by successive Nigerian governments to promote development and reduce the surge of militancy within the Niger Delta region. Statutory bodies such as the Niger Delta Development Board 1960, Oil Mineral Producing Areas Development Commission 1992 and the Niger Delta Development Commission (NDCC) 2002 were established for this purpose. Yet, these initiatives have not been able to eradicate ongoing disputes between the oil producing communities and the Nigerian State and international oil companies (outsiders). Instead, the region remains a hotspot for oil related conflicts. However, the Nigerian state adopted an amnesty initiative as a means of conflict resolution.

Debate has arisen on whether an amnesty initative instigated by a Westphalian state can be categorised as an indigenous dispute resolution mechanism. Odozobodio and Didiugwu[98] assert that an indigenous element of dispute resolution was incorporated into the Niger Delta amnesty initiative. They explain that this was undertaken through the use of the indigenous or customary method of "native

---

95. Frynas, n. 94.

96. BD Lundy, JJ Benjamin, J K Adjei (eds.) *Indigenous Conflict Management Strategies in West Africa: Beyond Right and Wrong* (Lexington Books, 2014).

97. W Eselebor, "Amnesty in the Niger Delta Region of Nigeria in Retrospect" in B D Lundy, J J Benjamin, JK Adjei (eds.) *Indigenous Conflict Management Strategies in West Africa: Beyond Right and Wrong* (Lexington Books, 2014) 242.

98. S O, I D, "From Militancy to Amnesty: An Exploration of Nigeria's Indigenous Conflict Management Strategy in the Niger Delta Region" in B D Lundy, JJ Benjamin, J K Adjei (eds.) *Indigenous Conflict Management Strategies in West Africa: Beyond Right and Wrong* (Lexington Books, 2014) 255, 266.

leaders" appeal. Indigenous leaders were able to persuade the youth leaders of the militancy movements to discontinue their armed struggle and to participate in the Federal Government's amnesty initiative.

Enyew explains that mediation by the traditional council of elders normally aims to restore the "previous peaceful relationship within the community as well as maintaining their future peaceful relationships by avoiding the culturally accepted practices of revenge."[99] Even as this should be seen as a positive development, it does not alter the fact that oil and gas dispute resolution and conflict management is largely controlled by Westphalian state institutions. However, such fledgling efforts have the potential to crystallise into something larger and can be similarly utilised at the transboundary level. The prospects of deploying such mechanisms at the subcontinent level is considered below.

PART 5: TRANSNATIONAL NATURAL RESOURCE MANAGEMENT IN SUB-SAHARAN AFRICA

The preceding part of this chapter considered the role that international and regional regimes on indigenous rights can play in the bolstering of the status of customary law and its indigenous institutions in natural resources management. In spite of the rights granted in regional and international regimes for local communities to utilise their customary law and traditional dispute mechanisms, natural resource management, especially in the area of energy exploitation, is predominantly under state control. Yet the Niger Delta Amnesty initiative demonstrates the positive way in which indigenous institutions may be utilised to promote Bhabha's "Cultures in Between"[100] and create a third space for Westphalian states and communities to dialogue and resolve conflicts. But many of these communities are not just confined to one Westphalian state. They cut across the formalist colonial boundaries that have been inherited by independent African states. The residential fluidity of these communities call for a new form of transboundary governance of natural resource management at the continental level.

A MULTI-LAYERED APPROACH TO TRANSNATIONAL RESOURCE MANAGEMENT

A number of the transboundary conflicts in Africa pertain to natural resource exploitation and management. The groundbreaking 2018 UNECA report[101] on transboundary disputes identifies the current transboundary natural resource

---

99. E Enyew, "Ethiopian Customary Dispute Resolution Mechanisms: Forms of Restorative Justice" (2014) 14(1) *African Journal on Conflict Resolution* 148.
100. Bhabha, n.46, 56.
101. UNECA, *Transboundary Natural Resource Disputes in Africa: Policies, Institutions and Management Experiences Report 2018*, Economic Commission for Africa, Addis Ababa, Ethiopia.

management framework in Sub-Saharan Africa as unfit for puprpose. The lack of normative and institutional processes to deal with natural resource management has been identified as a key limitation.[102] The report calls for a "multilayered governance regime" that would be responsive to the settlement of transboundary national disputes.[103] The report also canvassses for the development of legal frameworks that promote "sharing and cooperating in transboundary natural resources development."[104]

The UNECA report does not prescriptively stipulate what type of legal structures that the region should adopt to tackle natural resource conflicts. While it calls for a multi-layered governance approach to transboundary management of natural resources, it does not go as far as to prescribe the use of customary African law in the regulation of transnational resource management. Instead, it points to the successes that public international law has had in resolving boundary disputes within the continent.[105]

It is unclear why this pivotal report does not explictly call for the utilisation of non-Western norms as part of the multi-layered approach for dealing with transboundary disputes in the continent. Yet, the report identifies how the national policies of some African states have contributed to the "distortion and undermining"[106] of customary land norms and the exacerbation of natural resource conflicts within the region. Yet instead of advocating for the reinstatement of the local customary land norms, the report suggests that local grievances can be resolved by the development and use of "region-wide and transboundary natural resources management policies" framed within the public international law regime.[107]

The focus on a public international law approach could be based on the fact that most inter-state disputes in Africa are resolved through diplomatic channels or through the international adjudicatory processes as prescribed by public international law. This is the approach that has been adopted in transboundary maritime disputes such as the Cameroon and Nigerian dispute[108] and other transboundary disputes.[109] Yet transboundary disputes may not always take the format of inter-state disputes and may involve non-state actors such as local

---

102. UNECA, n.101, 7.
103. UNECA, n.101, 7.
104. UNECA, n.101, 8.
105. UNECA, n.101, 7.
106. UNECA, n.101, 33.
107. UNECA, n.101, 7.
108. *Case concerning Land and Maritime Boundary between Cameroon and Nigeria (Cameroon v. Nigeria)* Summary of the Judgement (*hereafter Cameroon/Nigeria case*) at http://www.icj-cij.org/docket/index.php?sum=496&code=cn&p1=3&p2=3&case=94&k=74&p3=5.
109. UNECA 2018 report, n 100, 29-31.

communities. Where this is the case, inter state mechanisms may prove to be ineffective in the long term.

The UNECA report accepts that transnational natural resource disputes could occur where two or more states have groups of the same ethnic identity living within their borders.[110] Again this scenario presented itself in the dispute between the Cameroon and Nigeria[111] where some of the indigenous groups that resided within the Bakassi peninsula shared historical ties and also self-identified with both states.[112] While the delimitation of maritime boundaries falls within state jurisdiction, the local communities affected by the outcome of the ICJ decision felt excluded from the decision making process that governed the delimitation process.[113] This may be due to the formalist approach adopted in the adjudication process, and also to some extent in the implementation of the Green Tree Agreement (a bilateral state treaty).[114]

It is not surprising that local communities did not feel part of the decision making process that fundamentally altered their status within the peninsula. The establishment of a mixed committee has however provided some opportunity for the local communities to participate in the decision making process and this is a welcome development.[115] The UNECA 2018 report[116] accepts that the resolution of such interboundary disputes involving communities may prove intractable if there is sole reliance on the formalist mechanisms of international courts and instruments developed on the basis of Western received law. This is why it calls for these disputes to be referred to African regional initiatives such as mixed commissions and African regional courts instead of being outsourced to international adjudicatory bodies far away from the continent.[117] While the recommendations for a wider use of these regional courts is a positive step, these courts are still formal Westphalian structures. This, however, does not mean that they will be unsympathetic to the rights of indigenous peoples as the Endorois and Ogoni decisions have shown. However, these formalist regional courts were not designed to replace the indigenous structures that the sub-national groups

---

110. UNECA, n.101, 24.

111. Cameroon/Nigerian case, n 107.

112. H Egede, "The ICJ Bakassi Decision: The rights of the indigenous communities and populations in the Bakassi Peninsula" in E Egede, M Ighiehon (eds.) *The ICJ Bakassi Decision: The rights of the indigenous communities and populations in the Bakassi Peninsula* (Routledge, 2017) chapter 5.

113. See a further discourse on this issue in F Kini-Yen Kinni, *Bakassi: Or the Politics of Exclusion and Occupation* (Langaa Research and Publishing, CIG, 2013).

114. *Agreement between the Republic of Cameroon and the Federal Republic of Nigeria Concerning the Modalities of Withdrawal and Transfer of Authority in the Bakassi Peninsula* (with annexes and summary of discussions), Greentree, New York, 06/12/2006.

115. The Abyei boundary dispute between Sudan and South Sudan provides another example of the weaknesses of utilising a formalist approach to resolve transboundary disputes over natural resources. For further analysis, see D Johnson, "The Heglig Oil Dispute between Sudan and South Sudan" (2012) 6(3) *Journal of Eastern African Studies 561-569.*

116. UNECA 2018 report n. 100, 85.

117. UNECA, n.116, 88.

can readily identify with or are able to freely participate in the adjudicatory processes of such institutions.

One could ask why the UNECA report focuses more on the use of public international law in the resolution of transboundary problems within Africa. This could be due to the fact that its commissioning body is a United Nations institution. It is to be expected that its preferred choice of law will be public international law and its institutions. Yet, in calling for a multilayered approach to natural resource governance, the UNECA report alludes to a possible role for other fields of law in transboundary natural resource management. To this end, is it possible for African social ordering norms to play a role in achieving an equitable management framework for the exploitation of natural resources at a transboundary level?

THE ROLE OF AFRICAN SOCIAL ORDERING NORMS IN TRANSNATIONAL NATURAL RESOURCE MANAGEMENT

The earlier part of this chapter has identified Afro-commutarianism[118] as the key social ordering system that governs many indigenous communities. This social ordering rule manifests itself in its regional variations of Ubuntu, Humwe and Omoluabi. South Africa is a good example of an African state that has effectively ingrained Afro-communitarianism in its dispute resolution mechanisms. This has been achieved through the recognition of Ubuntu as its key social ordering norm. The landmark case of *S v Makwanyane*[119] provides judicial recognition of Ubuntu at the highest level. In this case, the constitutional court of South Africa affirmed the paramount value of this social ordering norm in this manner:

> The concept is of some relevance to the values we need to uphold. It is a culture which places some emphasis on communality and on the interdependence of the members of a community. It recognises a person's status as a human being, entitled to unconditional respect, dignity, value and acceptance from the members of the community such person happens to be part of. It also entails the converse, however. The person has a corresponding duty to give the same respect, dignity, value and acceptance to each member of that community. More importantly, it regulates the exercise of rights by the emphasis it lays on sharing and co-responsibility and the mutual enjoyment of rights by all.[120]

The above-mentioned description of the Ubuntu establishes that the concept is all about communality and the right to human dignity as enshrined in international human rights law. However, unlike the Western concept of law

---

118. Onazi, n.48, 7.
119. *S v Makwanaye*, n. 44.
120. Makwanaye, n.44, para 224.

where individual autonomy is prioritized, the Ubuntu concept places more emphasis on co-responsibility and the inter-dependence of the members of a community. If Ubuntu and other African social ordering norms are applied to transboundary natural resource management, the focus will be on equitable management of resources that is based on the principles of community inter-dependence and communitarianism. This is unlike Lex Petrolea, a recognized form of transnational law which protects the investment of the international oil and gas sector.[121]

In contrast, Ubuntu and other African social ordering norms lean towards a communitarian approach to the exploitation of transboundary natural resources. At the national level, many African states have adopted the domanial approach to ownership of natural resources. Several African national constitutions assert that ownership of natural resources, especially petroleum and minerals, are vested in the state, which holds such resources in trust for its peoples.[122] Yet as part four of this chapter demonstrates, local communities also have the right to exercise internal self-determination over the resources situated within their territory.[123] These competing perspectives of sovereignty have created intra-state tensions between national states and local communities within these states.

Sovereignty challenges may also arise where there are transboundary disputes connected with straddling resources or with groups of the same ethnic identity that operate beyond one country.[124] The general approach to managing straddling deposits in Sub-Saharan Africa particularly when it pertains to petroleum deposits is the use of Joint Development Agreements (JDAs) or Unitisation Agreements. This is in line with the requirements of established principles of the Law of the Sea and in Oil and Gas Law.[125]

The Nigerian/Sao Tome Joint Development Zone is an example of how cross border straddling resources can be effectively managed between states. Yet as Oduntan[126] points out the issue of straddling deposits is still a flash point of potential dispute in the sub-continent and it is debatable whether the formalist structures of unitization and joint development processes can resolve such

---

121. N Mersadi Tabari, *Lex Petrolea and International Investment Law: Law and Practice in the Persian Gulf* (Routledge, 2016) 132.
122. Egede, n. 37, 142-144.
123. Economic and Social Council, *Prevention of Discrimination and Protection of Indigenous People: Indigenous Peoples' Permanent Sovereignty over Natural Resources*, Final Report of the Special Rapporteur, E/CN.4/Sub.2/2004/30 07/13/2004; Enyew, n. 90, 228.
124. UNECA 2018 report, n. 100, 85.
125. AE Bastida, A Ifesi-Okoye, S Mahmud, J Ross, T Wälde, "Cross-Border Unitization and Joint Development Agreements: An International Law Perspective" (2007) 29(2) *Houston Journal of International Law 355.*
126. G Oduntan, "The Emergent Legal Regime for Exploration of Hydrocarbons in the Gulf of Guinea: Imperative Considerations for Participating States and Multinationals" (2008) 57 *International and Comparative Law Quarterly* 253, 258, 293.

disputes particularly if they occur within the territories of local communities. This is why it is necessary to adopt a multi-pronged approach to natural resource governance in the region which allows for the utilization of local social ordering norms alongside other fields of law in transboundary management of natural resources.

The straddling resource scenario serves as a test case on whether true Afro-communitarianism exists in the sub-continent.[127] Questions would arise on whether African states with straddling deposits will apply these Afro-Communitarianism norms or if they would continue to rely on the formalist structures of joint development zones and unitization arrangements[128] situated in received Western law. Reliance on the latter arrangements is generally the preferred option. Africa's colonial past and its continuing interaction with globalization and neo-liberalism may account for the focus on formalist structures in the transboundary management of natural resources within the continent. This final point is explored below.

NEO-LIBERALISM AND AFRO-COMMUNITARIANISM: COMPETING INTERESTS IN THE TRANSBOUNDARY MANAGEMENT OF RESOURCES.

Neo-liberalism is considered a key obstacle to the adoption of Afro-communitarian norms in the regulation of commercial activities in Sub-Saharan Africa.[129] Neo-liberalism promotes an ultra-capitalist approach to economic liberalism. It prioritises the free market and personal property over other interests. Neo-liberalism is entrenched in many African states and has re-engineered the way and manner in which commercial activities are regulated in the sub-continent.[130] Although the current hierarchical system places natural resource governance under state control, most African states lack the capital and technical know-how to exploit their natural resources. The African extractive sector is heavily reliant on foreign direct investment. This has to some extent led to the liberalization of this strategic sector.[131] While state law still plays a key role in the regulation of this sector, the sector is still highly internationalized and transnational law such as Lex Petrolea (see part two of this chapter) continues to dominate the transboundary management of energy exploitation within the African continent and beyond.

---

127. Some doubts have been raised in other works on whether this level of interdependence and community really exists between African nations and communities. See V Simiyu, "The Democratic Myth in the African Tradtional societies" in W Oyugi and A Gitonga (eds.) *Democratic Theory and Practice in Africa* (East African Educational Publishers, 1987) 49-51.
128. Bastida, *et al*, n. 124.
129. R Edozie, *The Cultural Political Economy of Nigeria's Afri- Capitalism and South Africa's Ubuntu Business* (Springer, 2017) 163.
130. G Harrison, *Neoliberal Africa: The Impact of Social Engineering* (Zed Books, 2013) Chapter five.
131. C Roberts, "The other Resource Curse: Extractives as Development Panacea" in HG Besada (ed.) *Governing Natural Resources for Africa's Development (*Taylor & Francis, 2016) 67-71.

It is unclear how a neo-liberalized extractive energy sector will react to the emergence of another transnational legal ordering in the form of African social ordering norms. This is because Lex Petrolea is the primary form of transnational law that these oil companies recognize and are regulated by. It is unlikely that such companies would accept a role for indigenous African law to play in natural resource governance. This does not mean that these companies within the extractive energy sector are totally unfamiliar with the customary law of the communities where they undertake exploitation of resources. The key challenge is that the extractive sector is governed by civic law under the hierarchical legal system. For this reason, there is no compelling requirement for companies to have more than a superficial understanding of these norms. Yet as Frynas explains, an understanding of local customary law is "important to the understanding of oil related litigation because villages in oil producing areas still tend to observe customary law."[132] Yet the hierarchical system of law in African states limits the significance of customary law over oil litigation except in cases where the dispute of land is in contest.[133] In addition the framework of African domestic land use legislation has prioritized state ownership over communal ownership. The diminished value of customary law in matters of national economic interest confirms the revisionist theory that the present concept of African customary law merely exists to serve the interest of the African elite and not the primordial public.

Since customary law appears to have a limited role in natural resource management at the national state level, it is questionable what role it can play in the management of transboundary resources that extend beyond national jurisdiction. In addition, post-colonial legal systems have also localized the application of African customary law and to this end it is difficult to envision the deployment of such rules at the regional level. Himonga[134] responds to this question by reflecting on the transformative nature of Ubuntu and other social ordering norms. He explains that Afro-communitarian rules such as Ubuntu continue to apply to the continent because they are living and transformative norms. This is why such norms continue to exist even when formal customary law no longer represents the norms and values of a given society.[135]

If, as Himonga argues, African social ordering rules can exist outside of a formalist customary law system, why is there a continuing reluctance to deploy them in transnational resource management? Perhaps this has to do with the fact that the African neo-liberal establishment is more accustomed to Western received law. They therefore view African customary law through the prism of

---

132. Frynas, n. 93, 62.
133. Ibid.
134. C Himonga, M Taylor, A Pope, "Reflections on Judicial Views of Ubuntu" (2013) 16(5) *Potchefstroom Electronic Law Journal* 373.
135. Ibid.

received Western law and see no need to utilize indigenous African norms for the resolution of disputes. This may explain why it has been so difficult for the African legal establishment to move away from "their notional Western gaze"[136] and to consider how the normative elements of Afro-communitarianism can serve as a new paradigm for managing natural resources of a transboundary nature. A reorientation of the legal mindset is therefore required to steer policymaking in the multi-pronged approach to transnational natural governance as recommended by the UNECA report.

It is a positive development that the African Union (AU) level has instituted an "Ubuntu inspired African Continental Partnership on Education to achieve the goals of the AUC Agenda 2063."[137] The development of this partnership is seen as a correct step in developing a "re-visioned education on socioeconomic and political development of Africa."[138] However, it is unclear how far the AU has gone in promoting a similar initiative for law formulation at the continental level. This chapter maintains that even if social ordering norms are not regarded as a binding and formal transnational legal order, they can still be introduced as form of legal ordering at the continental level.

While some in the African legal establishment may find this form of legal ordering as "strange" the Bhabha third space construct provides an opportunity for sentimentalists and revisionists alike to consider how social ordering norms can advance a further re-engineering of the present rules on natural resource management in the continent. Recent scholarship[139] demonstrates that some within the African legal establishment openly recognize that these social ordering norms are an "important feature of African law."[140] However, it is unlikely that these norms will totally replace the current formalist legal system which is generally framed on legal positivism. But Bhabha's third space allows for a rethink on how at the continental level, policy makers can come together to engineer a new transnational law on transboundary natural resource management that embodies both received Western law and customary laws in a way that champions sustainable development and an equitable utilization of natural resources.

---

136. Edozie, n. 128, 19.
137. E J Takyi-Amaoko, N T Assie-Lumumba, "Towards an Ubuntu-Inspired Continental Partnership on Education for Sustainable Development in Africa- African Union Commission Agenda 2063 Strategy": In E Takyi- Amoako, N Assie-Lumumba (eds.) *Re-Visioning Education in Africa* (Palgrave Macmillan, Cham, 2018) 229-246.
138. Ibid.
139. O Amao, *African Union Law: The Emergence of a Sui Generis Legal Order* (Routledge, 2018).
140. Ibid., 11.

PART SIX: CONCLUSION

This chapter considered the role that African social ordering norms can play in the de-escalation of conflicts in theatres of conflict within Sub-Saharan Africa. Recent studies show that the nature of natural resource conflicts within this sub-continent is evolving. Many of the current disputes transcend national borders. Like other transboundary problems, both national law and international law are limited in their ability to combat natural resource conflicts of a transboundary nature. This is why the chapter champions a wider use of transnational law in the management of natural resources that transcend national boundaries.

The chapter argues that forms of transnational law such as Lex Petrolea are inadequate to resolve conflicts associated with local communities. It explores whether a homegrown African transnational law based on African social ordering norms can play a role in the management of transboundary natural resources. It considers whether these norms which embody the ideals of Afro-communitarianism and social justice can assist in the resolution of community disputes arising from natural resource exploitation. It examines the case for and against the use of these norms in transnational legal ordering. It discusses how the socio-legal approach to transitional law can strengthen the case for the utilization of these norms in transboundary natural resource management.

It explores Bhabha's third space construct and further develops on Silungwe's work to explain how the third space construct can be utilized to advance the case for a homegrown transnational law. This chapter argues that post-colonial African law makers and policy architects operate in both formalist and traditionalist structures of governance. As such, the third space construct provides the basis for unifying the divergent views on how to achieve transboundary management of natural resources within the Sub-Saharan African continent. Africa has come of age to utilize this third space construct to canvass for a greater utilization of African social ordering norms alongside received Western law and its formalist structures.

The Niger Delta amnesty initiative confirms the possibility of utilizing Bhahba's third space that allows for the convergence between Western received law and African legal ordering norms which promote dialogic interactions between African states and their sub-national groups. This third space will allow for these sub-national groups to exercise internal self-determination of their resources yet at the same time respecting their sovereign states' rights to territorial integrity, and their exercise in law making through formalist state processes.

The chapter calls for African States to recognize Afro-communitarian indigenous norms such as Ubuntu, Humwe and Omoluabi as a form of transnational customary law similar to Lex Petrolea (the transnational customary law for oil merchants). These social ordering norms shaped under the general framework of Afro-communitarianism can be afforded the status of the transnational customary law of African communities. The chapter calls for these social ordering norms to become part and parcel of any multi-layered energy governance framework as proposed by the UNECA 2018 report and other recent publications. This will ensure a wider role for homegrown African customary norms to shape and develop a more equitable natural resource governance regime for local communities within the African sub-continent.

Lightning Source UK Ltd.
Milton Keynes UK
UKHW051606301019

352587UK00004B/100/P